D0585085

CATHEDRALS *of the* WORLD

by Elizabeth Cruwys and Beau Riffenburgh

83

MAGNIFICENT CATHEDRALS FROM AROUND THE WORLD

BOHU
VLASTI
UMĚNÍ KE
BANKA
KU CHVÁLE
K SLÁVĚ
CTI-VĚNUJE
SLÁVIE

CATHEDRALS *of the* WORLD

AA Publishing

Copy editor: Rebecca Snelling

Designer: TT Designs, T&S Truscott

Produced by AA Publishing

First published 1997

Published by AA Publishing (a trading name of Automobile Association Developments Limited, whose registered office is Norfolk House, Priestley Road, Basingstoke, Hampshire RG24 9NY; registered number 1878835).

ISBN 0 7495 1208 3

A CIP catalogue record for this book is available from the British Library.

Origination by Daylight Colour Art Pte Ltd, Singapore
Printed and bound in Spain by Graficas Estella S.A.

HALF TITLE: A circular window in Notre-Dame Cathedral, Strasbourg.

TITLE PAGE, LEFT: Art nouveau window in St Vitus Cathedral, Prague.
RIGHT: Window detail from Notre-Dame Cathedral, Paris.

Contents

ABOVE: The blues of the windows in Notre-Dame Cathedral, Chartres, are unrivalled.
RIGHT: Deep reds and yellows feature in the south window of Chicago's Holy Name Cathedral.
BELOW: This magnificent fan-shaped window can be seen in Notre-Dame Cathedral, Strasbourg.
OPPOSITE: This window motif from St Etienne's Cathedral, Bourges, depicts the journey of the Cross.

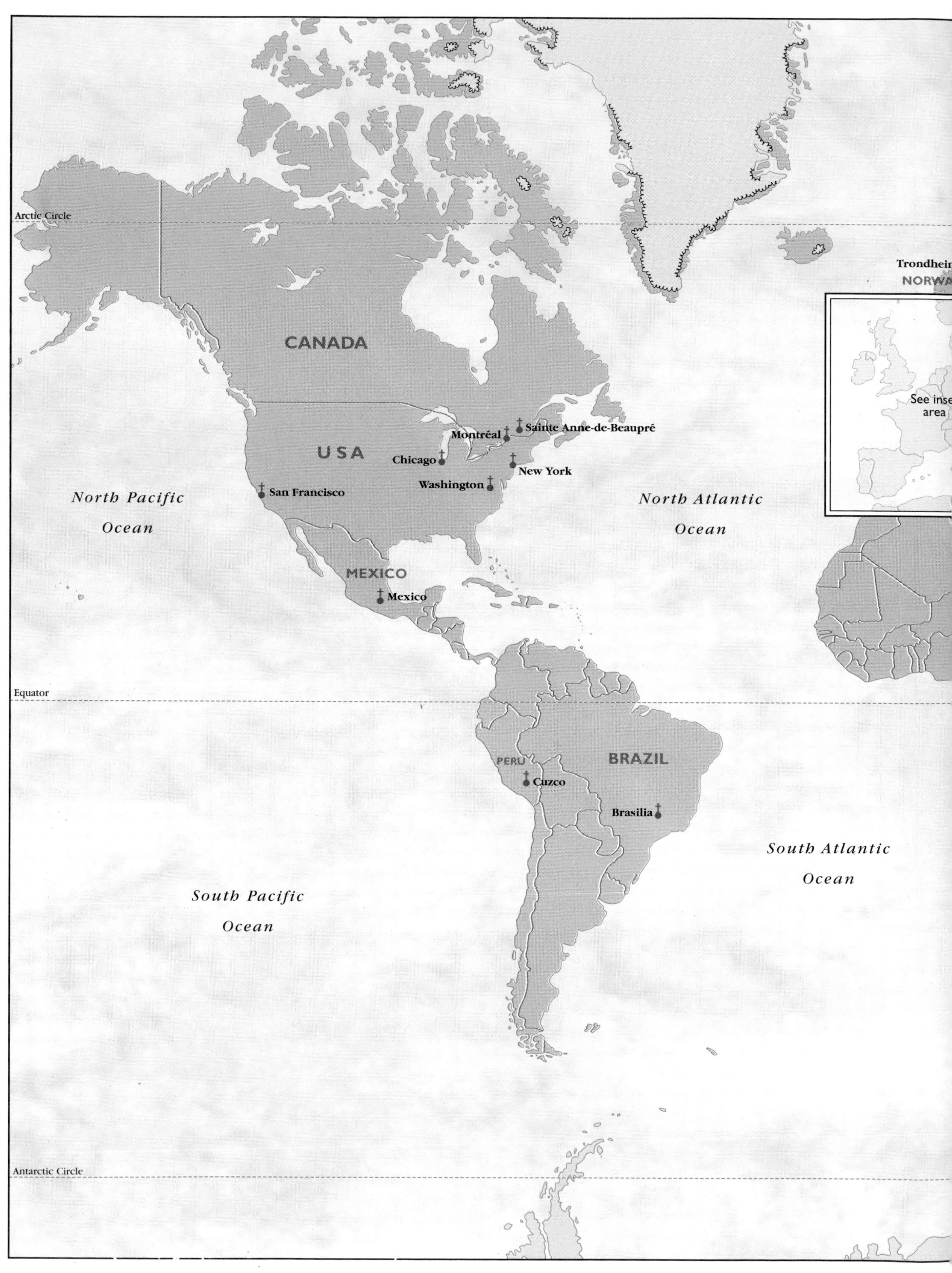

Arctic Circle
CANADA
USA
MEXICO
PERU
BRAZIL
Montréal
Sainte Anne-de-Beaupré
Chicago
New York
Washington
San Francisco
Mexico
Cuzco
Brasilia
North Pacific Ocean
North Atlantic Ocean
South Pacific Ocean
South Atlantic Ocean
Equator
Antarctic Circle

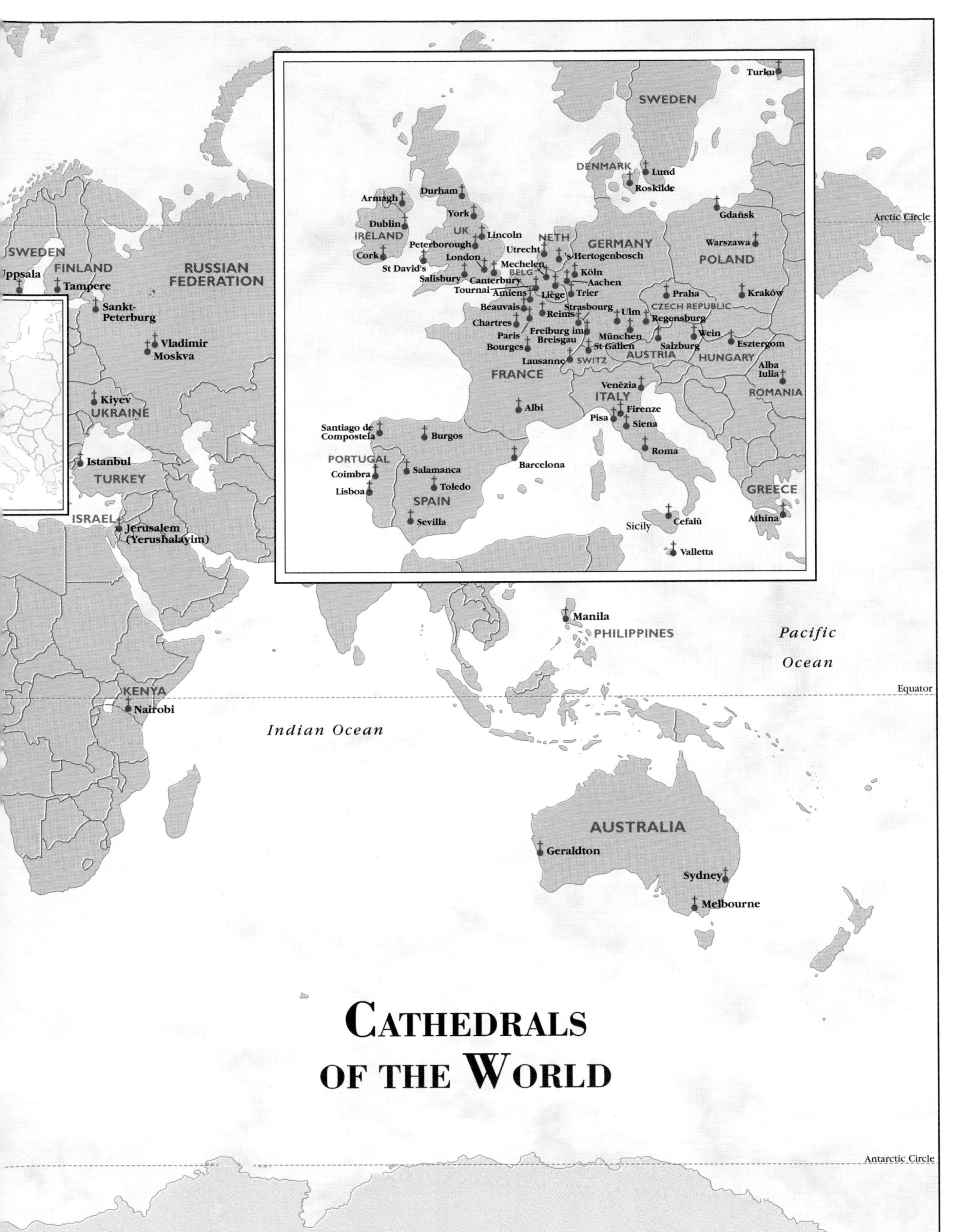

Cathedrals of the World

Introduction

What is a cathedral?

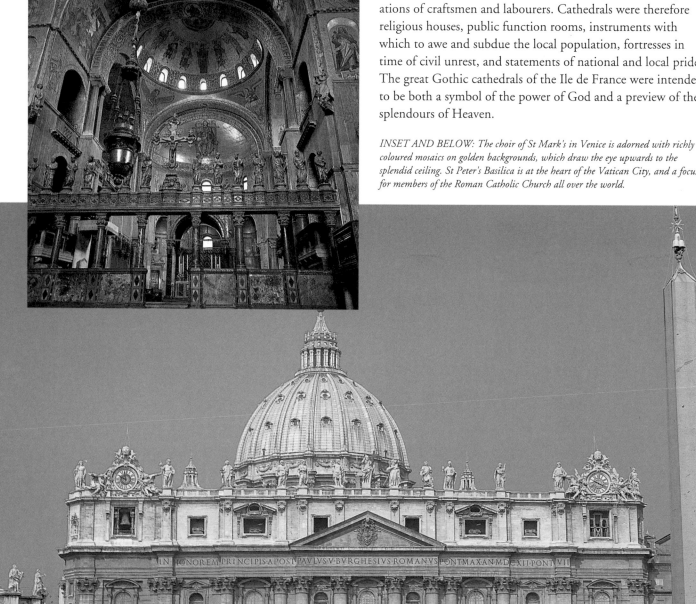

Cathedrals summon up a vast array of images in the minds of different people: airy Gothic buildings that strive to reach to the skies; sturdy Romanesque churches designed to dominate the local population or provide them with a fortress in time of need; or ethereal modern structures of glass and concrete that seem to defy the laws of gravity. Yet the actual definition of a cathedral has nothing to do with style, size or age. A cathedral is a church in which a bishop has his 'cathedra', a Greek word meaning throne or seat. In the Dark Ages, when Christianity was in its infancy in the British Isles and the population was scattered, a church was only a cathedral as long as it contained the bishop's throne. When the bishop and his retinue moved on, the cathedral reverted to being a church again.

Cathedrals fulfilled a variety of functions in the Middle Ages. They were not only places for religious gatherings, worship and, inevitably, political intrigues within the Church, but the focus of a community around which fairs, markets and secular activities were held. They also provided employment for generations of craftsmen and labourers. Cathedrals were therefore religious houses, public function rooms, instruments with which to awe and subdue the local population, fortresses in time of civil unrest, and statements of national and local pride. The great Gothic cathedrals of the Ile de France were intended to be both a symbol of the power of God and a preview of the splendours of Heaven.

INSET AND BELOW: The choir of St Mark's in Venice is adorned with richly coloured mosaics on golden backgrounds, which draw the eye upwards to the splendid ceiling. St Peter's Basilica is at the heart of the Vatican City, and a focus for members of the Roman Catholic Church all over the world.

A common misconception about cathedrals is that they are simply big churches, but size has nothing to do with whether a church has cathedral status or not. St Peter's Basilica in Rome is the largest Christian building in the world, but it is not a cathedral. At the other end of the spectrum is the Little Metropole in Athens, yet it was a cathedral for many years before the larger 19th-century replacement was built next door. However, having said that size is immaterial to a cathedral's status, many are enormous. Bishops were influential people in the Middle Ages and their cathedrals needed to reflect their elevated status. Cathedrals also had to be large in order to accommodate the huge numbers of people that gathered for religious and secular events. In addition, architects tended to confer a greater importance on cathedrals, and made them more elaborate than parish churches. And, of course, funding played a vital role. The medieval Church was a wealthy and powerful organisation which could usually afford great, glorious statements of its authority on Earth. However, the Church's purse was not bottomless and sometimes, when the money ran out, decades would pass before building could be resumed.

The building of some cathedrals took centuries to complete: the great Gothic Cathedral of St Peter in Cologne was started in the 13th century, yet its noble twin steeples were not built until the 19th century. Even in the 20th century, with modern building techniques, some cathedrals have taken many years to finish: work on the Washington National Cathedral in the United States began in 1907, and was only completed in 1990. So it is all the more astonishing that Salisbury Cathedral in England was completed in less than 50 years – almost no time for a cathedral – and so demonstrates a unity of style usually lacking in medieval cathedrals.

Cathedral architecture

Traditionally, cathedrals have been built in two styles: basilican and cruciform (or cross-shaped). The basilica style is the older form, the idea originating in the Roman halls of justice: simple, rectangular buildings divided with columns to make aisles, and a rounded (apsidal) end where the tribunal sat.

Early basilican churches followed this style, placing the altar at the apsidal end, with a porch at the opposite end. Many basilicas were adorned with a dome in the centre. At first these domes were simple, but, as building techniques developed, they became increasingly impressive, culminating with splendid domes like those at St Sophia in Istanbul, St Mark's in Venice and St Peter's in Rome.

Later, basilicas gave way to cruciform plans – either as Greek crosses (with four arms of equal length), or as Latin crosses (where the western arm is longer than the others). Cruciform churches had a main body (nave), arms to the north and south (transepts), and a choir, or sanctuary, in the east. All Gothic cathedrals are cruciform, but there was a revival of the basilican form of cathedral after the 16th century. Most churches and cathedrals face east, because the high altar was always placed nearest the rising sun – the symbol of Christ's resurrection from the darkness of death.

A glossary of architectural terms is included on page 190.

The cathedral through the ages

The first cathedrals were simple buildings, usually quite small because they were not required to hold as many people as later on in history. Many cathedrals were grafted on to pre-existing buildings to save money. In western Europe, a style of building called Romanesque began to develop. This was based on the style of building used in classical Rome – strong, round-headed arches and solid columns holding up the roof. It was in use in Europe from about 600 until around 1200. In Britain, Romanesque is often referred to as Norman, because it was the Normans who introduced it after the Conquest in 1066. As early medieval builders began to experiment, they found they could achieve quite grand effects by altering the style of vaulting in the roofs. Instead of the entire arch being used to support the ceiling vault, it was found that arches could spring from the tops of columns, and thus provide ribbing for a vaulted roof.

When pointed arches and flying buttresses were combined, Gothic architecture was established. It was pioneered in France from about 1100, and lasted until the 16th century. From the 12th century, cathedrals were made increasingly bigger, lighter and more extravagant. The zenith of this style is called High Gothic, and can be seen in the marvellous French cathedrals at Laon, Notre-Dame (Paris), Chartres, Rheims and Amiens, reaching its pinnacle in the unfinished Beauvais.

Gothic architecture was as much a philosophy as a building style. It was a series of ever-more-daring experiments with light and structure under the guidance of the brilliant Abbot Suger of St Denis' Abbey in Paris. Suger believed strongly in the power of symbolism and, to him, Christ was not only the keystone of Christianity, but of the symbols of His Church on Earth, that is, the cathedrals. Suger thought that the light that radiated within cathedrals was a symbol of Christ, and the pillars of the cathedral represented the Old Testament prophets, who, like the pillars supporting the cathedral, were the base upon which Christianity was built.

BELOW: The 17th-century cathedral of Cuzco, in Peru, presents a formidable twin-towered façade.

So, put simply, the goals of the architects of Gothic cathedrals became multifold; they not only had to reach the heavens, and by so doing pay tribute to God, but had to develop a building that, by its very nature, presented the symbols of Christ. Thus, the thick walls of the Romanesque buildings were replaced with increasingly fine flying buttresses, many of them exquisitely carved. As much wall space as possible was given over to windows, so that the interior of the cathedral was flooded with light. When the windows were filled with magnificent stained glass, the cathedrals became a glorious dazzle of blues, greens, golds and reds. Slender pillars soared to impossible heights, supporting delicately pointed ceilings in defiance of gravity.

In the 16th century, Gothic began to give way to the Renaissance style, which moved back towards classical forms of architecture. Renaissance started in the late 14th century in Italy, and there was an emphasis on individual expression. Renaissance architecture was developing when the Spanish empire was expanding to the New World. The Hispanic cathedrals at Cuzco and Mexico City are examples of how this style was exported overseas.

Classicism became even more pronounced in the baroque style – and later the exaggerated form of baroque called rococo – which followed the Renaissance in the 17th and 18th centuries. Among the finest baroque cathedrals are those in central Europe, such as the exuberant Salzburg in Austria, and the dazzling rococo St Gall in Switzerland. Many Romanesque and Gothic cathedrals underwent baroque restoration, especially inside. Perhaps the most notable example is Toledo in Spain, which boasts a noble combination of Romanesque, Gothic and Renaissance on its exterior, and a magnificently elegant baroque interior. One of the most impressive baroque façades is that of Santiago de Compostela, with its multitude of sculptures adorning every available inch of space.

After the devastation of wars from the 18th to the 20th centuries, cathedral building underwent another series of changes. Several cathedrals have been built in the 20th century in England, the best known being Coventry, Guildford, and the two in Liverpool. Liverpool expresses the extremes of choices open to architects: the Roman Catholic cathedral is a circular building of steel and concrete decorated with lovely stained glass; the Anglican cathedral looks like a late Gothic building. Each is impressive in its own right, yet they represent opposites on a spectrum ranging from a revival of traditional forms, to the use of modern techniques and materials to produce something original and different.

National styles

Architectural styles spread from country to country, so that the Gothic cathedrals of the Ile de France influenced architects from as far away as Australia, the United States and all across Europe. However, each country adopted the style to suit its own needs and priorities. For example, many countries drew inspiration from the fabulous dome of St Sophia's in Istanbul. Russian architects found that flat, saucer-like cupolas tended to collapse under the accumulation of winter snow, whereas the more rounded onion domes allowed snow to slide off before its weight became too great.

Other countries did not have the building materials that architects may have desired. Stone was rare in Denmark, and so

BELOW: Sunlight streams in through a window in Cuzco Cathedral; behind the high altar, crafted in solid silver, is the original wooden altar carved in traditional native style.

ABOVE. The unusual and ultra-modern design of Brasilia's cathedral features outstretched concrete ribs topped with spikes representing the Crown of Thorns.

brick was used. Since brick was not as versatile or as strong as stone, sacrifices needed to be made, and St Clement's Cathedral in Aarhus, dating from the 12th and 13th centuries, lacks the grace of the French Gothic, despite its 310-foot (93-m) spire and tower. Similarly, Roskilde, a late Gothic cathedral, is austere and angular.

Spain and Portugal did not lack stone, but their architecture was strongly influenced by four centuries of Muslim occupation. When the Moors were ousted from the Iberian Peninsula, many mosques were simply converted into churches. A prime example is the older of the two cathedrals at Saragossa, while the Renaissance cathedral at Cordoba actually stands inside a mosque. Seville maintained the magnificent Muslim minaret called the Giralda as part of its cathedral complex. The baroque appealed to the Spanish sense of the exuberant, and a wildly extravagant form known as the Churrigueresque was developed.

Meanwhile, the cathedrals of other countries were built as a statement of national pride. The great sun-blaze cathedral at Brasilia is said to be representative of the development of the country's powers in the international political arena, while the cathedral at Tromsø in Norway is popularly known as the Cathedral of the Arctic because its design is so in tune with its polar setting.

Cathedrals great and small

Cathedrals come in all shapes and sizes, and no two are exactly alike. Even the enormous Gothic Revival cathedrals in North America, although faithfully modelled on the Gothic buildings of the Ile de France, have their own distinctive characteristics and features. For example, Washington National Cathedral is unusual in that it has a chapel designed specifically for the use of children.

The largest cathedral in the world is that of St John the Divine in New York. This massive edifice looms out of the surrounding buildings like a sleeping giant, and its dimensions are staggering. It is 601 feet (180m) long, and has a floor area of 121,000 square feet (11,253sq m) and a volume of 16,822,000 cubic feet (476,3062cu m). The distinction of largest surface area goes to Seville Cathedral, which has a length of 414 feet (124m) and a width of 271 feet (81m). But while Seville Cathedral is noted for its huge horizontal dimensions, it boasts few pinnacles, spires or towers. The tallest spire in Christendom is the mighty 525-foot (158-m) tall Ulm Münster, built in the 19th century.

BELOW: The view over the rooftops of Seville Cathedral gives an indication of the vast proportions of the church below.

Amiens Cathedral is the largest in France, and was designed to hold about 10,000 people – the entire population of Amiens in the 13th century. The Cathedral of Santa Maria del Fiore in Florence was built after the end of the 13th century because the older Cathedral of Santa Reparta was not large enough. Beauvais Cathedral in France was intended to be immense, but lack of funds and a series of wars meant that it was never completed.

FIRES, EARTHQUAKES ...

It is sometimes said that Gothic architecture in France owed its development to fire. Indeed, several early cathedrals (notably Beauvais, Amiens and Rheims) were destroyed by fire, thus providing the opportunity for medieval architects and masons to create something more impressive than before. Christopher Wren's great baroque St Paul's Cathedral was built because its predecessor was damaged in the Great Fire of London, and the Chicago fire of 1871 destroyed many churches, opening the way for the city's fine Holy Name Cathedral to be raised. Lightning destroyed the 12th-century cathedral at Chartres, and, more recently, caused great damage at York Minster. The famous earthquake of 1755 caused the destruction of Lisbon Cathedral, while that of 1906 in San Francisco allowed the Church authorities to select land for the building of the handsome Grace Cathedral. Earthquakes also destroyed cathedrals at locations as diverse as Lincoln in England (in 1185) and Manila in the Philippines (in 1600, 1645 and 1863).

... WARS AND UPHEAVALS

Despite the ravages of natural disasters and accidents, wars and religious conflicts have inflicted far wider-ranging damage. The builders of some cathedrals, such as Albi in southern France and Durham in northern England, were well aware that their buildings might come under attack, and so they were constructed with thick walls, small windows and well-fortified doors that could be held against invaders. So, in the 12th century, a kind of building known as the fortress-cathedral began to emerge. These sturdy buildings were the antithesis of the lightness of the later Gothic period, and displayed the Normans' skill in castle-building as much as in church

BELOW: A lone figure among the war-time ruins of Coventry Cathedral seems to look to the future when the new cathedral will rise in its place; the part of the old cathedral which escaped destruction is preserved as a poignant reminder.

architecture. Other fortress-cathedrals include Cefalú in Sicily and Coimbra in Portugal.

Many cathedrals were the victims of religious and political upheavals. The Reformation in northern Europe meant that cathedrals in the Netherlands and Belgium, for example, suffered terribly at the hands of Protestant zealots; even when all the frenzy was over, the kind of Christianity that emerged was not conducive to building or maintaining great houses of worship. The French Revolution also took its toll. Many works of art and statuary were wantonly vandalised in France and Belgium in the 1790s, especially in the great cathedrals of Bourges, Reims, Notre-Dame in Paris and St Lambert's in Liège. Fortunately for posterity, the citizens of Amiens were so attached to their cathedral that they rallied to its defence, and it was spared the damage inflicted on so many other religious buildings in the 18th century.

Other cathedrals were damaged when they were used for purposes other than religion. Durham Cathedral, which formed part of a great fortress complex with the castle next door, and was under the control of the powerful and warlike prince-bishops of Durham, was used as a prison for 4,000 Scots in 1650. The Scots promptly used the choir stalls to make a great fire to keep themselves warm, and only spared the clock case because it had a Scottish thistle on it. They also smashed many of the cathedral's statues and much fine artwork. Many cathedrals in Russia and eastern Europe are no longer used as churches, and have been converted into museums. The wonderful 16th-century Cathedral of the Assumption in Vladimir (Russia) was subjected to use as a stable for horses during the Napoleonic Wars in the 1800s.

The two world wars inflicted still more damage. Rheims Cathedral took about 300 direct hits from shells during World War I, while Malines in Belgium was virtually on the front line. World War II was responsible for the wholesale destruction of cathedrals as far apart as Manila in the Philippines, St Michael's Cathedral in Coventry, and the Cathedral of St John in Warsaw. Many German cathedrals were also damaged, including perhaps the most famous survivor, Cologne, which emerged battered but still standing after the massive aerial bombardment by the Allies.

The cathedrals of the world have also suffered at the hands of the great enemy of everything created by man – time. Because of their age, many cathedrals are constantly in need of restoration and repair, and so charge entrance fees. While such charges can be regarded sceptically by some visitors, they are, as becomes obvious when they are considered, necessary to maintain the cathedrals not only for this generation but for those beyond. And surely cathedrals are among the most significant man-made structures of all time: they are not only architecturally diverse and remarkable, but frequently they house treasures of great beauty and historic significance.

The selection

One thing that should be noted is that not all the churches included in this book hold the official status of cathedral. One example is St Peter's Basilica in Rome. Another is the Church

ABOVE: St Patrick's Cathedral in Dublin is Ireland's longest church. The subtly coloured mosaic floor which leads up towards the choir is one of the glories of the cathedral.

of the Holy Sepulchre in Jerusalem, which contains a wealth of significant sites connected with the death and resurrection of Jesus. Control of the Holy Sepulchre was a prime goal of the First Crusade (1096–9), and it is still regarded as one of the holiest places in Christendom. The handsome St Patrick's Cathedral in Dublin is perhaps the best known religious building in Ireland, but the archbishop's 'cathedra' is in nearby Christ Church Cathedral.

Similarly, there are many wonderful cathedrals not included here. Inevitably, some of these omissions will be considered equal or superior to those that do appear. However, whereas there will always be disagreement about which cathedrals are the most important, the most beautiful or the most spectacular, it is generally agreed that as a whole they are an immensely important part of our heritage and culture and truly rank among the wonders of the world.

FRANCE

ALBI CATHEDRAL

This powerful fortress-cathedral is dedicated to St Cecilia, patron saint of music

THE ALBIGENSIANS

The Albigensians, a religious sect so named because many of its members were located in Albi during the 11th and 12th centuries, adhered to a philosophy which originated in Persia during the 3rd century and spread to Europe along the trade routes. This philosophy divided the world into two parts – the material and the spiritual – and its followers attempted to renounce all material aspects of life to attain spiritual purity. Their beliefs were deemed heretical by the Roman Church and the Inquisition and, through a series of sickening massacres conducted under the guise of a crusade, the Albigensians were eradicated by the early 14th century.

In 1277 the man enthroned as Bishop of Albi was a cruel and violent Dominican friar called Bernard de Castanet. He also held the dubious distinction of being the Inquisitor of Languedoc and the Vice-Inquisitor of France, and had been instrumental in bringing about the brutal suppression of a group of ascetics known as Albigensians (see panel). Although by the 1280s the official crusade against the Albigensians was over, indiscriminate persecution of local people continued and Bernard was forced to build his cathedral like a fortress to withstand attack from his many enemies.

A FORBIDDING EXTERIOR

Work began on 15 August 1282, but progress was painfully slow, and consecration did not take place until 23 April 1480 – although in fact most of the major building had been completed some 100 years earlier.

Albi Cathedral presents a formidable face to the gentle Languedoc countryside, with its 255-foot (78-m) tall great west tower and massive 15-foot (4.5m) thick vertical walls which rise sheer and cliff-like above the River Tarn. The walls are topped by machicolations that allowed defenders to drop missiles, boiling water and the like on to invaders,

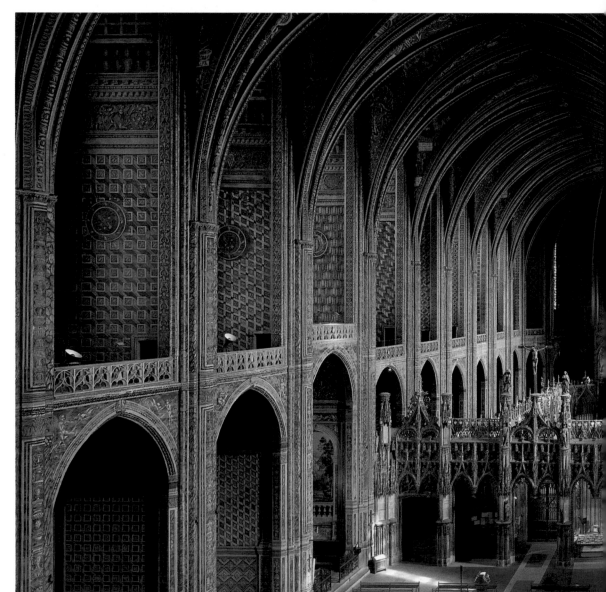

RIGHT: The soaring verticals of Albi Cathedral, viewed from the organ gallery. The richly carved rood screen dates from the 16th century, and extends across the width of the nave.

and great round buttresses were added to make undermining impossible. The roof of the cathedral is flat, providing a stark contrast to the elegant slopes and angles of French Gothic cathedrals in the north of France.

Yet, despite its forbidding appearance, further accentuated by the total lack of decoration on the purplish-red brick walls, Albi Cathedral is memorable, offering the visitor a unique insight into the violent, turbulent days of Bernard de Castanet and 14th-century southern France.

Decoration within

Cecilia, the cathedral's patron saint, is associated with sacred music, and her gentle character is better reflected in the cathedral's interior. Its lavish decoration came about largely as a result of the appointment of Louis of Amboise, a patron of the arts, as bishop in 1473.

The long narrow windows in the buttresses flood the building with light, illuminating the rich wall-paintings and carvings; the *Last Judgement* on the western wall depicts the fate of heretics and infidels. There are no aisles or transepts, and, although a finely wrought 16th-century screen divides the nave from the choir, the overall effect is that of a single, vast cube. Twelve square chapels open off each side of the nave, while at the eastern end another five chapels radiate off the apse. Blue and gold geometric designs adorn the vault of the nave, and on the dais (dating from 1529 to 1535) angels and pillars are carved in white stone.

ABOVE: The sheer walls of the cathedral rise from the south banks of the River Tarn. The remarkable structure was achieved by inserting flanking chapels between the internal buttresses, thus removing the need for supporting flying buttresses.

The choir ceiling rises in a series of graceful pointed arches, each one elaborately and delicately embellished with stonework and brightly coloured paintings. The walls, too, are similarly adorned with frescos, the work of Italian artists employed by Louis' nephew, Louis II, in the 16th century. They represent the best-preserved Renaissance work of its kind to have survived in France. Vividly executed stone statues of Old Testament characters – each one with a highly individual expression on its face – are found in the ambulatory, and the choir stalls have a fine frieze of Apostles and saints.

During the Revolution the choir was attacked and 70 statues were destroyed, but it nevertheless remains one of the best preserved in France.

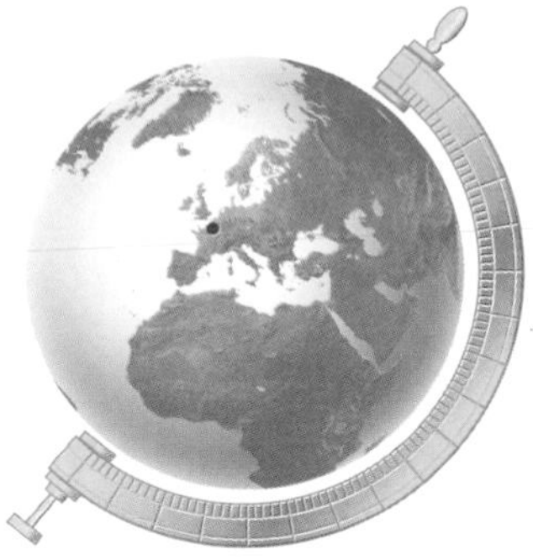

AMIENS CATHEDRAL

The noble 13th-century Gothic Cathedral of Notre-Dame is the largest in France

BELOW: The west façade escaped serious damage in World War I as it was protected by sandbags. Two towers, unequal in height, surmount a gallery of statues which represent the kings of Judah.

During the 10th century the invading Normans demolished the cathedral in Amiens which, subsequently rebuilt, burned down in 1137. A third building was then raised (it was consecrated in 1152), but this too was reduced to ashes when another inferno raged in 1218. Still standing near by was the little Church of St Firmin, which had weathered the blaze, and as it contained the relics of Firmin himself (Firmin was the first bishop of Amiens), it could not be demolished until the new cathedral was ready to receive them. Consequently, the nave of Amiens' fourth and final cathedral was built first, between 1220 and 1236, and the choir later. The old church was then destroyed and the north transept, or the northern part of the choir, built over the foundations.

A HUGE GOTHIC MASTERPIECE

Robert de Luzarches' cathedral is a masterpiece of Gothic architecture, the last of the Gothic cathedrals of the Ile de France to be built in the 13th century. Designed on a huge scale, it could hold the entire population of Amiens, which at that time numbered about 10,000 people. The length of the cathedral from east to west is 469 feet (143m), the nave stands 140 feet (42m) high, and it covers an area of 84,000 square feet (7,800sq m).

From every direction, Amiens is splendid. The slender spire that sits over the crossing enhances the overwhelming impression of height, as do the elegant flying buttresses that soar from arcade level to the roof. It has been said that the intention of Luzarches and his bishop, Evrard de Fouilloy, was to instil in the people a feeling of majesty and might, to create a symbol worthy of God.

The splendid nave has been described as the 'epitome of verticality', with the height of the arcade almost equalling that of the triforium and clerestory combined. This feeling of height is further enhanced by the light that floods down from the clear glass of the clerestory, by the slenderness of the piers and by the delicate vertical tracery in the windows of the apse.

A WEALTH OF TREASURES

Having admired the sheer size and magnificence of the nave and choir, there are numerous treasures to be discovered. Many French cathedrals suffered dreadfully during the Revolution, when carvings and sculptures were smashed by the thousand, but thanks to a group of influential citizens of Amiens who refused to allow the Revolutionaries access to their cathedral, the loss and damage here were minimal. However, the treasury did not escape plunder and, as elsewhere, most of the bronze and copper effigies were taken away to be melted down. Amazingly though, two effigies did survive; one, cast in a single piece of bronze, was of the aristocratic Evrard de Fouilloy who died in 1222.

The oak choir stalls, 110 of them, are reputed to be among the finest in France. Dating from the early 16th century, the misericords feature over 4,500 figures depicting scenes from the Old Testament and everyday life in Amiens.

Much of Amiens' stained glass, however, has been lost. The immense size of the windows meant that a large amount of ironwork was needed and in time this corroded and the glass fell out. Having been taken into storage while repairs were carried out, the glass was destroyed by a fire in the store room.

THE PENALTY FOR SPEED

The cathedral was virtually completed within 50 years, the final building stage being finished around 1269. As a result there is an impressive unity in style and this remarkable structure stands as a fabulous monument to church architecture at the height of the French Gothic period. Unfortunately another consequence of this rapid building was that within 100 years of its completion major repairs were necessary. The triforium in the nave proved to be unstable and had to be strengthened with tie rods, the north tower needed buttressing, and the north aisle of the choir needed reinforcing.

THE WEST FAÇADE

This supreme example of Gothic achievement, rich in medieval imagery, was started in 1220 and completed largely by 1236. Dominated by the huge rose window (added in the 15th century), it was based on Notre-Dame in Paris and has three elaborate portals, a gallery of recessed figures and two towers which have been criticised by architectural historians because they are not symmetrical; the one to the north is taller than the one to the south. Above the central portal is an intact medieval statue of Christ.

LEFT: The lofty interior of Amiens, viewed from the organ tribune. On the floor can be seen the 'labyrinth' of differently coloured stone; it is thought that following the winding pattern on one's knees may have been an exercise in penitence.

France

Beauvais Cathedral

Intended as the ultimate Gothic triumph, the glory of St Peter's Cathedral was short-lived

The visitor's first view of Beauvais Cathedral on approaching the city is every bit as awe-inspiring as the medieval masons could have hoped. Standing on a hill, it seems to float in mid-air above the houses that cluster around its base.

The first church to be built on the site was Carolingian and its nave can be seen next to the present cathedral. A second church was built to the east of the original building in the mid-10th century, but this was damaged by a fire in 1180 and again, more seriously, in 1225. At this time the building of Amiens Cathedral (see page 16) had begun and the Bishop of Beauvais, Milou de Nanteuil, was keen to rival it: the fight was on to produce the most magnificent cathedral in France.

Work began on the new choir and apse immediately but the bishop and canons had very little money available for the project, which may well have resulted in shoddy workmanship and the foundations being too shallow; whatever the cause, the building collapsed in 1227 and again in 1284. During the next 100 years building continued uninterrupted, albeit at a painfully slow pace, and the choir and the first bay of the nave were eventually completed. Another setback came in the form of the Hundred Years' War, during which time the already depleted funds of the bishop and chapter were drained completely.

Dreams and disaster

Work on the transepts resumed in 1500 and in order to help accrue funds it is reputed that the bishop allowed citizens of the town to eat butter and cheese during Lent if they made a donation. Then, in 1558, building started on the monumental tower and spire in a bid to outshine the dome of St Peter's in Rome (see page 58). With hindsight, of course, this proved to be a grave mistake as the building was

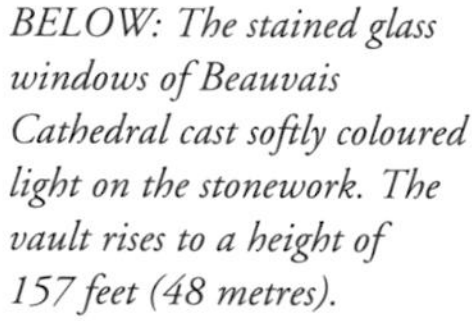

BELOW: The stained glass windows of Beauvais Cathedral cast softly coloured light on the stonework. The vault rises to a height of 157 feet (48 metres).

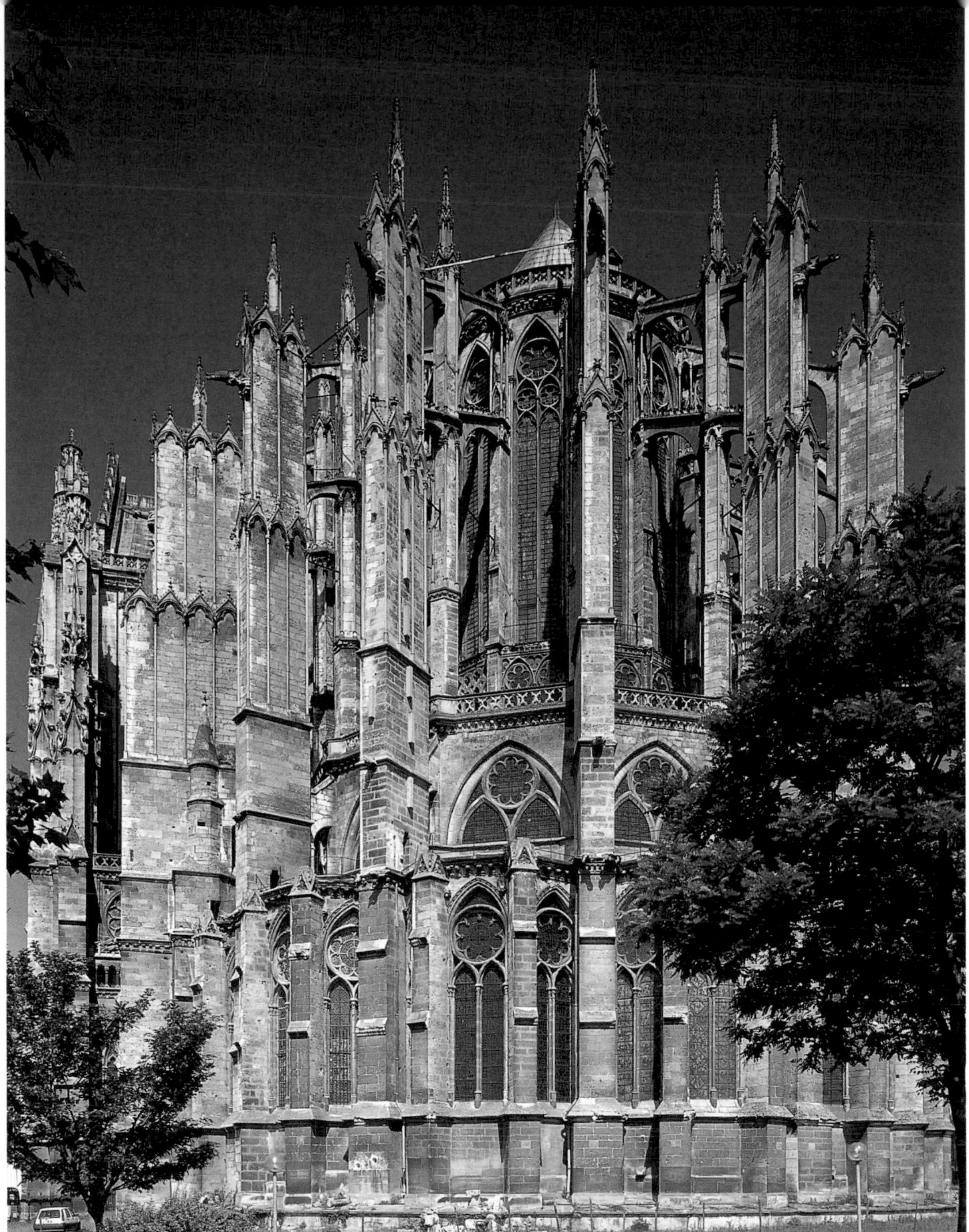

The Gothic ideal

The aim of Gothic cathedral architecture was to reach the skies – to build structures that were simultaneously majestic, powerful, ethereal and sublime; to instil a sense of awe among the people; to provide a glimpse into the wonders of heaven itself. Beauvais Cathedral was conceived as the very essence of the Gothic tradition – taller, lighter and finer than any cathedral yet raised in France. In reality, however, it was just too tall, too light and too fine, and on Ascension Day in 1573 the tower and spire that were built to reach the stars could not defy structural principles and came tumbling down.

LEFT: Still seeming to defy gravity, the towers and turrets of Beauvais Cathedral stretch up towards heaven. Although the centre of Beauvais was severely damaged by bombs in World War II, the cathedral was virtually untouched.

not strong enough to support such a structure. Nevertheless work continued and the tower and spire reached ever upwards, attaining an unprecedented 497 feet (149m) in 1569. Crowning it all was a *flèche* of oak supporting an iron cross.

Although now able to boast of being the highest cathedral in the world, it soon became clear that the structure was unstable, and more bays were added to the nave in an effort to support the massive weight from the western part of the tower. But even this device was inadequate and in 1573, just three days after the masons began reinforcing the supports, the tower and spire collapsed.

The choir was shored up immediately, but funds were low and it had been proved that architectural plans could not be successfully executed without due attention being paid to structural principles and types of building material; Beauvais' attractive but inappropriate chalk was simply unworkable.

Glorious remains

Despite its missing parts, Beauvais is glorious. The south and north ends of the transepts, added in the 16th century in the Flamboyant style, have great rose windows with fantastically delicate tracery, and the flying buttresses, built to equalise the thrust of the towering nave, stand sentinel around the cathedral, casting strange shadows over the tall, slender pointed arches of the windows of the apse.

Inside, clustered columns almost disappear as they taper high up towards the roof. The triforium, although relatively small, is exquisitely carved, while above it is the glorious clerestory, its massive windows allowing light to pour down into the cathedral. The glass is pale-coloured or clear, achieving that marvellous interplay of stone and light for which Gothic architects strove, every carving and facet of cut stone illuminated naturally by sunlight.

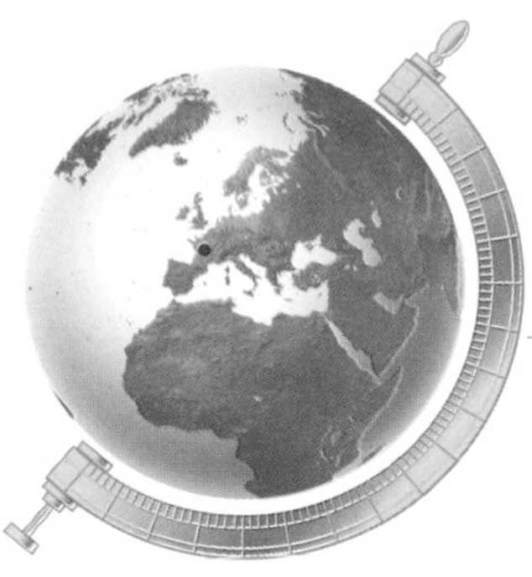

FRANCE

BOURGES CATHEDRAL

St Etienne's Cathedral has one of the most magnificent interiors in the world

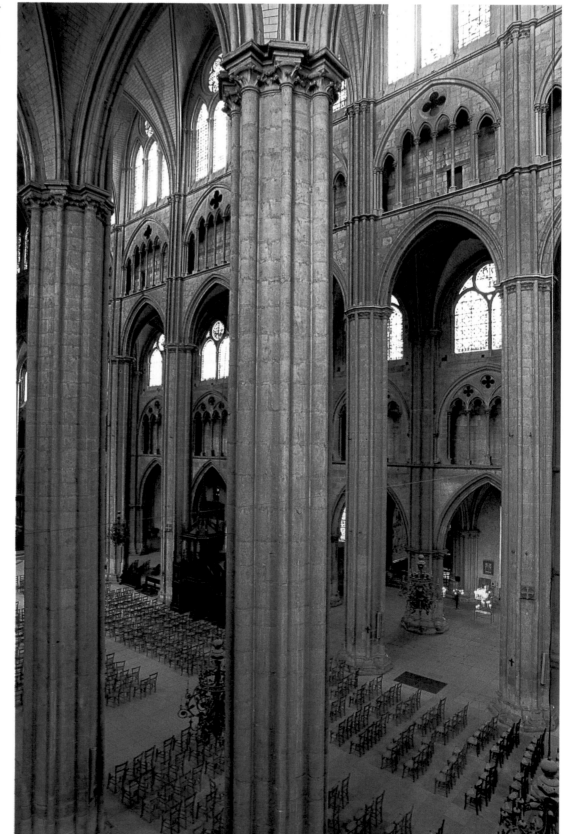

RIGHT: Looking down on the nave from the organ tribune gallery. The cathedral has four side aisles in place of transepts; this arrangement of double aisles in different heights is unique in France, and resembles the style of Milan Cathedral.

THE DUKE OF BERRY

One of the great benefactors of Bourges was Jean le Bon, Duc de Berry, or Berri (1340–1416), the third son of John II of France. A wealthy patron of the arts, he provided funds for much of the work on the west front and the stained glass, which some art historians claim is comparable to that of Chartres (see page 22). The duke built himself a spacious private chapel in the crypt, along with a handsome tomb in which he was later buried.

St Etienne's Cathedral has been subject to ferocious attacks at various stages of its 800-year history; the Huguenots vandalised it in the 16th century, in 1760 the clergy removed some of the 13th-century stained glass from the choir, and the French Revolution was responsible for the destruction and theft of some of its splendid furnishings. Yet, despite all this, the cathedral dominating the little town of Bourges has survived well and offers the visitor a wealth of interest, from the breathtaking size of the nave and the shadowy vastness of the crypt to the astonishing stained glass set in windows endowed with exquisite tracery.

An unusual plan

There has been a church on the site of Bourges Cathedral since the 3rd century, although work on the present cathedral did not start until around 1195. The Gothic work was carried out in three phases: the first (1195–1214) saw the completion of the huge crypt (the largest in the world and almost like a lower church in its own right), the choir and the ambulatory; the second commenced in 1225 and saw completion of the aisles, nave and façade, finishing around 1255; and the third, which began at the end of the 13th century, involved strengthening the nave piers and building the towers. In the 15th and 16th centuries the spaces between the buttresses were filled with little chapels.

The exterior of Bourges is unusual in several respects. First, the superb façade has five portals rather than the three seen in other Ile de France Gothic cathedrals. These handsome, recessed doors are topped by pointed arches pierced by traceried round windows. Over the central portal is a lovely 14th-century wheel-window – a round opening with ribs radiating outwards like a bicycle wheel. The façade is dominated by its two towers, but the northern one collapsed in 1506 and was rebuilt so that the two are no longer symmetrical. The southern one, too, proved to be unstable, and the huge buttresses that support it were added in the 14th century.

The body of the cathedral is also unusual as there are no transepts and the double aisles continue right round the nave into the choir and ambulatory. The aisles have an arcade, triforium and clerestory, and the arcade of the nave reaches the clerestory level of the aisles. The nave, 123 feet (37m) tall, is long and powerful with sturdy pillars that are nonetheless elegant. Light floods into the cathedral on three planes – from the windows in the outer aisle, the great windows of the nave clerestory, and from the aisle clerestory. From inside, the impression is one of a pyramid, the climax of the structure being the soaring nave clerestory.

ABOVE: The exterior of the cathedral presents a complex pattern of turrets and flying buttresses, here viewed from the south-east. The north tower was known as the 'Butter Tower', having been built with funds donated by citizens in return for being allowed to consume butter and milk during Lent.

The stained glass

Huguenots, clergy and Revolutionaries have done their worst, yet Bourges still proudly displays some of the finest stained glass in the world. Gothic architects wanted their cathedrals flooded with light, so they built massive windows which glass-makers were then free to use to edify the illiterate congregation, telling stories from the Bible, describing scenes from hell, or extolling various virtues with pictures in vivid colours.

One of the finest examples of stained glass at Bourges is the medallion from the window of the Prodigal Son (about 1215–20). The panels show the father dividing his goods between his two sons; the Prodigal leaving home; and the Prodigal encountering a prostitute. In the centre, the elder son is shown patiently ploughing the fields.

The oldest glass, dating from the 13th century, is in the choir and ambulatory. From this it is possible to trace the progression of the art right through to the 17th century. The 15th-century glass in the crypt and some of the chapels is especially fine.

BELOW: The brilliantly coloured stained glass windows were intended to provide moral teaching for the people. The 'reds of Bourges' are considered the equal of the famous 'blues of Chartres'.

France

Chartres Cathedral

Often deemed the most beautiful cathedral in France, Notre-Dame in Chartres is famous for its glass

ABOVE: Most of the stained glass windows date from the 13th century; the three west lancet windows are older, having survived the fire of 1194. The rose window is remarkable for its size, being almost 30 feet (9m) in diameter.

RIGHT: The south tower of Chartres Cathedral is the tallest Romanesque steeple in existence.

Chartres is a cathedral that inspires superlatives, and there are few architectural historians who have not waxed lyrical about its soaring aisles and delicate carving. These eulogies are richly deserved, for Chartres is truly one of the greatest of all French Gothic cathedrals. From a distance it seems to hover in mid-air above waving fields of corn, and it is only when the visitor draws closer that the city comes into view, clustering around the hill on which the cathedral stands. Its two contrasting spires – one, a 349-foot (105m) plain pyramid dating from the 1140s, and the other a 377-foot (113m) tall early 16th-century Flamboyant spire on top of an older tower – soar upwards over the pale green roof, while all around the outside are complex flying buttresses.

Risen from the ashes

The existing cathedral at Chartres is another of the French Gothic masterpieces built because fire had destroyed its predecessors. After the first cathedral of any great substance burnt down in 1020 (prior to this, other churches on the site had disappeared in smoke), a glorious new Romanesque basilica, which included a massive crypt, was built. However, having survived a fire in 1134 which destroyed much of the rest of the town, disaster struck yet again in 1194 when lightning created a blaze that left only the west towers, the façade between them and the crypt.

The people despaired when they believed that their sacred relic, the *Sancta Camisia* (see panel), had perished too. But three days later it was found unharmed in the treasury along with the priests who had taken it there for safety when the fire broke out and locked themselves in behind the iron trapdoors. The cardinal told the people that the survival of the relic was a sign from Mary herself and that another, even more magnificent, cathedral should be built in Chartres.

A Gothic jewel

Rebuilding, with the help of donations from all over France, began almost immediately and such was the enthusiasm for the project that the people of the city

voluntarily gathered to haul the stone needed from local quarries 5 miles (8km) away.

Work began first on the nave and by 1220 the main structure was complete, with the old crypt, along with the mid-12th-century Royal Portal which had also escaped the fire, incorporated into the new building. The plan is cruciform, with a 427-foot (128-m) long nave, and short transepts to the south and north. The east end is rounded with an ambulatory which has five semi-circular chapels radiating from it. On 24 October 1260 the cathedral was finally dedicated in the presence of King Louis IX and his family.

Even the elegance of the exterior does not prepare the visitor for the wonders that lie within. The spacious nave stands 121 feet (36m) high, and there is an unbroken view from the western end right along to the magnificent dome of the apse in the east. Clustered columns rise dramatically from plain bases to the high pointed arches of the ceiling, directing the eye to the massive clerestory windows in the apse.

Everywhere vivid colour splashes on to the floor from the superb stained glass windows. Dating from the early 13th century, the glass largely escaped harm during the religious wars of the 16th century; it is said to constitute one of the most complete collections of medieval stained glass in the world, despite 'modernisation' in 1753 when some of it was removed by the clearly well-intentioned but misguided clergy.

On the doors and porches medieval carvings of statues holding swords, crosses, books and trade tools parade around the portals, their expressions as clear today as when first carved 700 years ago.

However, in 1853 a screen given by Louis IX was demolished to make way for a pair of hideous wrought-iron gates and in the 1790s the Reign of Terror following the Revolution saw the destruction of many works of art.

SANCTA CAMISIA

In 876 Charlemagne's grandson, Charles the Bald, presented the cathedral at Chartres with a piece of cloth known as the *Sancta Camisia* (Sacred Tunic), said to have been the robe Mary wore when she gave birth to Jesus. This relic, which made Chartres one of the most popular places of pilgrimage in Europe, can be seen today in the cathedral treasury.

Not only was the *Sancta Camisia* a source of considerable income for the city, but the people believed it endowed them with special protection by the Virgin Mary. Perhaps it did: in 911, when Chartres was besieged by a Viking called Rollon, the bishop waved the relic from the city walls, whereupon Rollon promptly fled and was converted to Christianity.

LEFT: The medieval delight in intense colour was translated into the magnificent windows of Chartres, where stories of saints and biblical characters were depicted against a glorious blue that has never been surpassed.

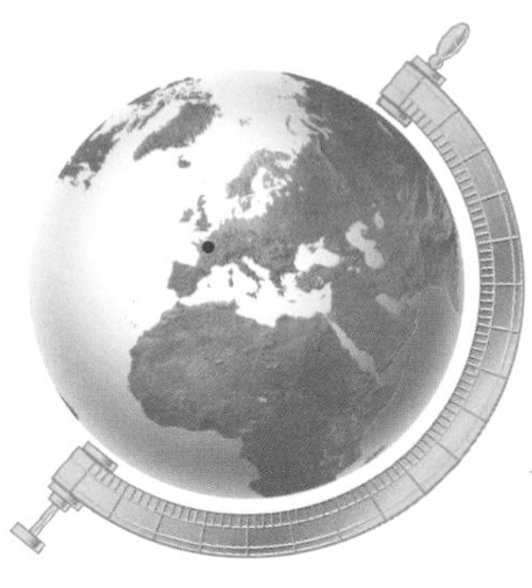

FRANCE

CATHEDRAL OF NOTRE-DAME

This magnificent early Gothic cathedral stands on an island in the centre of Paris

ABOVE: The rose window in the west front dates from about 1270 and is 42 feet (13m) in diameter. It depicts 80 Old Testament scenes.

The cathedrals of France have suffered horribly at the hands of various religious upheavals through the ages, but Notre-Dame, standing tall and proud on its island in the River Seine, has been more of a target than most. It provided a convenient symbol against which the French Revolution was directed in the late 18th century, and 19th-century restoration did more to compound the damage suffered at that time than to repair it. Under the direction of the archaeologist-architect Eugene Viollet-le-Duc (1814–79), many of the old and worn statues were removed and replaced with the now famous gargoyles.

Notre-Dame's position on the Ile de la Cité allows it to be admired from all angles: from the south and north the great rose windows of the transepts can be seen, beyond which rises the modern spire over the crossing; from the west the great façade looms up out of the cobbled square; while from the east, the lovely apse with its famous flying buttresses can be viewed. These buttresses have been irreverently compared to the oars sticking out from a Roman galley and to the legs of a giant spider, but their ungainliness cannot detract from the splendour of this beautiful early Gothic cathedral, its creamy-yellow stone reflected in the green waters of the Seine.

BISHOP MAURICE-DE-SULLY

The driving force behind the founding of the great cathedral of Paris was the charismatic Maurice-de-Sully. Probably born around 1120, he was the son of a peasant family who lived near Sully on the River Loire. Maurice came to Paris in about 1137 to study at the fledgling university before entering the Church. He earned a reputation for his sermons and, after becoming bishop in 1160, found himself in a position to mobilise funds with which to begin work on a new cathedral. Other churches on the Ile de la Cité were demolished in readiness, and Pope Alexander III came to lay the first stone in 1163.

THE BEGINNINGS

Bishop Maurice-de-Sully (see panel) had the foundation stone of Notre-Dame laid in 1163, after which building progressed rapidly. Archaeological excavations in the 19th century revealed foundations that were 30 feet (9m) deep: the architect (his name is not known) obviously intended that his cathedral was to be tall, like the cathedrals to the north. Within 20 years the choir

was sufficiently complete to be consecrated. The nave was built next, between 1180 and 1200, followed by the west façade and the two towers. In the mid-1200s the transepts were extended and two huge rose windows were added to each, one above the other, over handsome porches.

By the early 1400s work had begun on the eastern end of the cathedral, including the magnificent flying buttresses, but the radiating chapels, including the triple chapel at the chancel head, were added later.

Unlike the airy Gothic constructions at Amiens and Beauvais (see pages 16 and 18), the interior of Notre-Dame is rather sombre. Although the nave stands 100 feet (30m) tall and the clerestory windows are large, the sloping roofs over the aisles decrease the amount of light allowed in through their windows and parts of the nave are always swathed in mysterious shadow.

The ambulatory, dating from the earlier phase of building, is lovely, with simple cylindrical pillars supporting plain brick vaults. Like the nave, it is unevenly lit, bright shafts of light from the lancet windows contrasting with dark recesses.

The west front

The cathedral's west front is an impressive sight with its three great recessed portals standing below the rose window and its two sturdy towers. History reveals that at the time of its design King Philip Augustus of France had led a campaign against Richard the Lionheart of England and captured one of his castles and the façade, with its aura of strength and dominance, is said to be a symbol of this French victory. Below the great rose window is the Gallery of the Kings of Israel; all 28 figures are replicas as the originals were pulled down and smashed during the Revolution, because they were thought to be kings of France. Viollet-le-Duc's famous gargoyles, added in the 1850s and 1860s and said to represent the sins of man, peer down unpleasantly from unexpected places.

BELOW: The cathedral has been likened to a ship, moored to either bank of the Seine by the many bridges. The Ile de la Cité is the oldest inhabited part of the city and has been a centre of church and state affairs throughout its history. The delicate 'flèche' soars 300 feet (91m), flanked by the western towers.

SPIRE
AMBULATORY
LANCET WINDOWS IN TWIN TOWERS
FLYING BUTTRESSES
VAULTING
WESTERN FACADE
EASTERN APSE
ROSE WINDOW
RADIATING CHAPELS
ROSE WINDOW GALLERY
KINGS GALLERY
ROSE WINDOW
PORTALS
CROSSING
TRANSEPTS

REIMS CATHEDRAL

Glorious Notre-Dame in Reims was the coronation cathedral of medieval French kings

BELOW: The ornate west façade, by Bernard de Soissons, features recessed portals carved with over 500 statues. Above the rose window, 40 feet (12m) in diameter, is a gallery of tabernacled statues of French kings. The western towers soar to a height of 267 feet (80m).

The first church on the site was built in the late 5th century and recent archaeological excavations have revealed traces of this ancient building in the nave of the present cathedral, just east of the crossing. It was here that Clovis, King of the Franks, was baptised in 496 on Christmas Eve and thus the tradition of consecrating kings of France at Reims began.

Taking pride of place in the treasury today is the 12th-century gold coronation chalice, adorned with jewels, used for the communion of the kings of France at their coronation. An inscription on the base warns against its theft.

A new cathedral was started in 817 and underwent various stages of demolition and rebuilding until a fateful fire destroyed it, along with most of the city, in 1210. Building on a second new cathedral started on the anniversary of the fire in the following year, but progress was slow and although the choir was finished by the early 1240s, thereafter money began to run low and the nave and splendid west front were not completed until 1311.

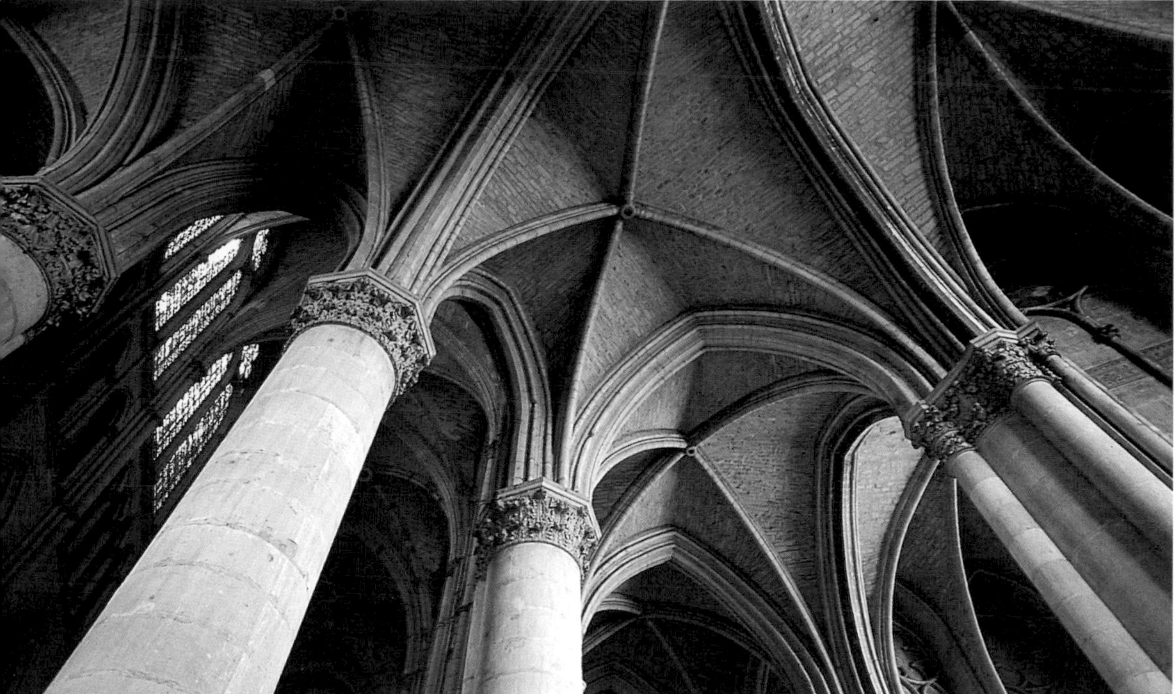

LEFT: The intersecting vault reaches a height of 137 feet (42m) above the cathedral floor, its weight transmitted by arches to piers which in turn are balanced by pinnacles and statues. Seen here are the ambulatory vaults, with foliage designs carved on the pillar capitals.

Thereafter the pace of work continued to be slow, with the northern tower not being totally finished until 1427.

Destruction and restoration

Besides the vandalism of the Huguenots in the 16th century and the ravages of the Revolutionaries in the 1790s (the citizens attempted to protect their cathedral, but were no match for sizeable gangs of heavily armed soldiers), Reims had to endure attacks from German shells and mortars during World War I. It was estimated that this noble Gothic cathedral took about 300 direct hits, and reports made as late as 1923 describe the piles of debris and smashed treasures that littered its floors, and the tangle of wreckage that formed its walls.

Since then, Reims has been subject to the very best of attention by French master craftsmen who have been working to restore it to its former glory. The delicate stonework on the splendid west front has been carefully repaired, so that now the statues and tracery stand out crisp and clear, a marked contrast to the worn and shattered face presented in the 1920s. However, only fragments of the stained glass remain in the choir and the north aisle.

Reims measures 453 feet (138m) from east to west and its ceiling rises to 125 feet (38m) above the pavement. The transepts are small, the accent being on the length of the nave and choir and their aisles, and the eastern end is encircled by an ambulatory with radiating chapels. Outside is a splendid battery of delicate flying buttresses.

Light floods into the lofty interior through the great windows of the nave clerestory and through the aisle windows, as well as through those in the apse and the circular windows in the western wall, giving the cathedral a light and airy atmosphere.

A gallery of saints

The west front is truly splendid. Three deeply recessed portals with pointed arches reach up to a massive central rose window, above which is a gallery of statues surmounted by two open-work towers creating an impression simultaneously powerful and delicate.

The façade's carved figures are its crowning glory. In all, there are about 2,200 statues of bishops, kings, knights, saints, demons and craftsmen. Most were executed between 1241 and 1290, although those on the north transept portals appear to be earlier. Three separate workshops were involved in the carving and as a result the sculptures display some intriguing variety. Widely acclaimed, Reims' statues were copied in Italy, France and Spain.

The façade also features friezes depicting scenes from Jesus' life on Earth. Perhaps the best known is the smiling angel that appears in the scene showing *The Annunciation*. Another smiling angel appears in a panel called *The Smile of Reims*. Joseph, in *The Visitation*, has a remarkably sly expression on his face; it is said to be representative of a French medieval peasant.

Joan of Arc

As the coronation cathedral of French kings, Reims has a special place in history. It was here, in 1429, that Joan of Arc (*c*1412–31), the Maid of Orleans, witnessed the anointing of the Dauphin as Charles VII, King of France, after having led the French troops to victory against the English during the Hundred Years' War. The story goes that at the age of 13 she heard the voices of saints telling her to rescue France from English domination.

BELOW: The figures of Reims are carved in a naturalistic style, with individual facial expressions.

FRANCE

STRASBOURG CATHEDRAL

Notre-Dame is a fascinating cathedral displaying French and German influences

FRANCE'S GLORIOUS GOTHIC

France is hailed as having many of the finest Gothic cathedrals in existence and for influencing the style of cathedrals across Europe. The man responsible for introducing Gothic architecture into France was Abbot Suger who, in 1135, started rebuilding the Abbey of St Denis, Paris, in a new and spectacular style (see page 24). Other cathedral builders followed suit, producing Notre-Dame in Paris, Laon and Sens. Later came the best known – Amiens, Beauvais, Bourges, Chartres and Reims.

But France also boasts many other Gothic cathedrals, each one a gem of architectural achievement in its own right. These include Rouen and Coutances in Normandy; Auxerre, Strasbourg and Troyes in the north and east; Albi and Narbonne in the south; and Tours in the west.

RIGHT: The shadowy nave and open triforium, seen from above the west doorway, showing the great rose window by Erwin von Steinbach (c1280). The diameter of the window is 45 feet (14m).

Positioned on the border between France and Germany, Strasbourg (Strassburg) has been passed back and forth between the two nations for centuries. It was made a free imperial city in the 13th century but was ceded to France in 1697 after the War of the League of Augsburg (1689–97) between Louis XIV of France and the Grand Alliance (the Holy Roman Empire, Spain, Sweden, several German states, England, and Holland). The city was taken back into German hands during the Franco-Prussian War in 1871, then finally returned to France after World War I.

A DUAL HERITAGE

Strasbourg's dual inheritance is reflected in its splendid cathedral which, although indisputably

French Gothic, has a tower bearing a strong resemblance to those of Ulm and Cologne in Germany (see pages 90 and 92). Like Notre-Dame in Paris (see page 24), Strasbourg Cathedral stands on an island, formed by a division of the River Ill. Also like its Paris counterpart, its position allows the cathedral to be admired from all sides. It is built of a pinkish-red sandstone known locally as *grès de Vosges*. Refacing of the stone, however, has given it an artificially smooth appearance.

From the exterior, the dominant features of Strasbourg Cathedral are its intriguing tower and spire. The tower has supports on its upper stages that resemble great ladders, while the spire has been said to have the appearance of a massive stone pinecone. Both of these were the work of German architects and, with the exception of Rouen, are the tallest in France. The façade and tower bases were begun by Erwin von Steinbach after 1284. Jean Gerlach (1341–71) continued the towers up to the platform, and Michel de Freiburg designed the belfry above the rose window in the 1380s. By 1419 the steeple was completed to the octagonal stage by Ulrich von Ensingen, and in 1439 Johann Hültz of Cologne had completed the spire. In Germany, Strasbourg's spire is only exceeded in height by those of Ulm and Cologne.

ABOVE: *The single spire above the west front is reminiscent of Freiburg im Breisgau. The façade features statues of The Wise and Foolish Virgins, as well as a double gable with four lion cubs – a copy of the original which is now housed in the nearby museum.*

Romanesque and Gothic

The first part of the cathedral to be built was the crypt, dating from the early 12th century and incorporating the only surviving part of an earlier church on the site. Work on the choir and transepts began in the mid-12th century, but building of the nave did not start until the 13th century. Two years after the nave was finished in 1275 work began on the west front which continued until 1339. The nave is Gothic at its most splendid, with soaring piers, an elegantly pointed vault and great windows that allow light to flood in from the clerestory and the aisles. By comparison, the later Romanesque choir and transepts are plainer.

Strasbourg's stained glass is one of its finest treasures, the rose-red sandstone with which the cathedral is built enhancing the rich sheets of vivid reds, blues, greens and yellows. The best glass can be found in the south aisle of the nave and in the two clerestories. The northern clerestory in particular is worth studying, with its procession of female saints led by the Virgin Mary, and the southern clerestory opposite displays an army of popes, deacons and bishops. The two Romanesque windows in the south transept depict scenes from the Childhood of Christ, his Ministry and Passion, and the Descent into Hell, followed by images of the Coming of the Holy Spirit and the fate of the damned at the Last Judgement.

The statues

The sculptures, displaying a strong French influence, were inspired by the great cathedrals of northern France – Reims, Chartres and Amiens. Wars and the crumbling nature of the sandstone have led to many of Strasbourg's statues being removed to be exhibited in the nearby museum. While these do not, perhaps, attain the same standard of artistic merit of those in the northern French cathedrals, the variety of quality and style make them a fascinating collection.

Inside the cathedral the most famous statues are *Vices and Virtues* and *The Wise and Foolish Virgins*, slender figures full of expression. Near the south portal is a carving, blindfolded and holding a broken staff, which represents the Synagogue, with the Church beside it holding a cross and chalice up in the air.

BELOW: *A detail of the cathedral's array of vivid stained glass windows.*

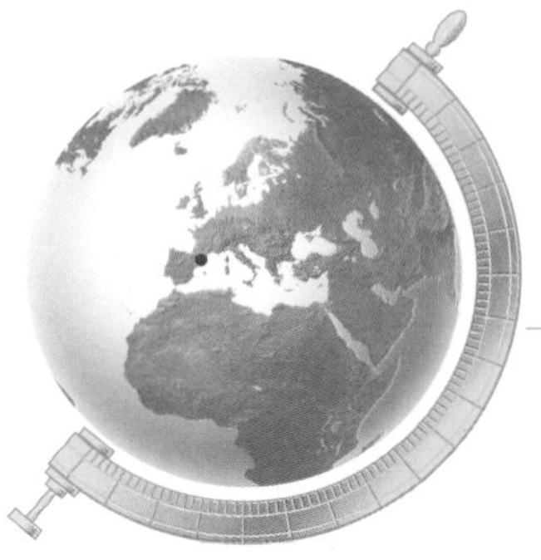

BARCELONA CATHEDRAL

The lacy spires of the Cathedral of St Eulàlia rise proudly over the city's lively Gothic Quarter

THE CATHEDRAL CLOISTER

The St Eulàlia Portal lies to one side of the busy Plaza Garringa y Bachs, a little square with a monument to those who died during the Napoleonic Wars. Entering through the Portal is like stepping into a different world: the cloister is an elegant quadrangle of delicately pointed arches surrounding a lush garden filled with gently swaying palms and powerfully scented magnolia trees, all enclosed by wrought-iron railings dating from the 15th century. Geese occasionally visit the garden, and the comforting babble of water from the fountains adds to a somewhat other-worldly atmosphere.

BELOW: Light streams in through the 15th-century glass windows and slender piers of the clerestory.

The glorious west front of Barcelona Cathedral, with its lofty Gothic arches and three soaring spires, was a long time in the making. Work started at the end of the 12th century, but it was not until the 19th century that the necessary funds became available with which to complete the handsome façade of the Cathedral of St Eulàlia.

The cathedral stands in the section of Barcelona known as the Gothic Quarter (Barrio Gótico) on the grandly named Taber Hill, really little more than a mound, but which affords some relief to what is otherwise a flat city. An ancient island in the urban metropolis, the Gothic Quarter is characterised by impossibly narrow streets, grand medieval residences and cramped plazas alive with activity, noise and colour.

THE MEDIEVAL CATHEDRAL

Work started on 1 May 1298 under the patronage of Jaime II, King of Aragon from 1291 until his death in 1327. The basic building of the cathedral took about 150 years, although the plans for three open-work spires were not completed.

The main part of the cathedral comprises a central nave with an aisle on either side of roughly the same height. Barcelona's building tradition was unusual in that its churches tended to be the hall type, well-suited to the large congregations favoured by the influential friars of Catalonia. At the eastern end of the nave is a fine apse with an ambulatory underneath an octagonal dome. The transepts are adorned with small, but handsome, 14th- and 15th-century towers.

The vast hall-like interior has a raised altar at the eastern end, under which is the crypt of St Eulàlia. The tomb of the saint is an exquisite piece of carving, executed in alabaster by a sculptor who was a disciple of the great 14th-century Italian artist Giovanni Pisano. Above the altar is the dome, with its notable multicoloured key-stones. It is said that the dome stands over one of Catalonia's three 'magnetic points'.

CHAPELS AND TREASURES

As at Albi in France (see page 14), there is a continuous line of chapels right around the inside of the cathedral. One of the most outstanding is the Chapel of the Transfiguration, designed by Bernat Martorell and built in 1447. Dedicated to St Salvador, it is regarded by many art historians as a masterpiece with its perfectly proportioned arches and superb carvings. Similarly, the lovely Capello del Santo Cristo de Lepanto (once the chapter house), built between 1405 and 1454, is said to be one of the finest examples of Gothic art – high praise indeed, situated as it is in a city bursting with superb Gothic architecture.

There are many other noteworthy features in this splendid cathedral, including the choir pews and benches executed by Pere Sanglada and Maciá Bonafé in the 1390s. On the north side of the cathedral is St Ivo's Portal, one of the earliest parts of the cathedral where the skill of the medieval masons can be seen in its exquisite carvings.

Many of the cathedral's finest treasures are displayed in the Museu de la Catedral, a museum housed within the cathedral which includes a splendid collection of paintings and sculptures spanning several centuries.

Building begins anew

In the 19th century a Barcelonan industrialist offered to finance the completion of the unfinished west front. It was designed by the architects Mestres Fontseré, based on a drawing dating from the 15th century by a master mason named Mestre Carlí. Building work included the handsome spires, the central one of which was added to the 15th-century lantern. Although the benefactor died before the work was finished, his son agreed to continue financing the venture and paid for the dome over the apse, which was finally completed in 1913.

BELOW: The striking west façade was completed relatively recently, in the 19th century; the cathedral is situated near the remains of the Roman city walls.

SPAIN

BURGOS CATHEDRAL

Santa María's Cathedral in Burgos is the burial place of El Cid and his wife

A glorious array of spires and pinnacles thrusting upward from the Gothic cathedral dominates the skyline of Burgos, the old capital of the kings of Castile. Burgos is a hilly city, and the cathedral is surrounded by a clutter of houses with tiled roofs that give way to more modern buildings on the outskirts, and then to the rolling fields and blue-grey hills in the distance.

Spain's first great Gothic cathedral

During the 13th century Spain underwent the process of 're-conquest', whereby lands were wrested from the Moors who had invaded them in the 8th century. Gradually, the autonomous provinces of Spain – Navarre, Castile and Aragon – began to recapture lost cities and, as they did so, they founded cathedrals as a statement of defiance and victory over the defeated Muslims.

The first of these great monoliths to Spanish Christian supremacy was Burgos, which was started around 1221. No less a person than the King of Castile himself, Ferdinand III (1217–52), ordered and paid for the early stages of this magnificent cathedral. Toledo (see page 42) and Palma de Mallorca were founded in the same decade.

The lower parts of the nave, transepts and a simple chapel with an ambulatory were built first, and records show that the first services were held there in the 1230s. By 1260 the main body of the cathedral had been completed, although work on the west front and the two towers was still at an early stage.

Three generations of masons

In the 15th century a German mason, one Hans of Köln (Cologne), was employed to finish the upper parts of the towers. After Hans' death, his son Simón began working on the fabulous Constable's Chapel at the eastern end of the cathedral, built for the constable of Castile, Pedro Hernández de Velasco, who is buried there. Few visitors will fail to be impressed by the delicacy of the stone carvings in this extraordinary chapel: figures of Christ, angels and the saints peer down from their niches high above, while coats of arms, flowers and geometric designs decorate the walls.

In the 16th century Simón's son Francisco built the lantern tower that stands astride the aisle crossing. Francisco took the Decorated style started by his grandfather to new heights, and his lantern is an intricate latticework of 12 pinnacles. With the western towers, the lantern and the spires of the Constable Chapel, Burgos presents a riot of Gothic stonework that is one of Spain's finest architectural achievements.

If the exterior of Burgos inspires awe, the interior equals it in craftsmanship and beauty. Some of the finest pieces are by the Renaissance sculptor Diego de Siloé and include the T-shaped Golden Staircase (Éscalera Dorada) in the north transept, sculpted in creamy-white marble with gilded metal banisters, and the retable behind the altar in the Constable Chapel. De Vigarni and de Vallejo, both highly respected artists in their time, contributed a wealth of Renaissance sculpture.

The cloisters

No visit to this splendid Gothic cathedral is complete without a stroll around the lovely late medieval cloister. Entrance is through a door on the south transept, richly decorated with 14th-century statues of King David, Isaiah the Prophet and the Virgin Mary. The cloister is two-storeyed and has strong, elegant pillars rising up to arches with lavish tracery. From their richly carved corbels the statues of King Alfonso X and Violente of Aragon gaze down.

El Cid

El Cid, or Roderigo Diáz de Vivar, was born in Burgos around 1040. He began his military career in full in about 1065, fighting for Alfonso, until the king exiled him in 1079 because he was accused of stealing part of the booty looted after a battle with Abdullah, King of Granada.

El Cid's military prowess became legendary, and he was eventually restored to royal favour. His greatest achievement was the capture of Valencia from the Moors in 1094, after which he was made Protector, and then ruler, of Valencia. He died in 1099, and was immortalised in a poem entitled *Cantar del mio Cid.*

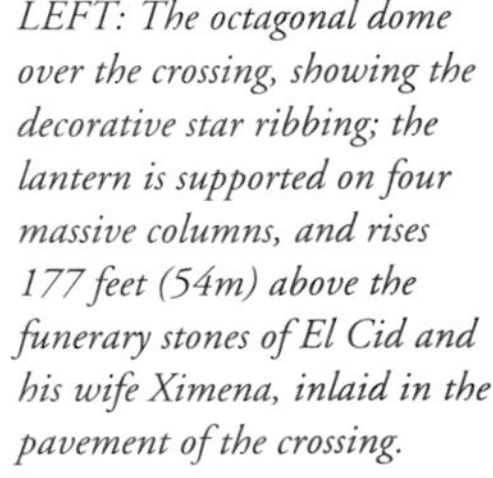

LEFT: The octagonal dome over the crossing, showing the decorative star ribbing; the lantern is supported on four massive columns, and rises 177 feet (54m) above the funerary stones of El Cid and his wife Ximena, inlaid in the pavement of the crossing.

FAR LEFT: The architecture of Burgos Cathedral reflects the French/German Flamboyant Gothic style, but has been tranformed with typically Spanish decorations. The pinnacled openwork spires are by Johan of Cologne.

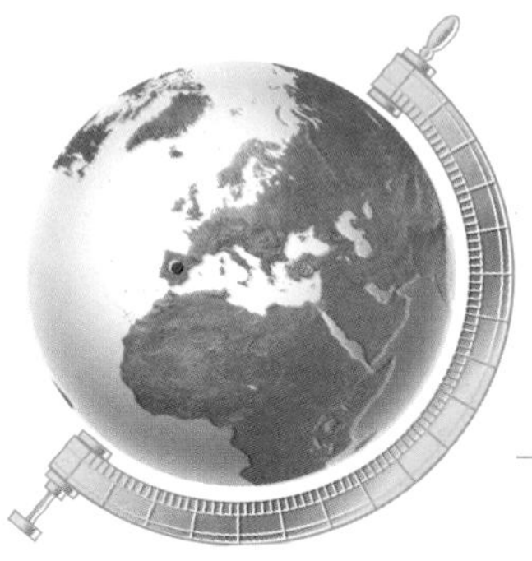

SPAIN

NEW CATHEDRAL, SALAMANCA

Two magnificent cathedrals stand side by side overlooking the River Tormes

BELOW: Although a new cathedral was built the old remained, its north transept having been replaced by a chapel of the New Cathedral. A passageway connects the two cathedrals.

Proudly displayed in the handsome New Cathedral in Salamanca is a bronze crucifix that was said to have been carried into battle by the legendary El Cid, the Spanish warrior who fought in many a war on the Iberian Peninsula (see page 35). The crucifix found its way here because El Cid gave it to his confessor, Bishop Jerónimo, who in turn gave it to the Old Cathedral which he founded in the 12th century. Four centuries later, Bishop Jerónimo's Romanesque Catedral Santa Maria de la Sede was superseded by a Gothic cathedral, and El Cid's crucifix was transferred from one to the other. Fortunately, Salamanca was blessed with a population who wanted to preserve the Old Cathedral and today the city boasts two cathedrals: the Old Cathedral (Catedral Vieja), and the New Cathedral (Catedral Nueva). They stand side by side and from a distance look like a single building, throwing up a forest of spires and turrets. The best view of them is from the far bank of the wide, slow-moving River Tormes where the cathedrals can be seen dominating the cluster of tiled-roofed buildings that climb the hillside.

A NEW CATHEDRAL

In 1512 Bishop de Bobadilla invited leading Spanish architects to submit plans for his new cathedral. Many designs were provided for the bishop's perusal, but the architect who finally won approval was one Juan Gil de Hontañón. Hontañón worked on Salamanca Cathedral until he died, at which point his son, Roderigo, took over. It was not unusual for sons to continue work started by their fathers: a similar situation occurred during the building of Burgos Cathedral (see page 34).

Construction of the New Cathedral started in 1513 and continued at least until the middle of the 18th century. Its outstanding feature is the massive south-west tower, rising 360 feet (110m) above the ground. The tower was faced with a protective sheath of stone after a devastating earthquake in Lisbon in 1755 demonstrated the potential fragility of the region's ancient structures. One of the earliest parts of the New Cathedral, it is a simple square, plain at the bottom and ornamented higher up. The uppermost part has corner pinnacles and round-headed arcades topped with an intricately carved dome and stone lantern. Designed by Roderigo de Hontañón, it bears a strong resemblance to the 15th-century tower that can be seen at Toledo Cathedral (see page 42).

ABOVE: This ornately carved screen displays the Churrigueresque style of some parts of the cathedral, which was popular in the 18th century; the wide range of styles, which also include 16th-century plateresque, is an indication of the long period of building.

THE FABULOUS WEST FRONT

The superbly carved west front, like the tower, is constructed of a locally quarried pale yellow-grey stone that glows a deep rose-pink at sunset. Following a richly ornamented style known as plateresque (said to be similar to the surface decoration employed by silversmiths, *platerías*), of which Salamanca city has many other equally fine examples, the edifice is a dazzling display of statues, carved heads and heraldic symbols. Among the best of the carvings are those that decorate the north portal, or the Door of the Palms, which takes its name from the frieze depicting Christ's triumphal entry into Jerusalem the week before his crucifixion. Twin Renaissance towers flank the west front, the central crossing being marked by a handsome cupola that was added in the 1730s.

NAVE AND CHOIR

The immense nave of the New Cathedral is lined with a decorative balustrade which stands on delicately patterned pillars; much lower are the galleried aisles. There are also galleries around the transepts, which are about 160 feet (49m) wide.

The choir was built at the eastern end of the nave between 1725 and 1733 and, like the cupola, was designed by the talented Churriguera brothers, a trio of architects – Don José, Alberto and Joaquín – born in Salamanca. Their extravagant, distinctive style has come to be known as Churrigueresque.

OLD CATHEDRAL, SALAMANCA

Still impressive, even though it has been superseded by the larger, grander New Cathedral, is the Old Cathedral at Salamanca, dedicated to Santa Maria de la Sede. Its most outstanding feature is its double-tiered Romanesque central lantern, built using a specialised form of pedentive first evolved in the Basilica at Santa Sophia in Istanbul. Like its sister cathedrals at Zamora and Toro, the dome from inside comprises carved ribs radiating from the centre, below which are rows of attractive round-headed windows.

The nave is almost perfectly symmetrical, with rows of Romanesque pillars down each side; it even surpasses that of Santiago de Compostela (see page 38), which is noted for the symmetry of its nave. The lovely 15th-century retable in the apse, one of the finest examples of early Renaissance work in the country, is well worth seeing.

SANTIAGO DE COMPOSTELA CATHEDRAL

The Cathedral of St James the Great was a major medieval pilgrimage site

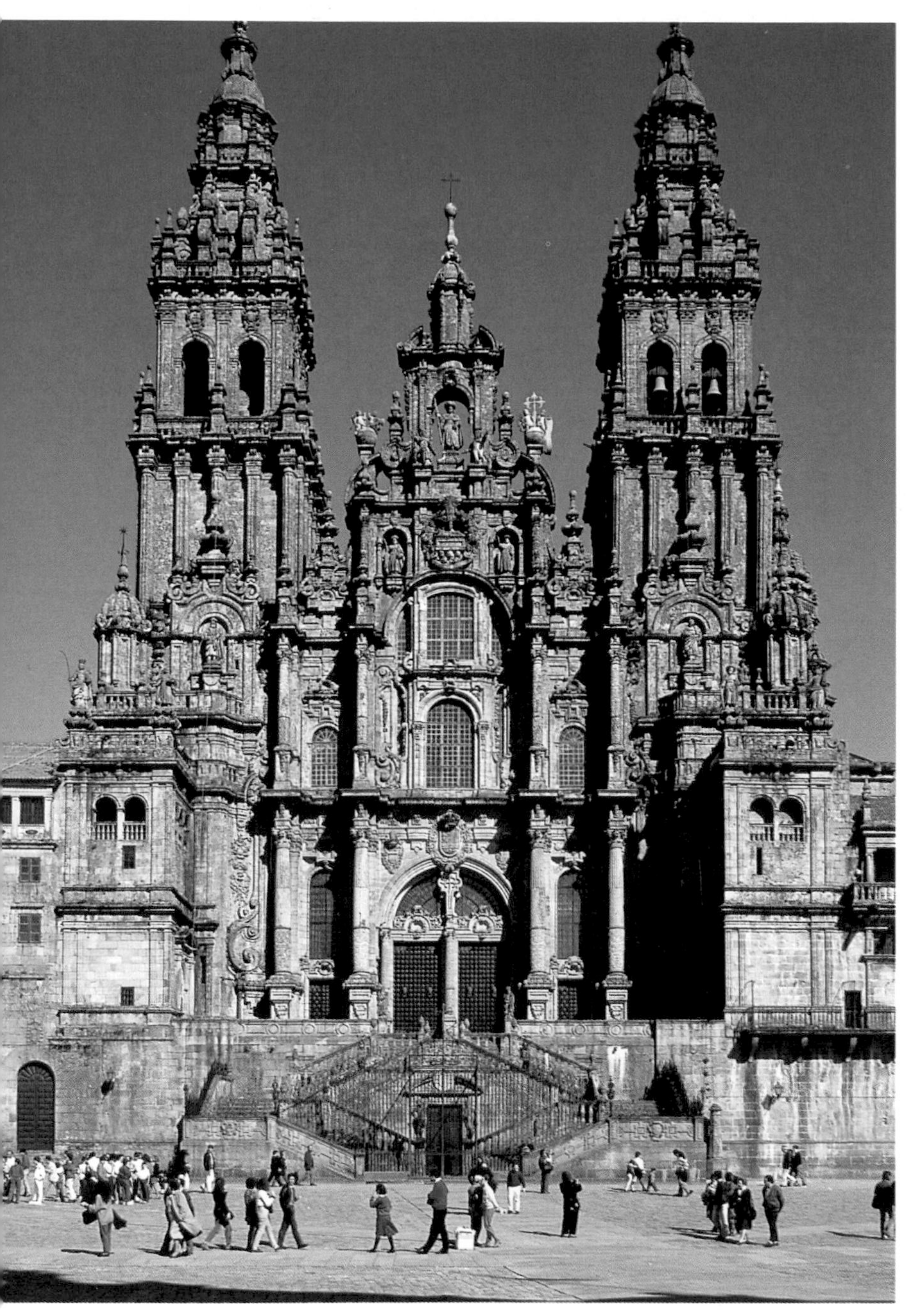

ABOVE: The cathedral is unique in Spain in that it can be seen from plazas on all sides. It was here that John of Gaunt had himself crowned King of Castile and León in 1386, after his invasion of Galicia.

Few sacred Christian sites have attracted as many pilgrims as the Romanesque cathedral at Santiago de Compostela. In medieval times it was said to be second only to Rome and thousands upon thousands of people made their way to the shrine of the Apostle St James (Santiago) the Great through France and across the northern reaches of Spain. A pilgrimage was a hazardous undertaking in medieval times: there were robbers on the roads, unscrupulous landlords overcharged for poor food and hire of a ragged blanket for the night, pardoners and relic-sellers preyed upon the vulnerable, and there was always danger of disease or injury.

EARLY DAYS

St James, like his brother John, was a fisherman and among the first of Jesus' disciples. After the resurrection James travelled extensively to spread the news and was thought to have preached in Spain. He was beheaded by Herod Agrippa I in 44AD, and in 813 a stone coffin said to contain his bones was found by a Galician peasant near Compostela. A shrine was raised over the coffin and housed in a small cathedral which was finished in about 900. By the 1070s the flood of pilgrims had become so great that a bigger, better cathedral was needed and in 1078 work began on one, largely financed by the pilgrims themselves. Progress was then made quickly under an architect called Bernard, who may have been a monk from Cluny in France, and by 1211 the first stages of this fabulous Romanesque cathedral were complete.

A BAROQUE FAÇADE

However, in about 1667 it was decided that the cathedral was insufficiently fine to do justice to such an important site and, throughout the 17th and 18th centuries, the entire building was re-cased in a frenzy of baroque exuberance. Today the west front has a glorious façade of pinnacles, balustrades and carvings. The handsome belfry over the south transept dates from 1676 to 1680. First impressions of the façade are that it takes after the French Gothic, but the decoration on the middle section is very characteristic of the style of the Churrigueras, a Spanish family of architects who developed a form of baroque all of their own (see page 37).

Although the outside of the cathedral was treated to a facelift, the interior was, mercifully, left untouched and remains today much as it was in the

13th century. The building was designed with pilgrims in mind and the ambulatory around the apse, and the arrangement of transepts and aisles, provided a specific route for them to follow as they made their way towards the focal point of the cathedral – the shrine of St James.

Once through Mateo's lovely Portico de la Gloria (see panel), visitors enter the nave, with its barrel-vaulted ceiling some 72 feet (22m) above. The simple grandeur of the nave, a massive 11-bay corridor flanked by cross-vaulted side aisles, makes a stark contrast with the fussy flutter of the baroque façade. Unusually, there is no clerestory, which makes the inside of the cathedral rather dark, despite the large windows in the aisles and a little light filtering down from the 14th- and 15th-century octagonal lantern tower over the central crossing. Yet the gloom merely adds to the unique atmosphere of the cathedral – mysterious and ancient – where the feet of weary, exultant or penitential pilgrims have trodden for more than 1,000 years.

PORTICO DE LA GLORIA

It is often said that the best feature of Compostela's fabulous cathedral is the central porch that lies just behind the baroque façade. Erected between 1168 and 1188 by a Spanish bridge-builder called Master Mateo, it is one of the best examples of design and sculpture from the Romanesque period and the beautiful carvings, protected by the façade, are perfectly preserved, every detail as clear today as it was in the 12th century.

The largest carving is of St James, seated, while all around him are the other Apostles, several saints, and some of the Old Testament patriarchs, each one different from the next.

The tympanum has carvings of a veritable orchestra of heavenly beings holding a range of medieval instruments.

THE PUERTA DE LAS PLATERÍAS

Earlier still than the Portico de la Gloria is the early 12th-century south transept doorway which leads out on to a square where silversmiths (*platerías*) work even today. In 1117 the inhabitants of the town revolted and set fire to the cathedral, damaging the south transept. The Puerta de las Platerías was repaired using statues rescued from the flames and bits and pieces from other parts of the cathedral. The result is a somewhat irrational design, comprising figures of many different styles, scale and quality.

LEFT: The Portico de la Gloria is approached by a quadruple flight of steps dating from 1606, below which lies a 12th-century Romanesque crypt.

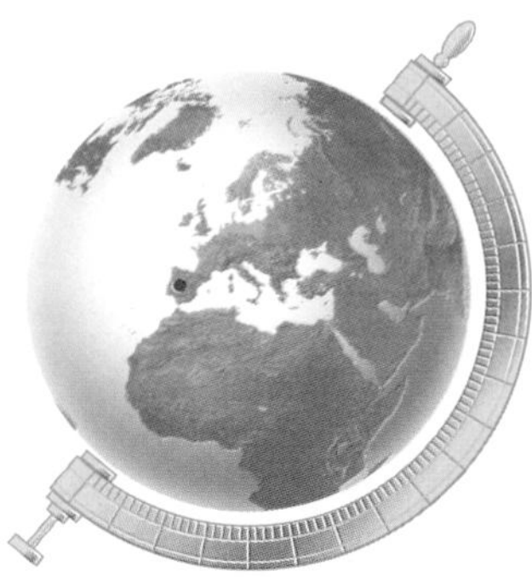

SPAIN

SEVILLE CATHEDRAL

Santa Maria de la Sede is the largest medieval cathedral in the world

ABOVE: The monument to Christopher Columbus, designed by Arturo Melida.

CHRISTOPHER COLUMBUS

In the south transept is an enormous monument to Christopher Columbus, built in 1899 to commemorate the occasion when the remains of the explorer were brought back from the West Indies.

Columbus, born in Italy in 1451, settled in Portugal after he was shipwrecked there in 1476. He believed he could reach the East by sailing westward and eventually convinced the King of Spain of this, who financed the voyage. He set sail with the *Nina, Pinta* and *Santa Maria* in 1492 and discovered the West Indies.

On his second and third voyages Columbus discovered Guadeloupe, Puerto Rico, Jamaica, Trinidad and mainland South America. He died in 1506 after his fourth voyage.

The sheer size of this massive 15th-century cathedral is breathtaking. It measures a staggering 430 feet (129m) from east to west, and 250 feet (75m) from north to south. The outside is dominated by the 12th-century minaret tower, the Giralda (see panel), left intact when the mosque that previously occupied the site was destroyed. Although the minaret, with its Renaissance belfry, stands a respectable 309 feet (93m) tall, the cathedral is more impressive for its length than its height. The skyline of the Cathedral of Santa Maria de la Sede is spireless, towerless and domeless.

THE MOSQUE AND THE CATHEDRAL

By the 8th century the Moors were firmly entrenched in the sun-soaked lands of Andalucia and were not expelled until late in the Spanish Reconquest. When they retreated, or became assimilated into the Christian culture that was sweeping through Iberia, the Moors left magnificent mosques behind them. The architects who designed the cathedral at Córdoba built their church inside the abandoned mosque, but those at Seville decided a completely new start was warranted and set about demolishing the mosque; all that was spared was the Giralda.

Building began in about 1402 and continued apace until 1506. The cathedral is an unusual shape – rectangular rather than cruciform – because the ground plan of the mosque was retained. At night, when the building is illuminated by pale yellow lights, it seems larger than ever, its great bulk casting shadows down across the flying buttresses and the many small chapels that virtually surround the nave. The intricate carvings, however, can only be fully appreciated by day when the sun blazes down on the exquisitely executed statues and filigree patterns that adorn the walls and doors.

THE MONUMENTAL NAVE

Few visitors will fail to be astounded at the sheer vastness of the great nave at Seville Cathedral. The notes from the meeting of the Church authorities and the architects in the early 1400s record that

their cathedral would be 'so good that there shall be none its equal', and in many ways their objective has been admirably achieved. Great clusters of pillars soar up to support the handsome vaulted ceiling some 125 feet (38m) above. The impression of height is further accentuated by the fact that these elegant stone columns seem far too slender to support the great weight of the roof.

Soft light floods into the cathedral through the stained-glass windows in the clerestory and through the fragile lantern. The lantern has been built three times: it collapsed in 1511, and again in the 1880s. The nave is flanked by double aisles, while many chapels can be found around the walls. The best known of these is the Capilla Real, or Royal Chapel, built between 1551 and 1575. It contains the tomb of King Ferdinand III of Castile (died 1252).

Other treasures include the paintings by Bartolomé Esteban Murillo and the Flemish artist Jakob Jordaens. The retable in the sanctuary, executed between 1482 and 1564, is one of the largest in Spain.

The Giralda

Built between 1184 and 1198, the Giralda is a sturdy tower 54 feet (16m) square with walls 8 feet (3m) thick at the base. Between 1560 and 1568 a Renaissance open belfry was added to the 12th-century minaret, capped with a revolving figure. This figure gave the Giralda its name, for the Spanish *girar* means 'to revolve'. The lower parts of the tower are typically Moorish, decorated with panels of intricate carvings flanking arched openings with balustrades. The upper parts rise in a series of ornate balconies.

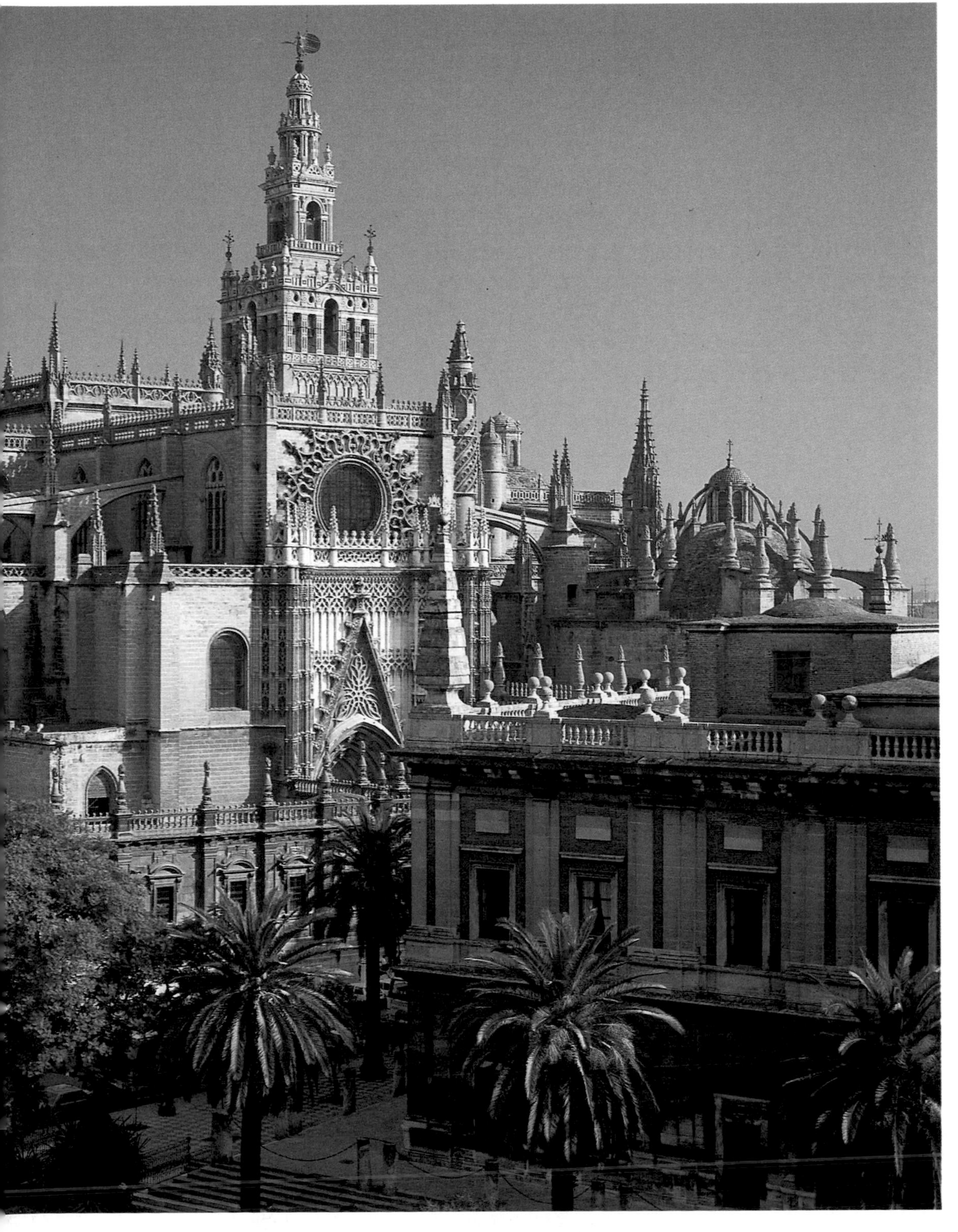

LEFT: The cathedral presents a complex pattern of pinnacles and buttresses surmounted by the 'Giralda' with its bronze figure of 'La Fé' (Faith). Seville Cathedral is the largest Gothic church in the world.

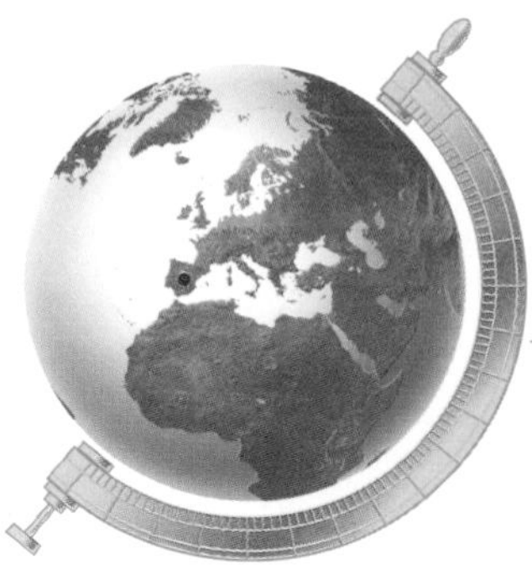

SPAIN

TOLEDO CATHEDRAL

Hailed as one of the finest of all Spanish cathedrals, La Catedral Primada houses a treasure-trove of art

EL TRANSPARENTE

Designed by Narciso Tomé in 1721, the astonishing marble sculpture in the Lady Chapel behind the main altar has stimulated some lively debates. Many art critics regard the clever interplay between the stone and the light that floods down from a specially constructed opening in the roof – El Transparente – as a work of genius; others dismiss it as an exercise in baroque vulgarity. A gang of fat cherubim are carved on the highest part of the tableau, while underneath is a scene from the Last Supper. Below is a sun, its rays picked out in gold, with all manner of celestial beings bathing in its light. At the bottom is a serene-looking figure of Mary and her Son.

RIGHT: The magnificent polychrome retable, with carvings in the Flamboyant style divided into five sections and depicting details of the life of Christ.

Seat of the Primate of Spain, La Basilica de Santa Maria de Toledo, or La Catedral Primada, is generally regarded as one of the most outstanding of all Spanish ecclesiastical buildings. It is the jewel in the crown of a settlement astride the River Tagus boasting so many buildings of architectural merit that the entire city has been declared a National Monument. Given that Toledo was once the capital of Spain and the region of New Castile was an historically important area, the cathedral is fittingly splendid. It houses an astonishing collection of works of art – perhaps more than in any other Spanish cathedral.

FOUNDATION OF A CATHEDRAL

Work first began on Toledo Cathedral in the 1220s, following the expulsion of the Moors during the Christian Reconquest. A church had been founded on the site in the 6th century by the first bishop of Toledo, St Eugenius, and when the Moors invaded in the 7th century it was converted into a mosque. Nothing remains of this early structure, however, since it was demolished by Ferdinand III, King of Castile, in the 13th century to make way for the new cathedral.

The first parts of the cathedral to be completed were the apse and its intriguing variety of chapels. The transepts do not project from the main body of the church, but stop short at the north and south portals. The magnificent nave was built next, while the western façade was built between 1418 and 1452. A great pointed archway with French-style recessed portals stands in the centre, and a tower and a cupola lie to the north-west and to the south respectively.

The tower is especially impressive. Standing about 295 feet (90m) tall, it was built between 1380 and 1440 in the Gothic style. The delicate spire, encircled with bands of horizontal pinnacles representing the Crown of Thorns, and the lantern were added between 1448 and 1452 by the Belgian architect Hanequin de Egas. To the south of the façade is the cupola; beginning as a square tower, it then becomes an octagonal structure and finishes off as a dome. It was designed in 1631 by El Greco's son, and its simple Renaissance design perfectly complements the more complex Gothic north tower.

ABOVE: Tourists approaching La Catedral Primada; the low roof is typical of churches in Spain, and contrasts with the tall and decorative north-west steeple.

Windows and art

Not only is the magnificent nave at Toledo impressive for its size and tall clusters of splendid columns with carved capitals reaching towards the pointed vaulting of the roof, but the spectacle of its 750 stained glass windows is breathtaking. The windows were installed between 1418 and 1560 which has resulted in a staggering array of colours, styles and subjects. These glorious windows – some soft greens and blues, others startling oranges, reds and golds – cast their colours down on an awesome collection of fine furnishings and decorations.

Among the best known treasures from this vast museum of priceless works of art are the retable in the Capilla Mayor (sanctuary), carved of larchwood between 1502 and 1504 and depicting several scenes from the life of Christ; the exquisite 15th- and 16th-century stalls; and paintings by artists as varied as El Greco, Goya, Titian, Bellini, Giordano and Van Dyck. Many of these works of art can be seen in the choir, which, as in most Spanish cathedrals, lies to the west of the central crossing. They include not only paintings, but sculptures in wood, stone, bronze and other metals.

El Greco

Born Domenikos Theotokopoulos in 1541 on the island of Crete, El Greco ('the Greek') settled in Toledo in about 1557 and remained there until his death in 1614. He painted most of his great masterpieces in Toledo and there is a museum to him in the city. One of his most famous works, the *Burial of Count Orgaz*, is in the Church of Saint Tomé.

Many of his paintings – easily identifiable by his use of strident colours and elongated, flame-like figures – can be seen in the cathedral sacristy.

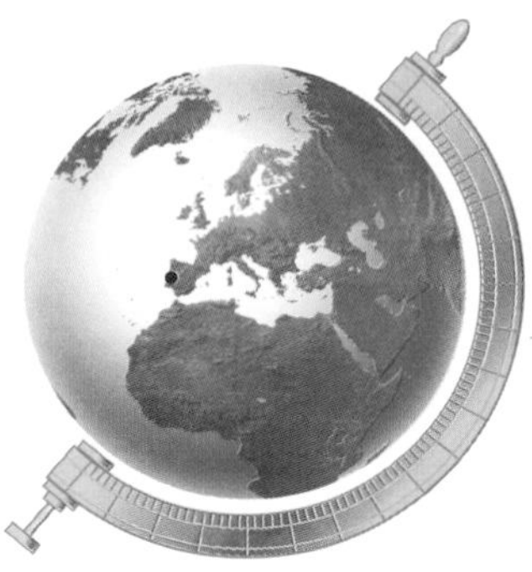

COIMBRA CATHEDRAL

Sé Velha in Coimbra is a handsome 12th-century fortress-cathedral

The Cathedral of Sé Velha stands in the ancient city of Coimbra, today almost overwhelmed by the newer buildings surrounding it. Small by cathedral standards, it has none of the elaborately decorated towers and spires that mark the later Gothic churches. Yet, despite its size and the encroachment of houses around its cobbled square, Coimbra Cathedral has a certain formidable grandeur with its thick, battlemented walls and narrow windows. But it is also a graceful building housing some lovely Romanesque carvings and a fine Byzantine-style cupola.

A CATHEDRAL STRONGHOLD

When the Moors were expelled from the Iberian Peninsula in the 12th century, Portugal, with its long, exposed western coast, remained vulnerable to attack. Consequently, when Church leaders began to raise cathedrals in the place of mosques they were forced to combine religion with defence. Coimbra is one of several cathedrals that has retained its fortified appearance and, like Albi in France, Durham in England and Cefalù in Italy, presents the world with a display of military, as well as ecclesiastical, power.

Visitors seeing Coimbra Cathedral for the first time might be forgiven for taking it to be a fortified house. It is built on a rectangular plan, with short, square transepts added on. The tops of the walls are crenelated and there are arrow slits in the apse at the eastern end. Like Albi, the windows are small and narrow, and they are few and far between on the lower parts of the walls. Immensely thick walls and a sturdy main door would have presented a serious obstacle to potential attackers, aided by the cathedral's position on the hill in the city centre.

THE BASILICA PLAN

Originally there was a church dating from the 10th century which stood on the site of the present cathedral and in the 1140s plans were drawn up to convert this early church into a basilica-plan cathedral. However, it was not until the 1160s that work began in earnest. The architect, Master Bernardo, was French and, not surprisingly, the plans were strongly influenced by the style of architecture in vogue in France. Most of the master masons were also French.

The basilica plan comprises a barrel-vaulted nave, supported by rows of sturdy Romanesque pillars, which is flanked by two aisles, each with a spacious gallery. There are two entrances: the first is the great round-headed portal in the west front, reached by a flight of steps; the second, added in the early 16th century, is on the north side between the north transept and the western end. The 16th-century gate is splendidly Renaissance, with some especially handsome carvings.

At the east end Coimbra Cathedral varies from the traditional basilica plan in that it has three apses, parallel but asymmetrical. A lantern sits above the southern apse, while over the crossing is a squat, military-style tower with polygonal corners. The tower is surmounted by a fine slender-ribbed cupola, tiled with ceramics, which is topped by a small lantern tower. The paucity of windows in the western end of the cathedral makes the interior dark, but the tower has round-headed windows that allow the light to pour downwards.

MANUELINE DECORATION

Portugal's Golden Age occurred during the period of exploration and expansion between 1480 and 1520. The king at this time was Manuel I (1469–1521), and as Portugal began to assert herself in the medieval world a form of architectural decoration was developed that was peculiar to Portugal and bespoke of her new confidence and authority.

The Manueline style (named after the king) was both exotic and extraordinary, and one of the finest examples of it is the 16th-century baptismal font at Coimbra Cathedral, a fascinating whirl of elaborate curves and fine detail.

BELOW: The cloister is reached from stairs off the south aisle. Dating from the 18th century, it has blind arcades topped by round bays.

ABOVE: The square tower is visible from the cloister; it is surmounted by a blue and white 'fish-scale' cupola and a weather vane in the form of an angel.

Renaissance sculpture

Coimbra has many treasures secreted within her sturdy walls, not least of which is some of the finest sculpture to be found in any cathedral in Portugal. Near the altar is a fabulous retable that was executed in wood by the Flemish artist Olivier de Gand between 1498 and 1503. De Gand's work in Coimbra contributed towards the city becoming a leading centre for Renaissance sculpture in Portugal, and during the 16th century many craftsmen learned their skills there.

The cathedral's two fine chapels, St Peter's and the Holy Sacrament, owe their exquisite decorations to the Renaissance period, and were created in an intriguing blend of styles combining influences from French and Portuguese artists.

PORTUGAL

LISBON CATHEDRAL

The lovely 12th-century Sé Patriarcal in the Old City is the seat of Lisbon's bishop

At 9.40am on 1 November 1755 many of Lisbon's (Lisboa's) citizens were at church celebrating All Saints' Day. The earth began to shake and heave and, 15 minutes later, the beautiful and ancient city centre lay in ruins; the few buildings that survived the earthquake were later damaged by after-shocks and subsequent tidal waves.

The appearance of the cathedral today – an unusual combination of sturdy 12th-century walls with Romanesque windows and intricate baroque ornamentation – is the result of the subsequent rebuilding and restoration of the Old City executed under the watchful eye of the social reformer Marquês de Pombal.

BELOW: Thoughtful restoration has meant that the distinctive Romanesque style of Lisbon Cathedral has been retained.

The cathedral is known as Sé Patriarcal, meaning that it is the seat of Lisbon's bishop.

TURBULENT BEGINNINGS

Lisbon did not become the capital of Portugal until 1256. Initially part of the Holy Roman Empire, it was invaded by German tribes who remained until ousted by a Moorish invasion in the 8th century. After the Moors were expelled in the 1100s, Portugal, like Spain, built churches and cathedrals in place of the Moorish mosques. For many years the people of Portugal feared the Moors would return, so many of the cathedrals built in the 12th and 13th centuries were heavily fortified. Some even operated in conjunction with castles to provide protection for cities.

A Roman temple, probably converted into a church some time in the 6th century, originally occupied the site on which Lisbon Cathedral now stands. Two hundred years later the Moors demolished the church and built themselves a mosque that survived until well into the 12th century. After the charismatic Christian rebel Dom Afonso Henriques took Lisbon, following a siege in 1147, the mosque was destroyed and a cathedral raised in its place.

Portugal, despite her proximity to Spain, did not achieve the architectural splendour of cathedrals such as Santiago de Compostela and León. Most of the country's earlier churches and cathedrals, specifically those at Lisbon, Braga and Oporto, were influenced by the architectural style that was developing in France. Lisbon Cathedral is more like a fortress than a house of God, with two great, squat bell-towers supplied with arrow slits for defence. These towers were also used as look-out points in times of unrest. The walls are thick, and there is a distinct absence of any windows on the lower floors that might make the cathedral vulnerable to attack. It was doubtless the strength and thickness of the walls that allowed the cathedral to withstand some of the destructive force of the 1755 earthquake so that although much needed to be rebuilt and restored, much of the medieval work survived.

Simplicity and elegance

Yet this powerful cathedral is not without beauty: the handsome west façade is dominated by a great rose window, a massive round-arched gateway, and twin towers with lovely mouldings on the arches of the upper floors. The interior of the cathedral, although the walls and ceilings are plain and there are few furnishings, possesses a certain simple majesty. Great clustered columns rise to the vaulted ceiling, their creamy whiteness accentuated by the bright sunlight that streams in from round-headed windows.

Although at first glance there appear to be few furnishings for the visitor to see, Lisbon does have its share of treasures. Many of these are stored in the cathedral treasury, which boasts an impressive collection of silver and ecclesiastical vestments.

Behind the altar, several gloomy crypts contain the remains of various Lisbon bishops and noblemen. They all have beautiful carvings, but the best is the tomb of a 14th-century nobleman, called Pacheco, and his wife. Pacheco's effigy shows him as a bearded soldier holding a great sword, while his wife lies next to him reading from a book of prayers.

The atmospheric cloisters in the overgrown graveyard contain Roman and Moorish pillars and are well worth visiting.

St Vincent

In Sé Patriarcal's sacristy lie the cathedral's greatest treasure – the relics of St Vincent, or São Vicente. Vincent, living in Spain in the 4th century, was a victim of Roman persecution and legend has it that after his death his body was protected from the ravages of wild animals by a flock of crows. Discovered some 500 years later in reasonable repair, the body was then spirited away to southern Portugal to escape the heathen hands of the Moors. When the ship carrying St Vincent's body sank, the remains were washed up at Cabo de São Vicente where they remained until the Moors had been ousted from the Iberian Peninsula. In the 12th century the relics were taken to Lisbon where they are displayed annually on St Vincent's Day – 22 January.

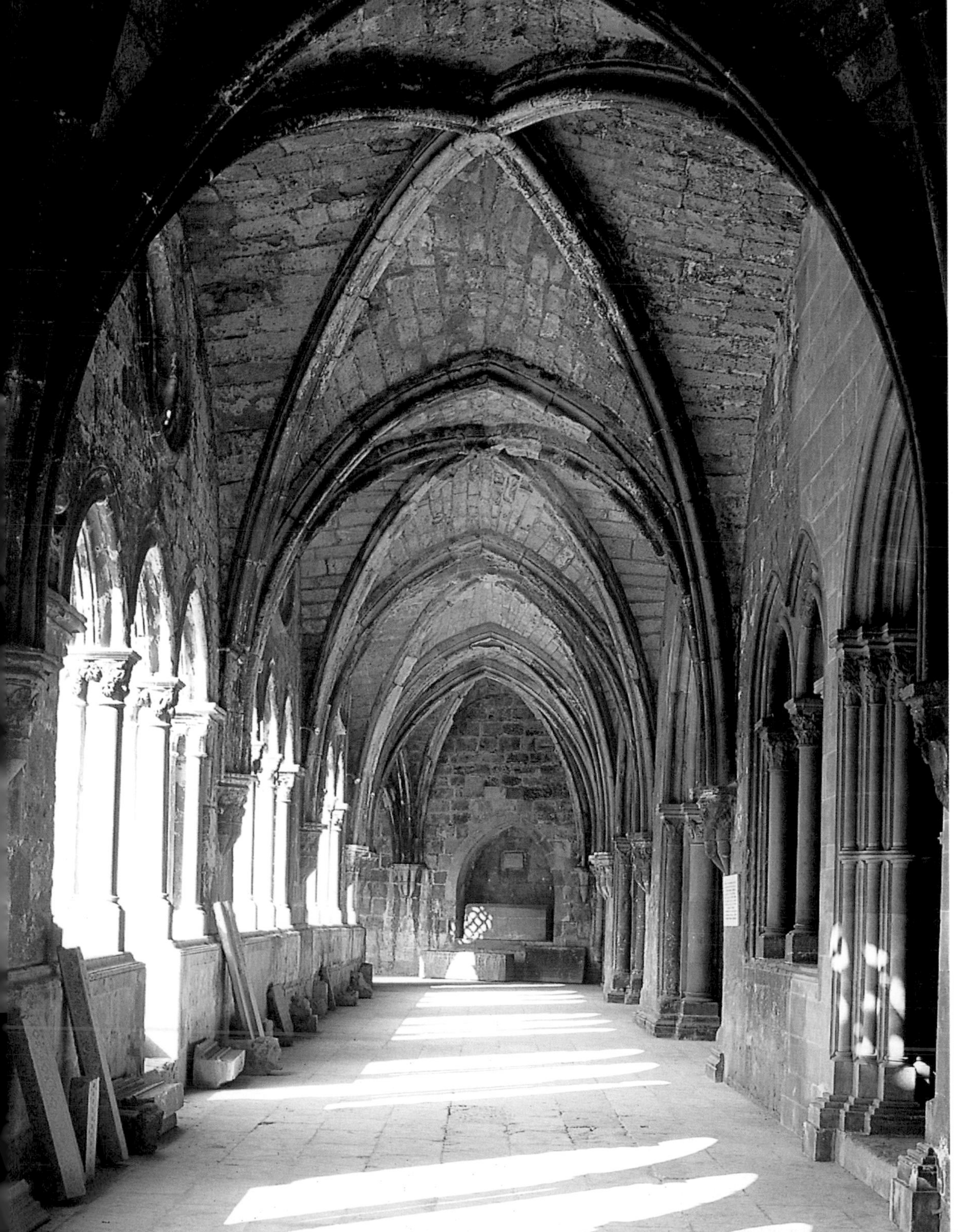

LEFT: The cathedral cloisters can be found by walking through the third chapel off the ambulatory. The lower gallery is supported by massive buttresses alternating with Gothic arches.

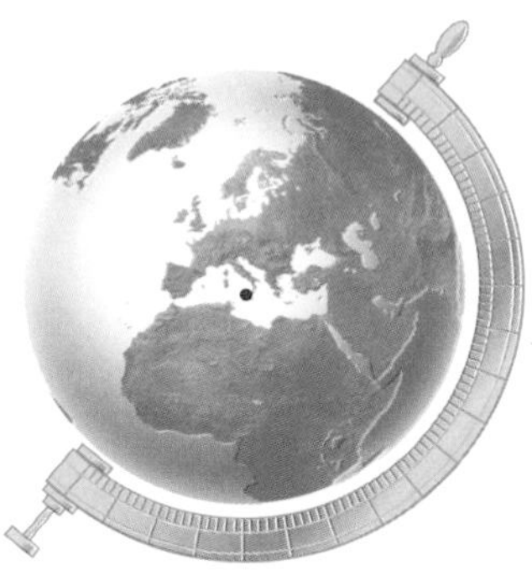

CEFALÙ CATHEDRAL

St Saviour's Cathedral in Cefalù is the grandest of all Norman buildings in Sicily

ABOVE: The Byzantine mosaic depicting Christ Pantocrator gleams with gold.

KING ROGER II

Roger was born in 1095, one of a race of powerful, acquisitive Norman barons who struck out from their own country to seek wealth and lands elsewhere. He was made Count of Sicily in 1105 and as soon as he was old enough began to create a strong kingdom for himself. He added Calabria to his realm in 1122, followed by Apulia in 1127. Roger was made King of Sicily in 1130, took Capua in 1136, and Naples in 1140. Pleased with his increasing power, he even attacked the mighty Byzantine Empire and pillaged the coastal cities of Dalmatia and Epirus. Despite his lust for power and wealth, Roger's court was an intellectual centre for Christian and Muslim scholars. He died in 1154.

In the mountains of northern Sicily, overlooking the sea, stands one of the finest Romanesque buildings in southern Italy. Built in honey-coloured limestone, the sturdy Cathedral of St Saviour in Cefalù appears more fortress than religious building and displays many of the features employed by the Normans when they built their castles. Windows are small and narrow and, as in any good fortress, scarce on the lower parts of the walls. The transepts and presbytery, reinforced with massive pilaster buttresses, and the immensely thick walls give this lovely cathedral a formidable appearance.

NORMAN AND BYZANTINE INFLUENCES

Sicily had been an outpost of several great empires throughout its history and the invading Normans had many predecessors. The Carthaginians had arrived first, followed by the Greeks, Romans, Byzantines and Saracens, all ruling this attractive island for varying periods of time and with varying degrees of success.

The Normans, who arrived in the 1090s and stayed for about 100 years, left an architectural legacy which includes not only Cefalù Cathedral, but the lovely Palatine Chapel at Palermo and the Benedictine cloisters at Monreale.

The cathedral was started in 1131 by Roger (see panel), who had just become King of Sicily. Although its design was inspired by the great Benedictine churches of Roger's native Normandy, at the same time it incorporated impressive defensive features and included the architectural styles of the Byzantines and the Saracens.

From the outside, the thick, plain walls of the cathedral give it an imposing appearance, despite the attractive blind arcades that decorate the upper

parts. The windows are either the round-headed arched type favoured by the Normans, or 'oculi' (round openings), neither of which are encumbered with unnecessary decorations.

Cefalù Cathedral took about 100 years to complete, although the bulk of the building was finished around 1150. It is about 240 feet (73m) in length from the apse to the narthex, or porch, and the transepts stretch out to a width of about 100 feet (30m). The nave is small compared to the massive narthex at the western end, and to the grand north and south transepts and sanctuary. The roof is tiled, with wooden supports underneath, with the exception of the south transept, which has a stone barrel vault. A simple arcade of Romanesque pillars separates the nave from the single aisles.

Gold mosaics

The main entrance to mighty Cefalù is through the splendid narthex. Flanked by two symmetrical square towers, the west porch has three arches: the central one is round-headed, while those on either side are pointed.

The interior is, as would be expected from the few windows, shadowy and mysterious, the fabulous gilt-tinted mosaics created between 1148 and 1170 by Byzantine craftsmen glittering dully.

Cefalù is famous for its mosaics, and there are many splendid individual pieces to admire, but the crowning glory is indisputably at the eastern end – in the choir and presbytery. Here a huge portrait of Christ Pantocrator (meaning 'all-powerful') fills the dome, one hand raised in blessing, while the other hand indicates an open book, picked out in blue and gold. Below it the walls are a mass of brilliant reds, greens, blues and golds depicting the Apostles, the Virgin Mary and a veritable host of other heavenly beings. Interweaving all are intricate geometrical designs and patterns in a frenzy of colours that is breathtaking.

BELOW: Cefalù Cathedral is dramatically situated at the foot of a steep slope which rises up from the sea. The name of the town derives from the small promontory above it, which has the shape of a head.

Italy

Florence Cathedral

Santa Maria del Fiore Cathedral is a magnificent tribute to Renaissance architecture

ABOVE: A detail of the exterior decoration of the dome.

Set like a ruby among the blue-green hills of Tuscany is the red-roofed city of Florence (Firenze), home to the Renaissance of classical architecture. Rising out of the very heart of this ancient city is the breathtaking Santa Maria del Fiore Cathedral (Holy Mary of the Flowers), a patterned marble building dominated by its vast rust-red dome. In Italy, Florence Cathedral is second in size only to St Peter's Basilica in Rome (see page 58).

From almost every angle the cathedral is spectacular. The free-standing campanile, or bell-tower, rises in a series of graceful arches to a shallow pitched roof some 325 feet (99m) above the ground. At the base of the octagon there is a cluster of symmetrical chapels at different levels, topped with red-tile roofs and with walls that seem to cascade downwards in steps of richly decorated blind arcading and lattice work.

A prosperous city

By the end of the 13th century the wool merchants and bankers of Florence had made the city wealthy, and the little Cathedral of Santa Reparata (see panel) was no longer deemed grand enough to reflect this new-found prosperity and status. As a result, the influential merchants commissioned a new cathedral in 1296, employing an architect called Arnolfo di Cambio who used both Norman and Gothic features in his plan.

First to be built were the wide nave, the aisles and the octagon at the eastern end, but work ground to a halt in 1310 when Arnolfo died and did not really get underway again until a new architect, Giotto di Bondone, was commissioned in the 1330s to design a bell-tower to stand at the south-west corner of the cathedral. However, Giotto died in

BELOW: The marble-panelled decoration of the exterior of Florence Cathedral is brilliantly coloured, taking the place of the sculpted decoration found on other cathedrals. Shown here are the dome and Giotto's Tower.

in 1337 and the tower, known as Giotto's Tower, was not completed until 1359.

Work then resumed on the rest of the cathedral. The final touches were completed on the nave in 1420 and the great octagon, built of green and white marble and adorned with the round windows and repetitive rectangular designs picked out in coloured stone that are used on the clerestory, received its upper storey.

The great dome

The problem of constructing the dome over the octagon was then posed as the authorities did not want the expense of erecting massive scaffolding. After some haggling and argument, the great Renaissance goldsmith and sculptor Filippo Brunelleschi was hired, as he claimed he could build the dome without scaffolding – although he would not say how this was to be accomplished.

Work began in 1420. Brunelleschi designed a light vault of herring-bone brickwork supported by slim horizontal and vertical ribs. The entire dome was then encased in red tiles to produce a vivid contrast with the red, green and white marble walls. Almost 140 feet (43m) in diameter, this great structure is topped by a tiny white marble lantern erected after 1446.

When the magnificent dome had been completed, Brunelleschi was persuaded to stay on to supervise the rest of the building work. By his death in 1446, the great Cathedral of Santa Maria del Fiore stood virtually complete. The west front, built in the late 14th century, was demolished in 1588 and rebuilt in the 1880s by Emilio de Fabris.

In contrast to the magnificently decorated exterior the interior is refreshingly plain, although many 19th-century architectural historians, used to the excesses of the Gothic Revival, found it too much so. Rows of angular pillars separate the nave from the single aisles and the roof is simply vaulted. The inside of the dome is picked out in gold mosaic, although the main attraction is a sculpture of the *Descent from the Cross* by Michelangelo. This was started around 1547 but was never finished.

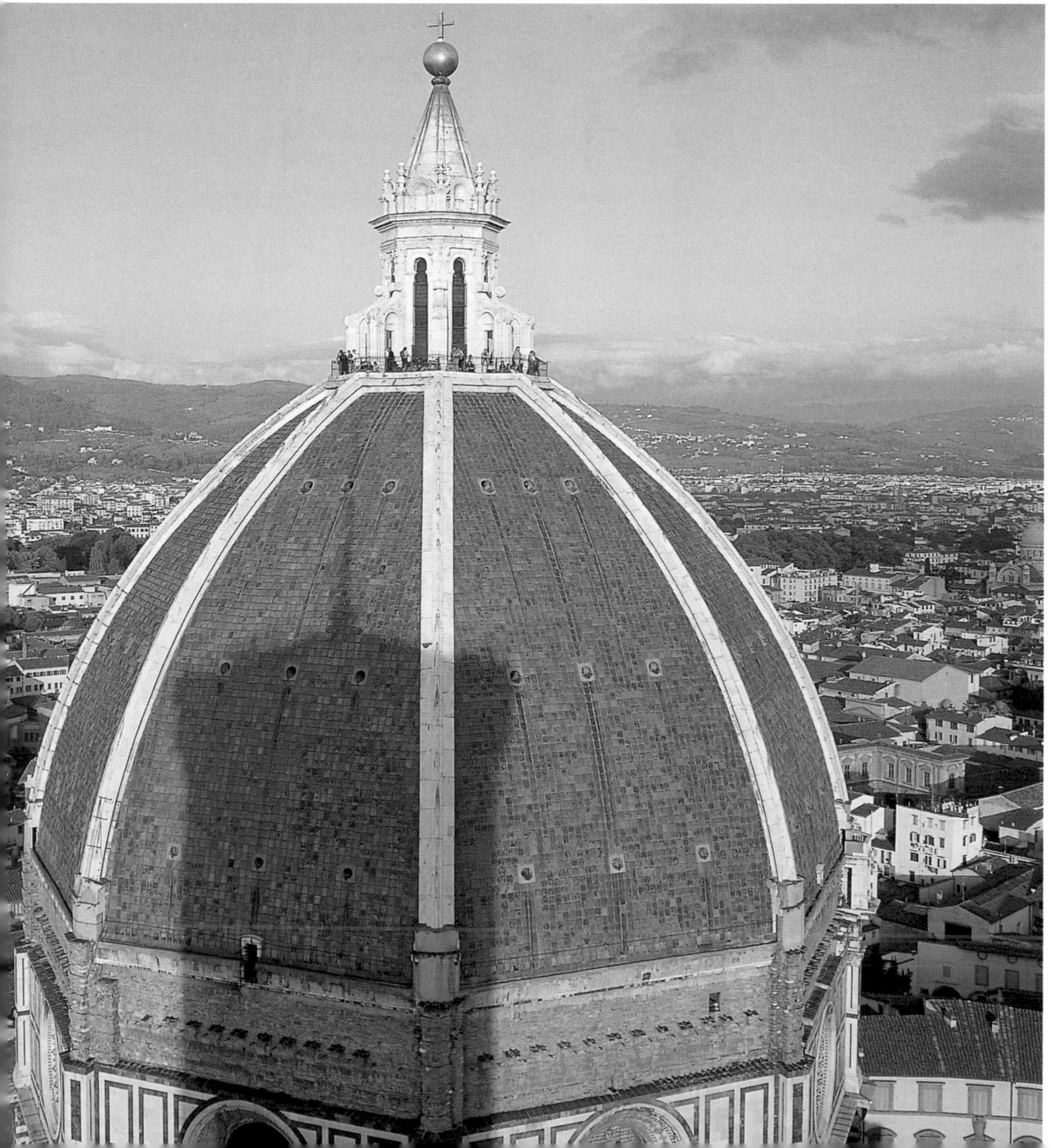

The old cathedral baptistry

When the new cathedral was built the baptistry of the Cathedral of Santa Reparata was retained. Dating mostly from the 11th century but with 5th-century origins, it is a fine three-storeyed octagonal building of contrasting green and white marble. It is remarkable as the oldest surviving building in Florence and for its sets of wonderfully detailed bronze doors.

An architectural landmark

The massive red-tiled dome of the cathedral is described in John Julius Norwich's *Great Architecture of the World* as 'a crown of glory to the Renaissance' and 'a miracle of design and engineering'. It certainly stands as an important landmark in Italian architecture as the techniques in use by Gothic builders would not have enabled Brunelleschi to build the dome he envisaged. To solve the problem, he undertook an extensive study of the vaulting methods used in imperial Rome – specifically the 2nd-century Pantheon.

Having showed that Gothic architecture could be enhanced by the revival of classical techniques, he then went on to derive the 'Latin cross plan' from Roman basilicas. Examples of this in Florence can be seen in San Lorenzo and Santo Spirito churches, and the Pazzi Chapel in Santa Croce.

LEFT: The astonishing dome dominates the city, rising to the height of the surrounding Tuscan hills.

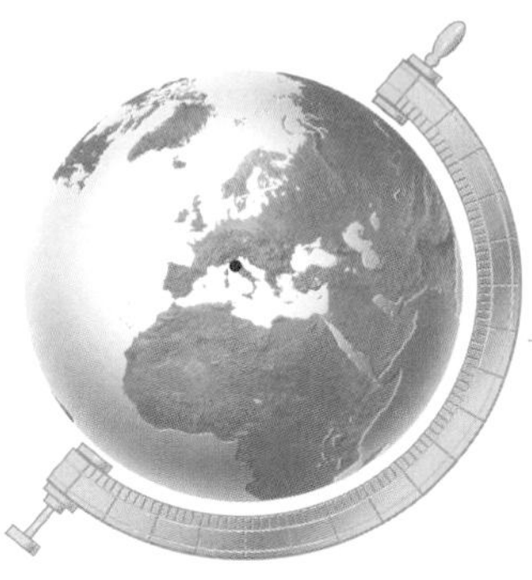

PISA CATHEDRAL

The Cathedral of Santa Maria Maggiore is unfairly eclipsed by the famous Leaning Tower

BELOW: Typical of Baroque architecture is the arrangement of a group of buildings to create a 'stage-set' effect. The massive basilica is surmounted by an elliptical dome of later date.

Nowhere else in the world is there an ecclesiastical complex quite like that at Pisa. Standing in a neat, emerald oblong of immaculately tended lawn in the centre of the city are three buildings of dazzling white marble. The largest of these is the Cathedral of Santa Maria Maggiore; to the west, separated by a swath of green, stands the lovely baptistry; and to the east teeters the famous campanile, known to the world as the Leaning Tower of Pisa.

A UNIQUE COMPLEX

The cathedral, baptistry and tower took almost 300 years to complete, yet retain a remarkable unity of style as, although the actual design of each building is individual, they are linked by the recurring use of tiers of open-arcading and round-headed windows. The cathedral is the most important of the three buildings – the other two were intended to complement, not dominate, it – but it is around the Leaning Tower that tourists cluster, allowing the visitor to contemplate the cool, graceful interiors of the cathedral and baptistry in relative peace.

Building of the cathedral itself was started in the 1080s under an architect called Busceto. During this time the city became a training ground for artisans and craftsmen who came from all over Italy to study, so it is likely that a considerable amount of talent was available. Progress was rapid, and by the 1150s the bulk of the cathedral had been completed.

THE CATHEDRAL

The cathedral that emerged was based on the style of the basilicas so popular in Rome. There is a rounded apse at the east, similarly rounded apses at the end of each transept, and both nave and choir have double aisles. Outside, the cathedral's main focus is the fabulous west front. Tiers of blind arcades rise in four storeys above the three doors. The lowest tier runs the width of the cathedral, and the upper ones grow narrower to end in a pediment. This superbly symmetrical façade is reminiscent of Greek temples, although the coloured religious reliefs around the bronze portals and the statue of *Virgin and Child* at the gable summit counteract pagan overtones.

In contrast to the bright whiteness of the outside are the darker colours of the interior. Simple round piers with carved capitals rise to starkly banded arches – an effect favoured by Tuscan architects and achieved by using alternating layers of different coloured stone. The ceiling is low, lending the nave a dimness which mitigates the starkness of the banded stone.

On entering the west door a superb mosaic in the apse catches the eye; it depicts Christ between the Blessed Virgin Mary and St John the Baptist.

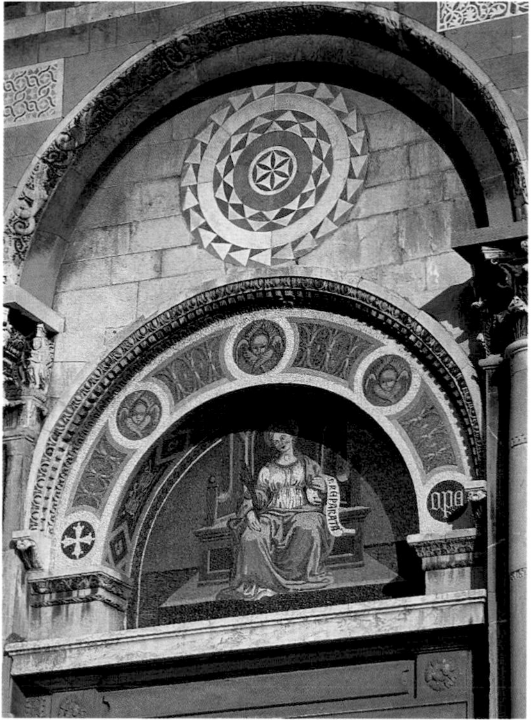

LEFT: This decorative panel forms part of the entrance façade, and is located above one of the portals at the side of the main doorway.

THE LEANING TOWER

Towards the end of the 13th century the half-finished campanile was very obviously beginning to list. At this point, only the bottom four storeys had been built, so the upper sections and the belfry were raised at an angle to the lower levels in order to compensate for the lean. Unfortunately, this merely served to make the tower lean at two slightly different angles and, so far, plans to straighten it, or prevent it tilting further, have failed.

The tower, 180 feet (54m) tall – the foundations are only 10 feet (3m) deep – and about 50 feet (15m) in diameter, was started in 1173 and completed about 200 years later. It comprises a blind-arcaded bottom floor, six open-arcaded upper floors and a belfry.

THE BAPTISTRY

This exquisite circular building, measuring about 115 feet (35m) across, was started in the 1150s. On the outside, the lowest of the three storeys has simple blind arcading with narrow windows set high in the walls; the middle storey has an open arcade (like that on the Leaning Tower) with double-headed arches that reach upwards to elegantly carved points; while the upper floor is plain, but with small windows and the same pointed arches as the middle floor. The whole is capped by a pale red dome.

DISASTER IN 1596

A disastrous fire in 1596 deprived the cathedral of some of its most valued ornaments, including a pulpit of 1311 and the original cupola over the central crossing. It is likely that the fire was started by careless workmen, although a more prosaic explanation offered at the time was that it was started by the spontaneous combustion of pigeon droppings.

SIENA CATHEDRAL

Distinctive black and white stripes characterise the Cathedral of Santa Maria in Siena, both inside and out

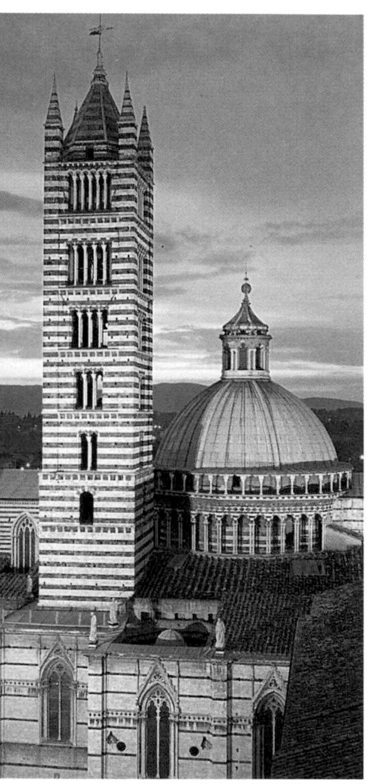

ABOVE: Rising from the south transept, the campanile dominates the group of buildings. An unusual feature is the six stages of windows, which increase in size progressively.

RIGHT: The highly ornate façade, dating from 1370, has three portals with 'gablets' which are balanced by the three gables above. The facing is of white marble, picked out in red and green.

Siena Cathedral is a startling building. The glorious west front, designed by Giovanni Pisano, is a superb example of Italian Gothic architecture, complementing the simpler Romanesque nave and the tall striped campanile. Reached by a flight of steps that runs continuously around three sides, the cathedral stands in an open square, dominating the buildings that surround it.

EARLY HISTORY

It is known that there was an early church on the site now occupied by the cathedral, but the present building dates from the 1220s. In 1245 Nicolà Pisano was commissioned to build a west façade, but for some reason this was demolished only 40 years after its completion and Pisano's son, Giovanni, was commissioned to design another.

By the late 1340s plans were continuing apace when an unexpected and entirely unwelcome development came in the form of the Black Death which swept across Europe. About a third of the city's population died and the building of the new cathedral was abandoned for 20 years.

In the 1360s artists were hired to complete the stained glass windows of the choir and to start the beautiful decorated pavement in the nave. By the end of the 14th century the transepts had been enlarged, the choir and presbytery extended, and the handsome cupola completed over the unusual hexagonal crossing. The basic design of the cathedral is cruciform.

THE BELL-TOWER AND CUPOLA

The bell-tower, or campanile, is one of the most memorable features of this remarkable cathedral. Constructed in the 13th century, it is built of alternating dark and light bands of marble. Marble was in plentiful supply in Tuscany, unlike the northern parts of Italy, and the Tuscans made good use of it. The narrow tower appears to be taller than it actually is and rises in tiers featuring an ever-increasing number of arches, starting with one on the lowest level, and reaching six on the uppermost level. The entire structure is neatly finished with a striped pinnacle at each corner and a pyramidal roof.

The campanile quite overpowers the lovely Romanesque cupola over the crossing, despite the size of the latter which is about 52 feet (16m) across and 180 feet (54m) tall. The cupola is similarly dominated by the clerestory, also banded in black and white, which was apparently added after the cupola was completed. Life-sized statues of saints, dating from the 15th century, stand at strategic points on striped plinths all around the roof.

PILLARS AND PAVEMENT

Sturdy zebra-striped pillars dominate the nave, vying for attention with the remarkable marble pavement which stretches along its entire length. This is one of Siena's glories, and besides various geometric designs includes over 50 detailed scenes from the Bible and classical literature. Among the most vivid of these are the *Death of Absolom* (Absolom was hanged in a tree by his long hair), and the gruesome *Massacre of the Innocents*. The final paintings were added in 1547.

The pillars rise 60 feet (18m) to sturdy Romanesque arches and a vaulted ceiling that is painted blue with a silver glitter of stars. The stained glass in the great rose windows in the east and west ends of the cathedral splash their own vivid colours down on to the pavement and the overall effect can be overwhelming, presenting a dazzling array of mismatched patterns and colours.

The Pisanos

One of the most influential sculptors in Italy in medieval times was Nicolà Pisano (1220–78), who was largely responsible for reviving the antique Roman forms of architecture that eventually led to the Renaissance movement in the 15th century. Among his best-known works is the monumental octagonal pulpit, on which he worked with his son Giovanni (1250–1320), in Siena's cathedral.

Giovanni introduced an element of the French Gothic into his sculptures, especially in the pulpits he designed for the cathedral at Pisa (see page 52) and for St Andrea's Church in Pistoia. A similar style was used in his design of the magnificent façade of Siena Cathedral.

Sienese Architecture

When the cathedral was started in about 1226 the ancient Tuscan city of Siena was at the height of its powers and influence. A university was founded in 1240 and several palaces sprung up, the best known of these being the Palazzo Pubblico (1297–1310). The tower on this palace, called the Torre del Mangia, is Italy's tallest campanile at 335 feet (101m).

LEFT: The cathedral is justly famous for its splendid decorated marble floors, which took almost 200 years to complete.

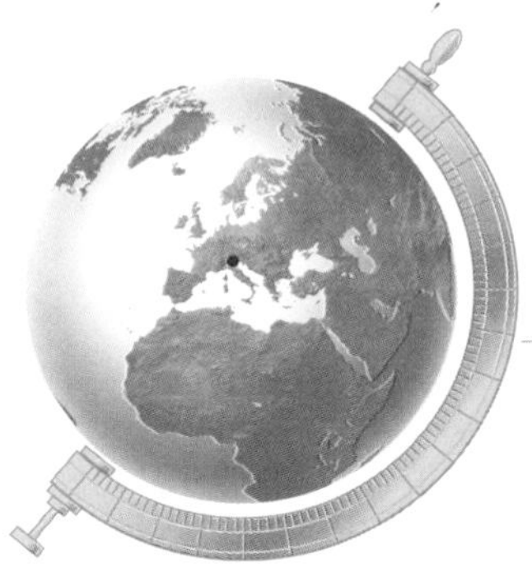

ITALY

ST MARK'S CATHEDRAL

The cathedral, a glittering cluster of domes, stands in St Mark's Square in the beautiful city of Venice

BELOW: The façade of St Mark's Cathedral is covered with fine sculptures and a mist of colour from the alabaster, marble and gold mosaics. It is also embellished with numerous 'trophies' brought from other lands.

The island city of Venice (Venézia) was founded in the 5th century in the myriad of vivid blue lagoons and swampy islands that lie in a northern pocket of the Adriatic Sea. Strategically placed as a trading point between the great Byzantine Empire to the east, and the European powers to the west, Venice eventually became one of the most powerful maritime forces in the world.

The city's architecture reflects its dual cultural heritage and St Mark's Cathedral displays both Byzantine and western Christian influences.

The first basilica, no more than a chapel built inside the Doge's Palace, was replaced in 832 by a Byzantine-style church, which in turn was succeeded in 978. Further building took place in 1063 and then between 1071 and 1084 under the Doges. This then formed the basis of the cathedral seen today, albeit embellished with nine centuries' worth of wealth and architectural splendour.

'THE BALLROOM OF EUROPE'

St Mark's Square (Piazza San Marco) is, quite justly, considered one of the most magnificent architectural achievements of the western world. Described as 'the Ballroom of Europe' by Napoleon, the exuberant 14th-century Doge's

Palace and the 15th-century campanile in St Mark's Square serve as worthy companions to the glorious domed and pinnacled façade of one of Italy's most famous cathedrals.

Visitors could spend hours admiring the fabulous western façade of St Mark's, and still not take in all it has to offer. A riot of domes and spires point heavenward, every one of them richly decorated with sculpted turrets, elegant statues or glittering crosses. The lower part comprises a narthex 170 feet (51m) across, with five great recessed portals alternating with tiers of marble pillars. The semi-circular areas over the portals are filled with brightly coloured mosaics and reliefs depicting scenes from the Bible. Above the narthex is the 15th-century upper façade with its gables and pinnacled niches containing 17th-century mosaics.

Byzantine domes

The cathedral, built in the shape of a Greek cross, measures 250 feet (75m) from east to west and 205 feet (62m) from north to south. Above the nave, choir, both transepts and crossing is a set of five domes over a 16-windowed drum, a supreme example of Byzantine Christian architecture. The largest dome, over the crossing, is 42 feet (13m) across, while the others are smaller (33 feet/10m in diameter). These great domes, supported by enormous piers and arches on pedentives in much the same way as the dome of St Sophia in Istanbul (see page 154), are each crowned with a bulbous lantern – shaped something like a clove of garlic – resplendent in their 13th-century gilding.

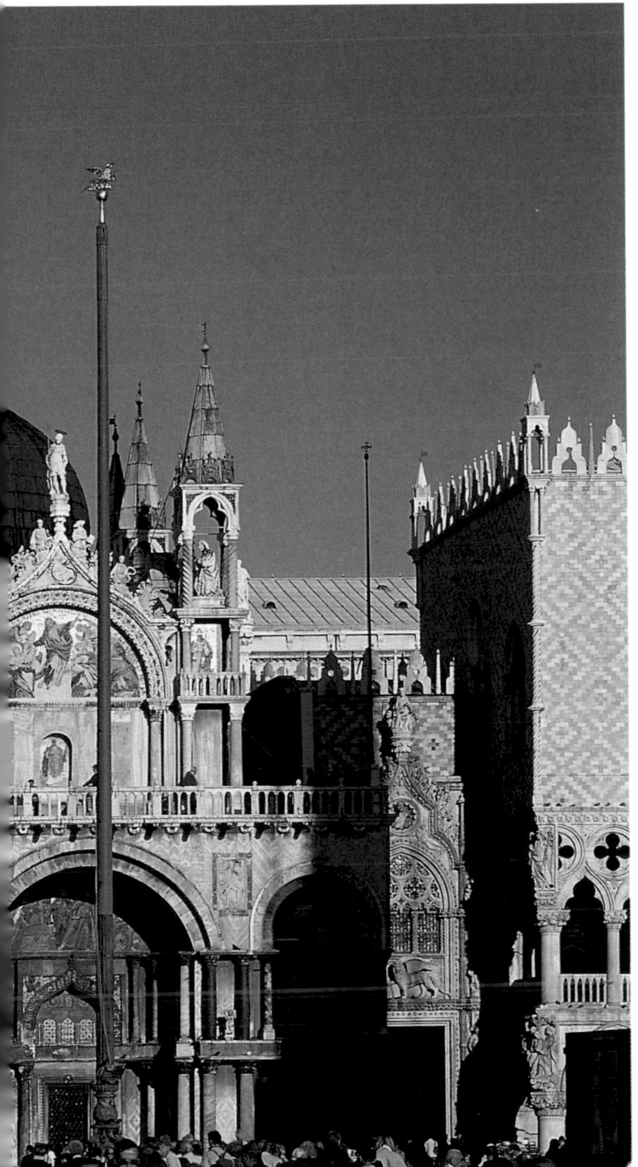

LEFT: It was the innovation of brick vaulting rather than wood which allowed the use of coloured marble and mosaic in a continuous surface over the interior of the vault and dome, performing the same function as medieval stained glass.

Gold and more gold

Inside the cathedral all the walls glimmer with the dull yellow of gold, broken here and there by the sharper glitter of coloured glass, forming mosaics that seem to cover every available fraction of space. Scenes depicted include incidents from the lives of various saints, stories from the Bible, and Christ performing miracles. These mosaics date from several different periods – as reflected by the varying styles and quality – but those dating from the 12th, 13th and 14th centuries are thought to have been executed by craftsmen from the Byzantine Empire, illustrating yet again the close connections of Venice with the East.

It is not only the spectacle of unbroken decoration that is impressive about St Mark's. The interior rises majestically to a height of almost 100 feet (30m) under the crossing, and is crammed with all manner of fascinating, priceless and ancient treasures. Perhaps the most ostentatious is the gaudy *Pala d'Oro*, dating from the 10th century but refashioned in medieval times. It includes 1,300 pearls, 300 emeralds and hundreds of semi-precious stones.

Theft and pillage

In the late 820s two Venetian merchants stole the bones of St Mark the Evangelist from Alexandria and brought them to Venice. This was merely the first episode in a history of dubious acquisitions that resulted in St Mark's Cathedral being filled to the brim with an assortment of priceless works of art.

Soldiers of the Second Crusade (1202–4) gathered in Venice to be ferried across the sea to the Holy Land, but when the crusaders were unable to pay the Venetians, they decided to attack the Byzantine city of Constantinople instead. The Venetians agreed to accept a share of the spoils and the four bronze horses from the Hippodrome that adorn St Mark's façade were just one of the treasures seized in that deplorable frenzy of looting, mayhem and murder.

BELOW: The four bronze horses over the central doorway, copies of the originals which are now in a museum.

ITALY

St Peter's Basilica

St Peter's in Rome, the largest church in the world, is Catholicism's most sacred pilgrimage site

RIGHT: The twisted 'Solomonic' columns of the 85-ft (26-m) baldacchino *are made of bronze from the Pantheon.*

St Peter's Piazza

In the 1650s Pope Alexander VII ordered the baroque sculptor and architect Gian Lorenzo Bernini to design a grand approach to St Peter's. It was not an easy commission: he had to ensure that as many people as possible could see the Pope both from the basilica itself and from the Vatican Palace. In the end, Bernini designed a covered portico that swept outwards in two symmetrical curves which were low enough not to impede the view of the basilica itself.

When the 1,100-year-old Basilica of St Peter in Rome (Roma) began to show signs of wear and tear in late medieval times, the popes began to consider rebuilding it. However there was a problem – the church contained the tomb of St Peter himself and any building replacing it needed to be a truly glorious affair, one worthy as the seat of the Pope lying at the very power centre of the Christian world.

A succession of architects

Pope Nicholas V proposed plans to rebuild the crumbling basilica in 1450, but very little happened until 1503, when Guiliano della Rovere was elected Pope Julius II. He commissioned one of the best Italian architects of the day, Donato Bramante (1444–1514), to design the new St Peter's.

Bramante's plans were grandiose, taking the form of a Greek cross, symbol of the 'Universal Christ'. Julius was satisfied with them and work began with the laying of the foundation stone in 1506. When Bramante died, Raphael (1483–1520) succeeded

LEFT: St Peter's presents the first of the great Baroque interiors, with its use of gilt stucco and coloured marble.

him, although few of his plans were realised. By 1547, so little progress had been made that Pope Paul III persuaded Michelangelo to take over. Michelangelo agreed on the proviso that he be given a free hand. Nervously, Paul acquiesced, and the 72-year-old artist began work.

Michelangelo realised there were certain flaws in Bramante's original plans and set about improving them. He kept Bramante's basic dimensions, but opened out the corners to produce a simpler, more unified, interior.

The crowning glory

The dome was intended to be the highlight of the basilica, a massive, but elegant, pale-grey monolith rising from its colonnaded drum. In fact, only the drum – 140 feet (42m) in diameter complete with 16 windows to allow light to filter down – was finished before Michelangelo's death. Although he left clear instructions for the completion of the dome, his successor Giacomo della Porta did not follow them precisely, and made it taller and more pointed than Michelangelo had intended.

Forty years after Michelangelo's death Carlo Maderna was commissioned to take up where the great artist had left off. Sadly, Pope Paul V interfered with Maderna's plans, insisting on an extension to the eastern part of the nave and the creation of a new eastern façade which masks the magnificent dome from the Piazza (see panel).

A papal palace

The interior of St Peter's has been described throughout the ages as transcending the grand, the beautiful and the vast into the sublime. Indeed, there are few churches that can claim such a great collection of masterpieces. Michelangelo's painting in the dome is sufficiently magnificent to defy description, while huge mosaics decorate every altar and every chapel. The subtle creams, greens and pinks of the floor are complemented by the glittering glory of the patterned ceilings and walls, while exquisite carvings in stone and wood are everywhere.

Handsome monuments to popes abound, some enormous and grand, like that of Clement XIII (died 1769) by Antonio Canova, others smaller but expressive, like that of Urban VIII by Bernini. The tombs of other popes lie in the 14th-century crypt below the newer building.

Michelangelo

Michelangelo di Lodovico Buonarroti Simoni was born in Caprese in 1475. In 1503 he embarked on his stormy relationship with Pope Julius II, who first commissioned him to build a papal tomb (never completed), and then to work on the Sistine Chapel.

Although Michelangelo spent a good deal of his life in Rome, his heart was in Florence where he did some of his best work, including the sculpture of *David*, and the painting *Holy Family*.

He returned to Rome in 1538, where he was appointed architect of St Peter's Basilica, on which he worked until his death in 1564.

BELOW: Michelangelo's design for the exterior features the world's largest Corinthian pilasters supporting an enormous attic. The Doric columns of Bernini's piazza support an entablature with over 60 statues of saints.

TV ES · PETRVS · ET · SVPER

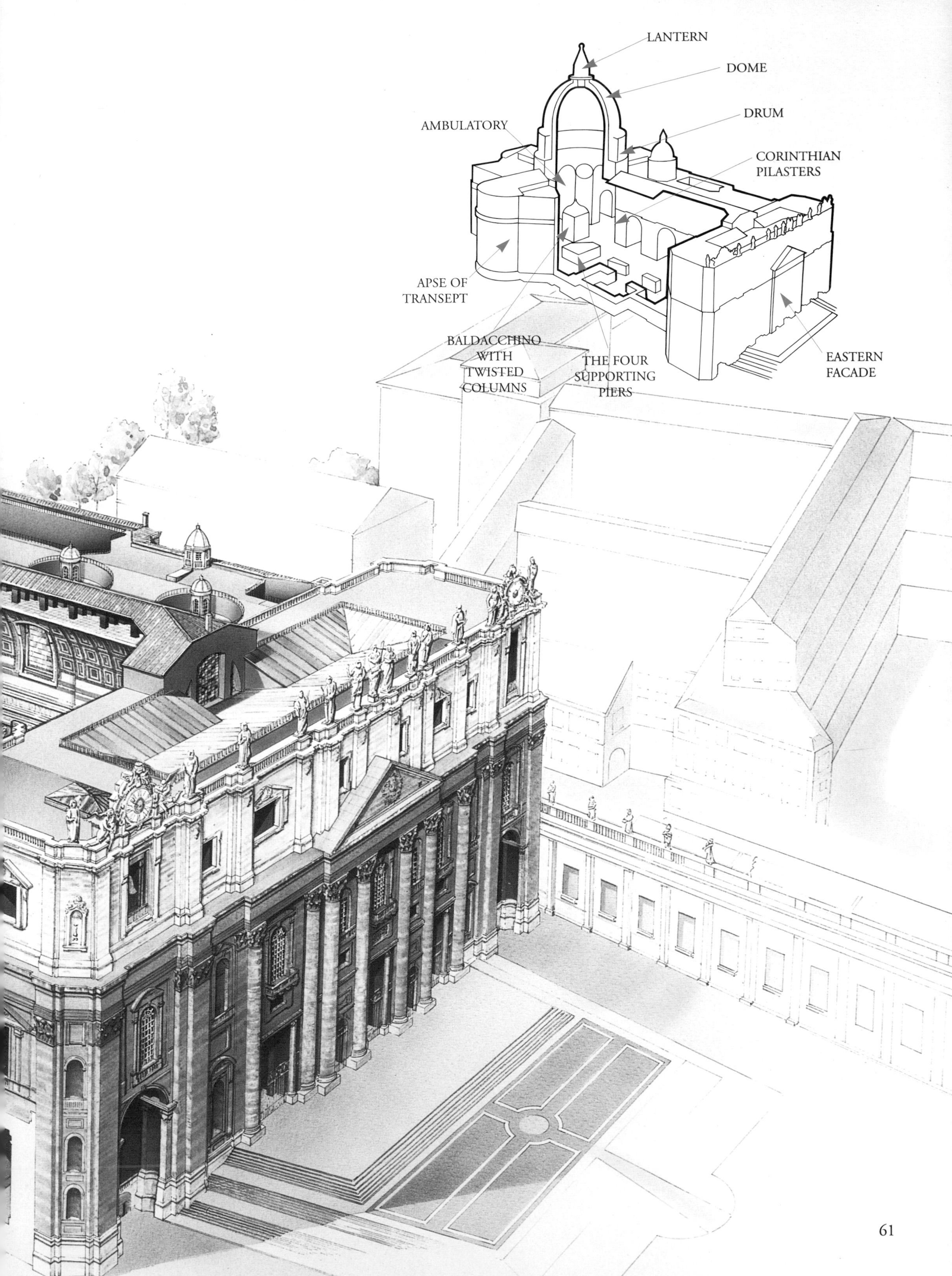
LANTERN
DOME
DRUM
AMBULATORY
CORINTHIAN PILASTERS
APSE OF TRANSEPT
BALDACCHINO WITH TWISTED COLUMNS
THE FOUR SUPPORTING PIERS
EASTERN FACADE

AUSTRIA

SALZBURG CATHEDRAL

The Cathedral of St Rupert and St Vergil is a noble baroque building in the heart of Salzburg

AUSTRIAN BAROQUE

Of all Austria's contemporary ecclesiastical buildings, Salzburg Cathedral has been described as the most perfect example of the baroque style. When it was being built, Austria was at the very beginning of what was to be its greatest period of architectural achievement – Austrian baroque.

Three architects are usually associated with this era: Johann Bernhard Fischer von Erlach designed public buildings and palaces, such as the Karlskirke and parts of the Hofburg in Vienna; Lukas von Hildebrandt concentrated his skills on designing palaces and produced the magnificent Belvedere Palace on the outskirts of Vienna; and Jakob Prandtauer was solely a builder of monasteries, most of which were in the Danube Valley.

The baroque period in architecture flourished from the late 1500s to the early 1700s, and few nations in Europe adapted their architecture, music and art so readily to this particular style as the Austrians. Two glorious celebrations of the baroque can be seen in the magnificent cathedrals in Salzburg and Linz. Like Vienna, the capital, Salzburg is rich in baroque buildings, and the entire city exudes an aura of the elegance and refinement of the days when the composer Mozart was born, and the great Habsburg Empire was at its peak.

AN ANCIENT SITE

The Irish monk St Rupert founded a bishopric in Salzburg around the year 700. In the 770s, St Vergil, another Irish-born monk, became bishop and founded the first cathedral here. In the 10th century this little cathedral, and the rest of the city, was seriously damaged after a series of raids by the Magyars invading from the east. The cathedral was partly rebuilt, but no major repairs took place until the end of the 12th century. It started as a simple basilica, with a nave and two aisles on either side, and a handsome lantern tower rising above. Other alterations and extensions were completed during the following 400 years, but at the beginning of the 17th century the building was almost entirely demolished to make way for a spectacular new baroque cathedral of honey-yellow stone and green copper domes.

BAROQUE SPLENDOUR

The citizens of Salzburg felt that something impressive was needed for their city, a cathedral that would reflect the grace and elegance of the baroque. They turned to Italy for inspiration and plans were drawn up by the Italian architect Vincenzo Scamozzi (1552–1616) for what would have been an astounding structure. But these plans were rejected and the Salzburg elders and churchmen approached another Italian, Santino Solari, to provide an alternative design. Solari's elaborate plan *did* meet with the citizens' approval, and work began almost immediately, in 1611.

RIGHT: A gloriously ornate roof boss exemplifies the Baroque magnificence of Salzburg Cathedral.

ABOVE: The west façade with its two symmetrical towers is of pale Salzburg marble. The cathedral lies within a group of churches and bell-towers in the area of the Old Town.

In contrast with the earlier cathedral Solari's building took the form of a Latin cross, the western arm being longer than the north and south arms of the transepts and the eastern arm of the choir. Magnificent apses were placed at the end of the cross's arms and there was a great dome over the crossing, but no aisles.

The western façade is especially handsome, with two superbly proportioned square towers separated by an ornate pediment almost as tall as the towers themselves. At each level there is a simple square- or round-headed window, the lintels of which are elaborately embellished. The towers are topped by a simple balustrade, behind which are octagonal drums with circular windows. The drums each support a delicate dome and a lantern.

Light and colour

Despite the height and narrow width of Salzburg Cathedral, the interior is as well-lit as any of the best French Gothic churches. Most of the light comes from the square windows that pierce the drum below the cupola over the central crossing, and from the clear glass windows of the apses in the choir and transepts.

The interior is further brightened by the exquisite frescos and stucco work which lend a dazzling array of colours to the walls and ceiling. During the day the sunlight bounces off the decorative panels and brilliant white pillars, while in the evening, when the cathedral is lit by hanging candelabra, the colouring is more subtle, with soft shadows and gentler hues.

AUSTRIA

ST STEPHEN'S CATHEDRAL

A 14th-century Gothic hall-church cathedral in the centre of Vienna

ABOVE: This lifelike painted figure can be found at the base of an arch in St Stephen's Cathedral.

RIGHT: The cathedral shows the results of architectural developments during eight centuries.

ALTE-STEFFL

The towering steeple adjoining the south transept is known affectionately by the Viennese as Alte-Steffl ('Old Steve'). Built between 1368 and 1433, it has been claimed as 'the supreme monument of the German Gothic style', and, considering its princely proportions and handsome carvings, it is difficult to dispute this. The architect in the latter stages was the German-born Master von Prachatitz, a talented sculptor and stonemason.

The tower is square at the base then becomes polygonal before tapering into a circular spire. Adorning it is layer after layer of filigree stonework, rising to a delicately carved cross some 448 feet (134m) above the ground.

The unique profile of St Stephen's Cathedral soars over the beautiful city of Vienna (Wien), its slender tower rising above its distinctive steep-pitched roof, designed to withstand the heavy falls of winter snow. Decorating the roof are vividly patterned tiles, in places displaying the eagle motif of the imperial Habsburgs.

In 1857 construction began on a great boulevard – the Ringstraße – which was designed to replace the old city ramparts. Enclosing most of Vienna's venerable buildings, it forms a circle with a canal branching off from the Danube. Here St Stephen's stands in noble company near the Hofburg (the former Imperial palace), the late 19th-century Rathaus and parliament buildings, the Opera House and the 14th-century university.

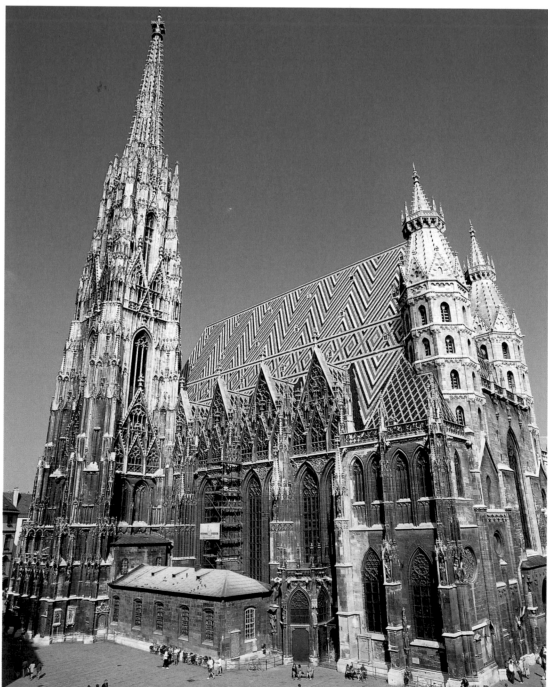

Austrian Gothic

In the 1140s a simple cathedral was built on the site now occupied by St Stephen's, much of which was demolished in the 13th century to make way for the second larger and grander building. With it, a move was made away from the original basilica plan to that of the hall-church, a vast nave with aisles of almost equal height and width ending with three apses – a style that was used subsequently as a model for other Austrian churches. All the light comes from the massive windows in the aisles and apse, as the nave has no triforium or clerestory. There are about 30 chapels leading off the aisles and the apse, many of which feature handsome marble altars.

When the nave and choir were completed work began on the towers. The lofty southern tower was completed by 1433, and building work on the short northern tower was started in 1430. This was completed in the mid-16th century when a cupola was mounted.

The roof is enormous, and shows a clear Germanic influence in the rich patterning of the tiles. The exotic designs vary from rows of brightly coloured diamonds to simple zig-zags, picked out in bright reds, greens and whites.

The west front is dwarfed by the towering free-standing southern steeple (see panel), and comprises two small polygonal towers over an especially fine portal. This is the oldest part of the cathedral, the only surviving part of the pre-13th-century building. The symmetrical towers are built of a creamy-coloured stone that contrasts somewhat starkly against the rest of the building. Both are lit by small, round-headed windows and taper off into carved spires.

A rich interior

After suffering severe damage during World War II the interior was little more than a shell, but painstaking restoration has since returned it to its former glory.

The sculpture and furnishings in the cathedral are among the finest in central Europe, with several famous artists having contributed to the work. The organ was built by Anton Pilgram in the early 16th century, while the glorious high altar was designed by Jakob Pock. Pilgram also carved the pulpit (1510–15), a splendid monumental piece with amazingly delicate and complicated lace-like designs. In the panels, cleverly sculpted figures depict the Latin fathers St Gregory, St Jerome, St Augustine and St Ambrose delivering sermons, some with pious, benevolent expressions, others breathing fire and thunder – another interpretation is that the figures represent the four 'humours'. Pilgram's portrait can be seen carved on both the pulpit and the organ base.

Also dating from the early 16th century is the tomb of Emperor Frederick III, a glorious affair in the style of Lucas van Leyden (a painter and engraver born in the Netherlands in 1494, and influenced by Dürer).

Underneath the cathedral are the catacombs, a labyrinth of dank tunnels which are open to the public at certain times.

BELOW: The vivid patterns made by the glazed tiles of the roof. Visitors who climb the 312 steps of the south tower are rewarded with a magnificent view of the city.

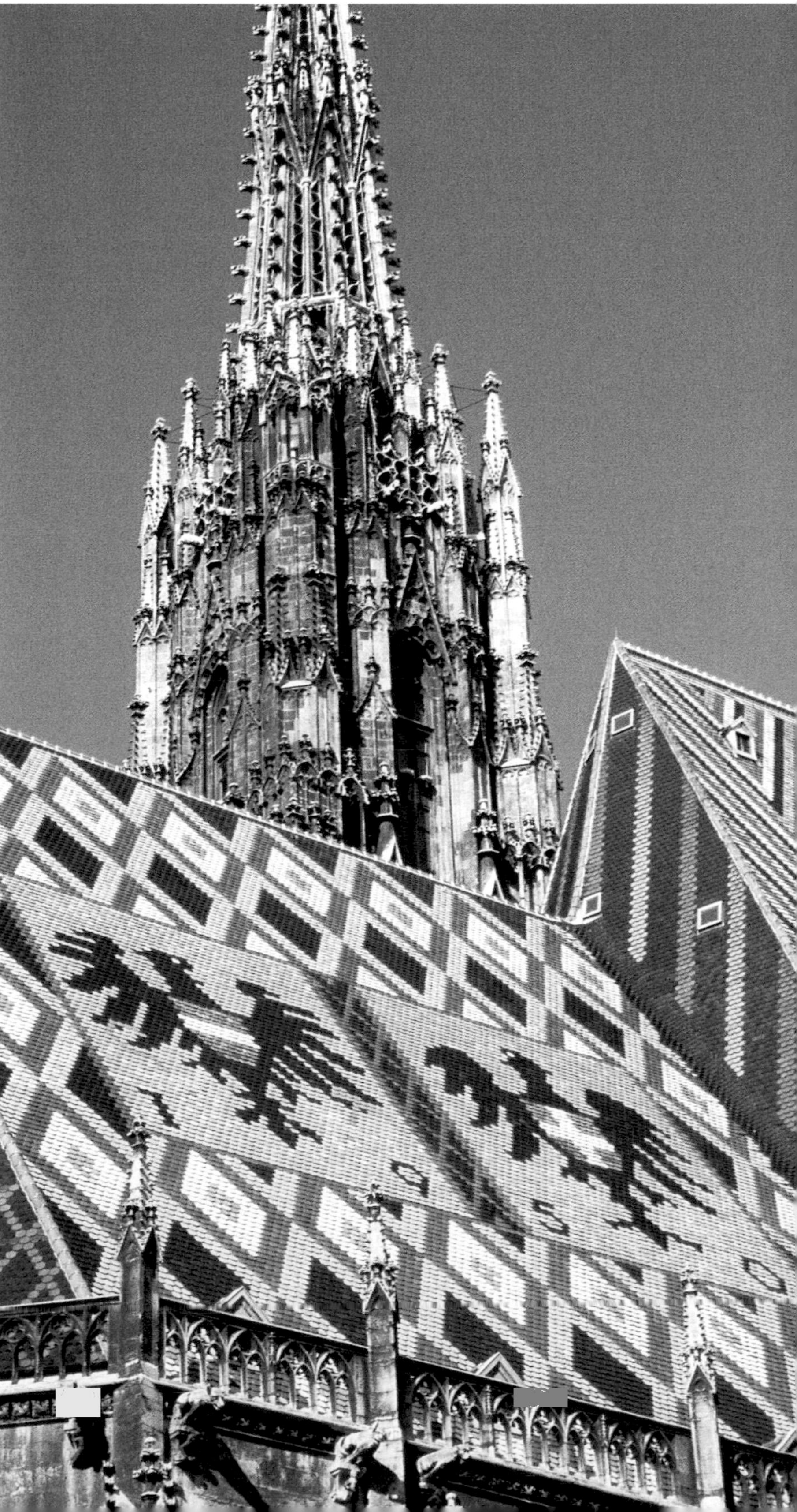

SWITZERLAND

LAUSANNE CATHEDRAL

The 13th-century Notre-Dame Cathedral is Switzerland's most impressive Gothic building

The noble Gothic Cathedral of Notre-Dame in the ancient city of Lausanne offers a stark contrast to the glorious rococo flamboyance of St Gall's Cathedral in the north-east (see page 68), and the sombre Romanesque Cathedral of Mariä Himmelfahrt in Chur, in the east of the country. Switzerland's largest and most splendid Gothic church, Notre-Dame stands prominently on a hill in the sprawling Old City, overlooking the sparkling, deep-blue waters of Lake Geneva.

BELOW: Looking upwards near the entrance to the cathedral, visitors find graceful roof vaulting lit by bright stained glass. The interior displays a pleasing unity of design.

CHANGING FORTUNES

Not surprisingly, the cathedral was not the first building to occupy this strategically important site, and until the 8th century there was a Roman fortress here. In about 800, during the reign of Charlemagne, this was partly demolished to make way for a big Lombardian church with a nave and two aisles. This lasted until around 1000, when it was demolished in order that a larger church with a fine porch and baptistry could be built. In 1173 Bishop Landry de Durnes ordered that a new cathedral should be raised, and work started in the Romanesque style.

Building did not continue for long, however, and there followed a substantial break in proceedings until the 13th century, when the work resumed. By this time Romanesque architecture had gone out of fashion and Lausanne Cathedral was completed in the Gothic style. The name of the later architect is not known, but it is clear that he gained his inspiration from the magnificent cathedrals of northern France.

For over 200 years the bishops of Lausanne enjoyed a position of considerable power, adding other buildings – a palace, offices, storerooms and halls of accommodation for their monks – in a cluster around the cathedral. Then, in 1536, troops from Bern advanced on Lausanne and ousted the bishop and his retinue: the cathedral became a simple parish church and its choir was used for scientific lectures and various other secular activities.

In 1873 Viollet-le-Duc (who died in Lausanne in 1879) began a programme of restoration, but much destruction had taken place during Protestantism, leaving the interior bare of treasures.

PERFECT PROPORTIONS

The plan of Lausanne Cathedral is simple; the nave is flanked by two aisles, and there is an ambulatory, a transept and a handsome west façade with twin towers. With its forest of piers and pillars of different sizes and designs the nave is especially fine, while the transepts have two-storey chapels with tiers of slender Gothic arches rising to beautiful vaulted roofs. At arcade and clerestory levels the pointed windows are filled with brightly coloured glass, depicting scenes from the Bible, which splash the creamy stone floor with blues and reds.

Lausanne has some of the finest Gothic portals in Europe and among the best of these is the 16th-century door in the west front. Above the inner portal a statue of the Virgin Mary sits above a wall of delicate lattice-work. The Apostle Portal on the south side of the cathedral still possesses fragments of the original paintwork that decorated it. There are statues of the 12 apostles standing in an open vaulted hall, while over the portal itself are carvings of the Virgin Mary being taken to Heaven ard crowned by her son.

One of the most striking features of this elegant building is its well-balanced proportions. The cathedral is about 328 feet (98m) in length, but the architect has cleverly conspired to ensure that it is evenly lit – there are no blinding shafts of light, and no dismal corners. Whether admiring the cathedral from the inside or the outside, there is no single feature that draws the eye to the detraction of the whole. In a word, the cathedral is harmonious, and a fitting monument to the anonymous architect who designed it 700 years ago.

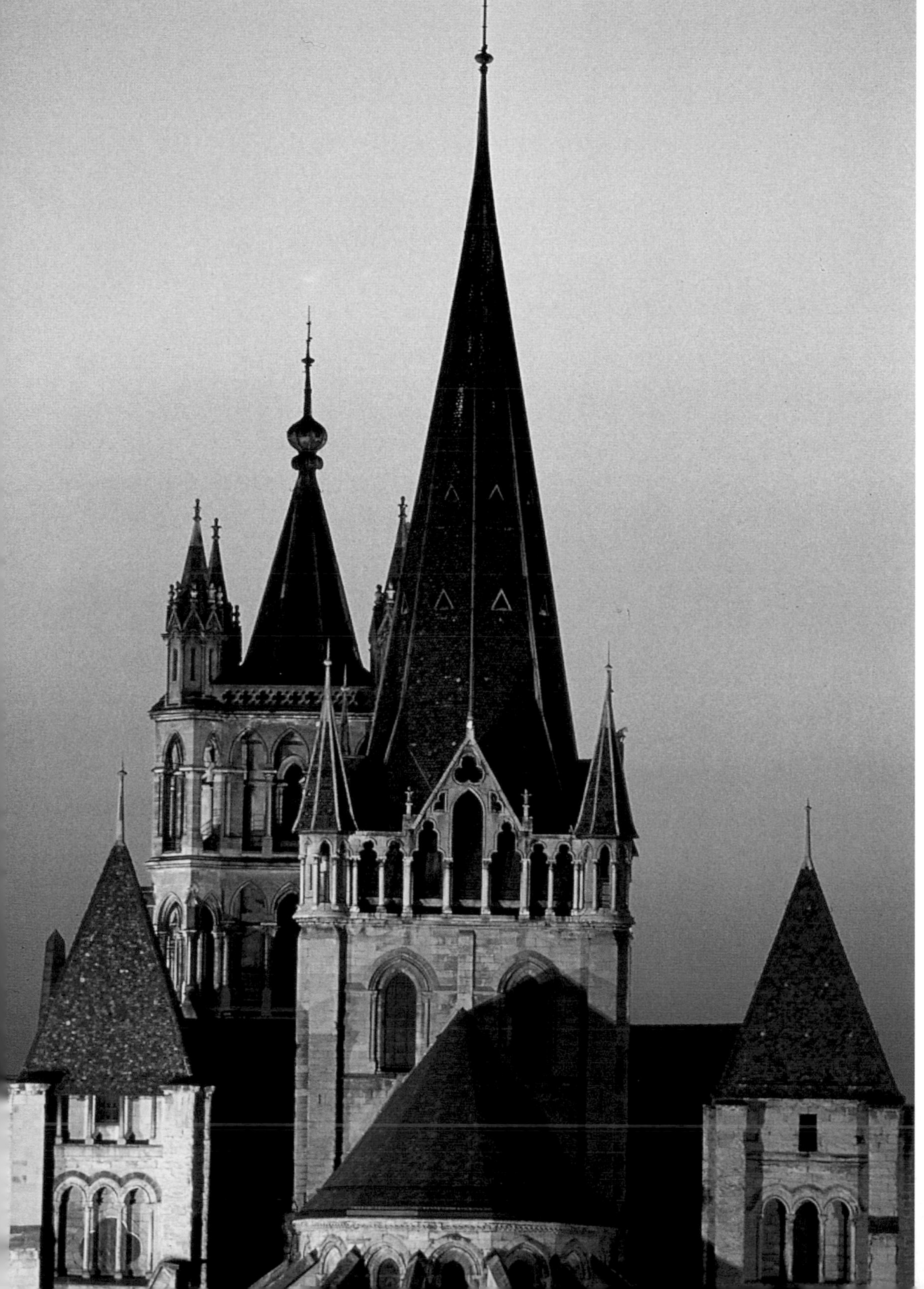

The Rose of Lausanne

Perhaps Lausanne Cathedral's finest feature is the lovely 13th-century rose window in the south transept which allows coloured light to flood into the transept as far as the nave in a dazzling display of reds, golds, greens and blues.

The tracery forms an intricate pattern of squares and circles arranged in a complex geometric design based on a cruciform arrangement. The round glass discs, centred around an image of Christ in Glory, are surrounded by scenes from the Creation, signs of the zodiac, and pictures of the four rivers of Paradise.

The window is said to be the work of the northern French artist Peter of Arras, one of the best-known glass-makers of the early Gothic period.

LEFT: The cathedral's spires are dramatic at dusk; each has its own spiral staircase within. Lausanne is one of the last towns to maintain a night watch, and a town crier shouts the time hourly from the cathedral between 10pm and 2am.

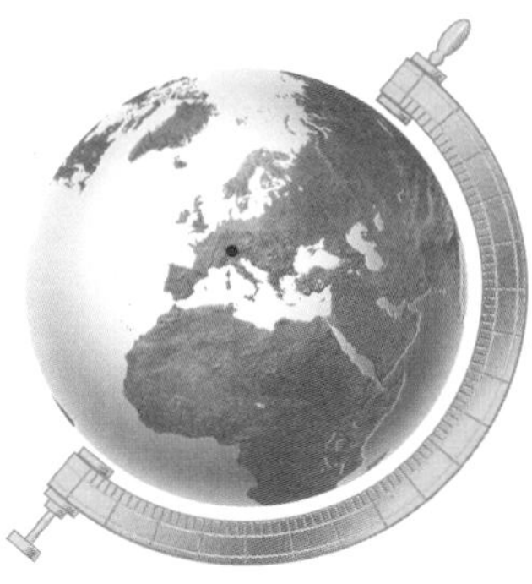

SWITZERLAND

ST GALL'S CATHEDRAL

This exuberant baroque cathedral stands on the site of a 7th-century hermit's cell

SWITZERLAND'S CATHEDRALS

Switzerland boasts a dozen or so cathedrals in all, ranging from the superb baroque exuberance of St Gall to the rather sombre Chur. Switzerland was subject to a variety of architectural influences, which is not surprising given its location on the borders of Italy, Germany and France.

Basle Münster, generally regarded as the finest of the Swiss cathedrals, is one of the oldest, consecrated in 1019. Its portals were carved by German sculptors in the 12th century, the statues inside were executed by Italian artists, and the spires bear a resemblance to those of Notre-Dame in Paris.

Besides St Gall, other post-Reformation cathedrals include Lucerne, rebuilt in Renaissance style after a fire in 1633, Lugano, and parts of Fribourg.

RIGHT: The glorious Baroque interior is justly famous, and includes magnificent grilles enclosing the high altar, which dates from 1810.

The Cathedral of St Gall is a fabulous celebration of baroque architecture, its interior a battle of startling whites, subdued greens and blazing gilt, while its rose-cream exterior is more sober, dominated by twin towers that look out across a spacious square.

The town of St Gallen, just south of Lake Constance, takes its name from the cathedral which, until 1846, was an abbey church.

St Gallen and the Benedictines

Gallen, or Gall as he was called in his native Celtic tongue, was a scholar and hermit who travelled from Ireland to Switzerland in about 615 in search of solitude. He built himself a tiny cell in a thick forest where he lived until his death around 640. After he died word spread about Gall's reputed holiness and learning, and a Benedictine monastery was built on the site of his simple dwelling.

By the end of the 8th century this had become an important religious site and plans dating from 820 show that it was a well-organised foundation with a church, refectory, sleeping quarters and a kitchen range. The monastery continued to grow in wealth and influence into the 10th century, so much so that it was in danger of attack by Saracens who were raiding in the area and the monks had to raise a sturdy wall to repel the invaders.

When the Reformation swept across Europe in the 16th century, Switzerland followed the teachings of the French Protestant reformer John Calvin, who was a virtual dictator in nearby Geneva from 1541 until his death in 1564. The Benedictines in the great monastery of St Gall were dispersed, and the abbey buildings put to other uses.

Grace and simplicity

In about 1755 work began on a new abbey church with a German architect by the name of Peter Thumb (1681–1766). He based his design on a basilica plan, with the unusual addition of short apsidal transepts. The main building phase only took 15 years to complete, but Thumb died about four years before the work on the cathedral was finished.

The exterior of his church, although indisputably baroque, shows a restraint in keeping with the city and with Switzerland's traditionally sober architectural history, and exudes a sense of grace and simplicity. The eastern end is dominated by twin towers surmounted by bulbous ribbed cupolas with elegant lanterns. They rise in three stages of roughly equal height, all decorated with subtly proportioned oculi and round-headed arches. A smaller lantern stands at the apex of the roof above the attractive polygonal apse.

St Gall is unusual in having its principal façade to the east, since most cathedrals and churches have a dominant western front, including a ceremonial entrance, or great west door.

The body of the cathedral is characterised by rows of plain, tall, round-headed arched windows picked out in white to contrast with the deeper pink of the surrounding stone. The transepts take the form of a magnificent rotunda that bulges outwards halfway down the nave and provides a sense of space after the narrowness of the nave and choir.

A riot of green and gold

The sobriety of the outside of St Gall's does not prepare the visitor for the explosion of colour – predominantly a vivid array of greens and golds – that decorates the ceilings, pillars and walls. The frescos on the inside of the rotunda were executed by Christian Wensinger (1710–97).

Every arch is highlighted with patterns of red and gold, while the vaults seethe with mysterious green clouds and heavenly beings. The pillars, above and below the capitals, drip with foliate carvings picked out in pale green or glittering gold, and statues, icons and monuments positively effervesce with ornamentation in a display of rococo unsurpassed anywhere else in the country.

BELOW: The eastern façade with its two towers, which is embellished with a low relief on the pediment depicting the Coronation of the Virgin – a modern (1933) replica of the original work.

LIÈGE CATHEDRAL

Formerly the Collegiate Church of St Paul, the cathedral is especially noted for its exquisite carvings

RIGHT: The Cathedral of St Paul is not so grand as the former Cathedral of St Lambert, destroyed in 1794, but its simple style shows influences of French and German architecture.

Like Durham Cathedral in the north of England, Liège Cathedral was the seat of powerful prince-bishops in medieval times. Their wealth and influence meant that the cathedral gained an outstanding number of treasures such as the relics of St Lambert and lovely medieval stained glass windows.

It was unfortunately true, however, that the same wealth attracted attention from forces uninterested in the preservation of ecclesiastical history: the medieval Cathedral of St Lambert was totally destroyed when troops from the French Revolution spilled across to occupy Belgium at the end of the 18th century. When the religious fervour had abated, the Collegiate Church of St Paul was designated the new cathedral at Liège.

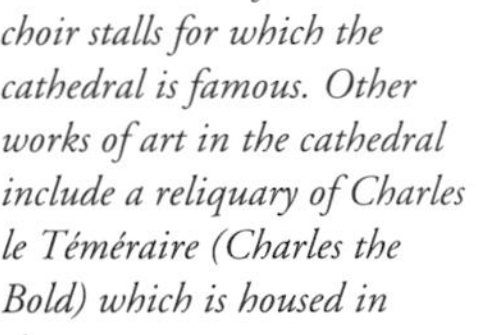

BELOW: One of the carved choir stalls for which the cathedral is famous. Other works of art in the cathedral include a reliquary of Charles le Téméraire (Charles the Bold) which is housed in the treasury.

ST PAUL'S COLLEGIATE CHURCH

St Paul's, a simple, large cruciform church in the centre of Liège, had a handsome chapter house and a large cloister. Although it was founded during the middle of the 10th century by Bishop Heraclius, virtually all that remains dates from the 13th century or later. The choir, transepts, chapter house and parts of the nave, erected between 1232 and 1289, represent the earliest work. The original east end was replaced by a lovely polygonal apse in 1334 and the clerestory and vaulting in the nave date from the 16th century.

The western tower dominates the appearance of the cathedral from the outside. Its lower part is ancient, but the upper parts, including the spire and four bell turrets, date from 1813 and were possibly modelled in the style of the spire of the destroyed St Lambert's Cathedral.

The cathedral underwent intense restoration in the mid-19th century, and again after it was damaged by a flying bomb during World War II.

A BEAUTIFUL INTERIOR

The inside of the cathedral is most attractive. Round pillars topped with polygonal capitals support a high arched roof still sporting its original 16th-century painting executed in the arabesque style. The painting is a masterpiece of scrolls, birds and flowers, all linked in an intricate design. The predominant colour of the ceiling is green, while the stone pillars, arches and rib-vaulting are either slate-grey or a honey-yellow.

The tall nave is separated by pillars from double aisles, although the outer aisles have been divided into a series of chapels. The choir follows the simplicity of the nave and is lit by three slender, immensely tall lancet windows in the eastern end. These windows still possess their original 16th-century stained glass and are well worth seeing. The windows in the eastern wall of the two transepts are also very fine and have been compared to those of Westminster Abbey. The great west window is very intricate, but the best window is the one in the south transept, dating from 1530, that depicts the Coronation of the Virgin. This was designed when the art of making stained glass windows was at its very peak and is a glorious celebration of colour and geometric design. Depending on the time of day, it can appear either as a blazing sunset of reds, oranges and ambers, or, in low light, as a more subtle blend of shades.

The stalls in the choir are said to be among the finest in Belgium. The canopies drip like lace over the exquisite carvings of the Resurrection of Saints (on the south side), and the Translation of the Relics of St Hubert (on the north side). These were designed by Durlet of Antwerp. Also of note are the brass screen that separates the nave from the choir, the handsome reredos, and the towering pulpit dating from 1844.

LIÈGE'S TREASURES

Among the cathedral's treasures is a reliquary of St Lambert that is said to contain his skull. This, along with a fine collection of ecclesiastical vestments and plate, is in the cathedral treasury which is entered from the south side of the cloisters. The rest of the saint's remains are displayed in a shrine, dating to 1896, which is housed in the main cathedral.

RIGHT: The altar, seen against the inspiring backdrop of one of the cathedral's many beautiful stained glass windows.

BELGIUM

MALINES CATHEDRAL

The magnificent western tower of St Rombout's Cathedral dominates Malines

Mystery surrounds the exact period in which the mighty cathedral at Malines (Mechelen) was built. It is known that an abbey was founded here in the 8th century by an Irish monk, Rombout, who travelled through Europe converting people to Christianity. He was canonised after he was martyred. At some point in the early 13th century work began on the nave and the transepts. A fire destroyed much of this early work and the building underwent an extensive rebuilding programme in the 15th century.

However, St Rombout's did not become a cathedral until 1559 when religious disturbances resulted in the reorganisation of Belgian bishoprics. Malines became an archbishopric, and remained so until the French Revolution spilled over into Belgium in 1794. Subsequently the Archbishop of Malines was arrested for failing to comply with the demands of the Republic and was driven into exile. A revolution in 1830 saw Belgium emancipated, and Malines was made the seat of the Primate of Belgium.

BELOW: The interior of St Rombout's Cathedral. Malines is at the centre of Belgium's carillon tradition, and the bells in the cathedral belfry are a splendid example. The Royal Carillon School is near by.

The nave is elegantly Gothic, with simple, round columns rising up to the handsome tracery of the clerestory windows. A series of panels between the clerestory and the main arcade was decorated in the Classical period by plaster mouldings. These have not proved popular with architectural historians on the basis that they are incongruous with the rest of the building.

The choir is thought to have been started in the 1340s and the vaulting completed in the 1450s. It is dominated by an enormous baroque altarpiece, topped by a large statue of St Rombout, designed by Fayd'herbe. He was a student of Rubens and his carvings are an explosion of intricate patterns, featuring flowers, plants and geometric designs.

The cathedral is rich in works of art, including the pulpit which has carvings of the Conversion of St Paul. It stands on a rock base, and the handrail has been carved to look like a fallen tree, complete with a mass of carved twigs, leaves, flowers and various creatures crawling up the branches.

In the south transept is a painting of the *Crucifixion* by Van Dyck, dating to about 1627 and considered to be one of his finest works. The 18th-century English portrait painter, Sir Joshua Reynolds, criticised the artist for making Mary Magdalene's hair look too silky. Several pictures of St Rombout and his life can be seen in the transept. These were presented by various churchmen on the occasion of the Papal Jubilee in 1775.

Of the stained glass, the most interesting is that in the Chapel of the Blessed Sacrament, designed to commemorate the First Eucharistic Congress of 1930 that was held at Malines. It features symbolic representations of the nations that took part.

The western tower

The most outstanding feature of the cathedral at Malines, despite the fact that it was never completed, is its magnificent western tower. Built between 1452 and 1578 to a design by Wauthier Coolmans, the plans show that he intended the great tower to be topped by a slender spire that would have reached a staggering 548 feet (164m). Although the existing tower is only 320 feet (96m) high, it lacks nothing from its missing spire. Every line emphasises the vertical, achieving a simultaneous impression of strength and lightness which prompted Vauban, Louis XIV's brilliant military engineer, to call it the Eighth Wonder of the World. Visitors must climb 558 steps to reach the top, yet the foundations on which the tower rests are only 9 feet (3m) thick. The tower houses two carillons, each of 49 bells, which were hung in the 15th and 16th centuries.

LEFT: The stunning 18th-century pulpit is carved in a highly naturalistic style to resemble a fallen tree.

Rubens and Van Dyck

Sir Anthony Van Dyck (1599–1641), one of Belgium's greatest painters, was born in Antwerp. He studied under Peter Paul Rubens (1577–1640) and travelled extensively to study painters in other parts of Europe. Knighted by Charles I of England, his painting greatly influenced English portrait artists in the 18th century. As an artist Van Dyck was prolific and his paintings decorate many cathedrals and churches in Europe.

Rubens was even more prolific; he painted at least 40 church ceilings, as well as many altarpieces. One of his most famous paintings, *The Descent from the Cross*, hangs in Antwerp Cathedral. Several of his paintings are in the Church of St Jean in Malines.

BELOW: One of the carved statues of apostles in the main arcade; this one represents St Andrew.

Belgium

Tournai Cathedral

Notre-Dame in Tournai is often considered to be the most splendid cathedral in Belgium

The treasury

The cathedral treasury is well endowed with ecclesiastical valuables. Of special note are the two lovely 13th-century reliquaries, an early 6th-century Byzantine cross carved from ivory, a painting by Rubens depicting souls in purgatory, a diptych of St Nicaise, and a chasuble said to have belonged to the English saint Thomas à Becket, who visited Tournai in 1170 (the year he was murdered in Canterbury Cathedral [see page 110]).

Another English churchman associated with the cathedral is Cardinal Wolsey, Henry VIII's Lord Chancellor. Tournai was under English rule between 1513 and 1518, during which time Wolsey occupied the bishopric.

Cathedral-building in Belgium

Belgium's cathedrals have been subject to many architectural influences over the centuries. French and German styles are apparent at Tournai, Brussels, Ghent, Liège and Malines, while English (St Michael's Cathedral's façade, Brussels), Spanish (Antwerp), and Italian (St Aubain and Namur) influences have also played their part.

It was not until the Flemings attained a degree of financial independence that a local style began to break through, as can be seen, for example, in the tower at Malines (see page 72).

In the pretty medieval town of Tournai the five great Romanesque towers of the Cathedral of Notre-Dame soar into the sky. Each one (there were originally seven) stands 270 feet (81m) tall.

Tournai Cathedral underwent a serious programme of restoration between 1850 and 1860, under the direction of Lemaistre d'Anstaign. D'Anstaign scraped years of whitewash from the walls and pillars to reveal the stonework underneath, restored the tracery to the upper windows, and added the stained glass. Unlike many other restorations in this period, d'Anstaign's was sensitive to the origins of the building, enhancing the harmony with which Gothic and Romanesque combine in this magnificent cathedral.

Early history

Tournai's history stretches right back to the Dark Ages. Clovis, King of the Franks, was converted to Christianity in 496 and it is thought that he founded a church in Tournai, then the capital city of the Frankish Empire, at about the same time. In the 800s Clovis' church was rebuilt as a basilica, but was known to have been attacked, and perhaps destroyed, by Viking raids in 881.

The cathedral that stands so majestically today was started in the 11th century on a design similar to those at Speyer and Worms in Germany. Its striking towers, dating to between 1150 and 1250, rise above the town in four tiers of graceful, round-headed arches. Each one is topped by a neat, slate-grey pyramid added in the late 1500s, and is adorned with a metal cross. The central tower, although the same height as the others, is broader and has a larger pyramidal spire. These towers were so imposing that the one to the north of the nave was once used as a prison.

The nave dates from the 12th century and, like the towers, rises in four tiers of arches. Although the pillars have ornately carved capitals they have no bases and the arches are plain without mouldings. The white plaster of the upper part of the nave contrasts vividly with the plain blue-grey limestone of the walls below.

A remarkable choir

The Romanesque choir was evidently considered to be too plain in the 1240s, for it was replaced with one built in the Gothic style by French stone masons working for Bishop Walter de Marvis, who was responsible for many churches built in the area in the mid-1200s. It is vast – almost as long as the nave itself – and stands about 110 feet (33m) tall and 100 feet (30m) wide, excluding the five chapels around the apse. The Renaissance furnishings were designed by the Flemish artist Cornelis de Vrient

LEFT: The circular apse or 'chevet' and three of the five towers. In the foreground is a statue depicting the Parable of the Blind.

(1514–75) in 1572. However, the flamboyance of this later style does clash somewhat with the simplicity of the rest of the cathedral. A huge marble screen separates the nave from the choir, also designed by de Vrient. It resembles a great bath-tub and has huge square pillars rising to an arched pediment; there are also four enormous candlesticks.

By the time de Vrient worked on Tournai Cathedral it had been through the Reformation and a series of religious wars that had seen many of the fine carvings destroyed in a frenzy of Protestant zeal. In 1566 many cathedral documents were also taken away and destroyed, including the original deed of gift from King Chilperic. (Chilperic or Childeric I, King of the Franks, who died in 481, was the father of Clovis, who was converted to Christianity.) Tournai, along with many other Belgian churches, suffered in 1794 when it was overrun by French Revolutionary troops. It was systematically sacked, anything of value was spirited away and painted glass and statues were remorselessly smashed.

BELOW: A view of the impressive choir. The nave, with its large open triforium, is Northern French in style. The cathedral is built mainly in black marble from the surrounding region.

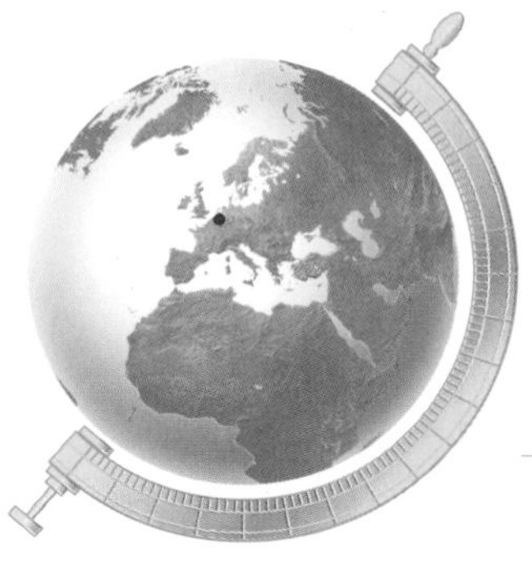

'S-HERTOGENBOSCH CATHEDRAL

St John's Cathedral, the Netherlands' finest ecclesiastical building, is famous for the carved figures scrambling up its walls

RIGHT: The highly decorative stonework which adorns the cathedral provides an unusual example of the 'Brabantine' Flamboyant style, a development of French Gothic architecture.

Unlike its sister cathedral in Utrecht (see page 78), St John's in 's-Hertogenbosch was not as affected by the movement against the beautification of churches and cathedrals during the Reformation. It became Protestant in 1629, and continued to be so until Napoleon's rise to power in the late 18th century. When the emperor invaded the Netherlands, he made his younger brother Louis King of Holland, and returned 's-Hertogenbosch Cathedral to the Catholic Church.

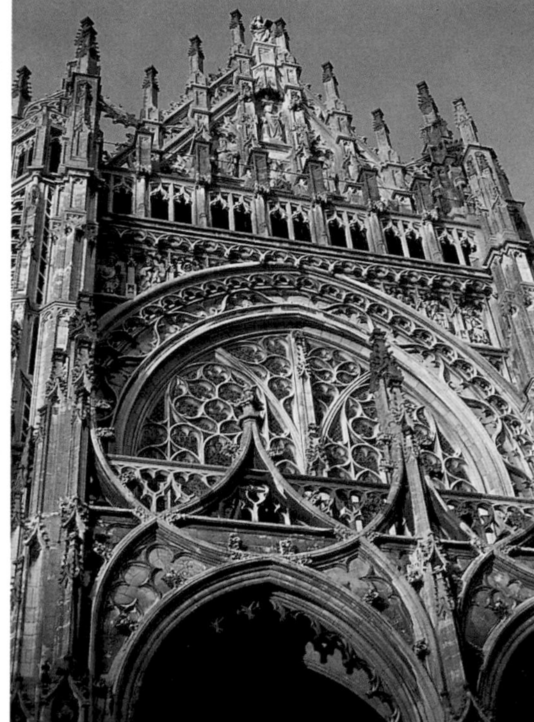

A NEW CATHEDRAL IS RAISED

The first church on the site was raised around 1200, although nothing survives of this building except the lower part of the tower. It was dedicated to St John, or St Jan, as he was known locally. A few years before, the Flemish Duke of the province of Brabant, Henry I, built a hunting lodge near by which later developed into a formidable fortress. The little town thus became an important military centre and a larger, more impressive ecclesiastical building was required. Work on a second cathedral was started in the 13th century and the Lady Chapel and baptistry survive from this time. However, the cathedral that visitors see today dates mainly from a rebuilding programme that took place between 1336 and 1550.

The outside of the cathedral is a riot of richly carved stone and clusters of pinnacles. Visitors looking upwards will see a swarm of curious creatures sculpted on to the steep copings and the flying buttresses. These were said to be climbing the cathedral in order 'to escape from the demons pursuing them'. It is a pity they are so high up, for these stone manikins possess a fascinating variety of remarkable facial expressions. All these pinnacles and spires give a strong sense of the vertical, drawing the eye ever upwards towards the heavens, as was the intention of late Gothic architecture. Yet the sturdy western tower is capped by octagonal drums with little domes, and the central crossing has a lantern tower with a cupola.

BELOW: The Altar of the Passion, a 15th-century triptych. In the central panels, sculptures embellished with gilt depict Christ carrying the Cross, the Crucifixion, and the Descent from the Cross. The six surrounding paintings act as shutters which can be closed to protect the altar.

A TOWERING NAVE

The interior of the cathedral is every bit as impressive as the outside. The 15th-century Flamboyant nave, characterised by slender and elaborate curves, towers some 110 feet (33m) above the floor, its delicately arched roof supported by 150 pillars.

To either side are the aisles – two to the south and two to the north – and five transepts, all decorated in the Flamboyant style. The elegant Lady Chapel has a lovely 13th-century statue of the Virgin Mary that was said to be capable of performing miracles in medieval times and continues to be a focus of pilgrimages. The font, standing in the south aisle, is sculpted in bronze and dates from the 1490s.

Hieronymus Bosch

Bosch was born in 's-Hertogenbosch in about 1450 as Jerome van Aken, but took the pseudonym Hieronymus Bosch in honour of the city in which he spent most of his life ('s-Hertogenbosch was officially called Den Bosch for many years). In 1486 Bosch joined the Brotherhood of Our Lady, an organisation dedicated to Catholic ideals.

His paintings were strongly allegorical, featuring fantastic creatures and half-human monsters in a style said to be the forerunner of surrealism. Some of his contemporaries considered his disturbing paintings heretical, but Bosch was staunchly religious, as were his patrons (who included King Philip II of Spain). It is more likely Bosch intended his work to warn against the consequences of evil.

He worked on some of the paintings in 's-Hertogenbosch Cathedral, the best of which are the grisailles in the north transept. These were originally intended to be panels for a door, but were removed and placed inside the cathedral to preserve them. A statue of Bosch stands in the city's market square.

The carillon

The cathedral boasts a splendid carillon of 48 bells, the oldest and heaviest of which was cast by a bell-founder called Jacob Noteman in 1641. It weighs 1,588 pounds (3,500kg). Two of the smaller bells date from 1644 and 1663. Many of the others came from a bell-founder (Gillet and Johnstone of Croydon) in England. The carillon can be heard daily, and it is pleasant to sit in the market square and listen to the bells after visiting the cathedral.

LEFT: The narrow verticals of the nave pillars curve around the magnificent altar.

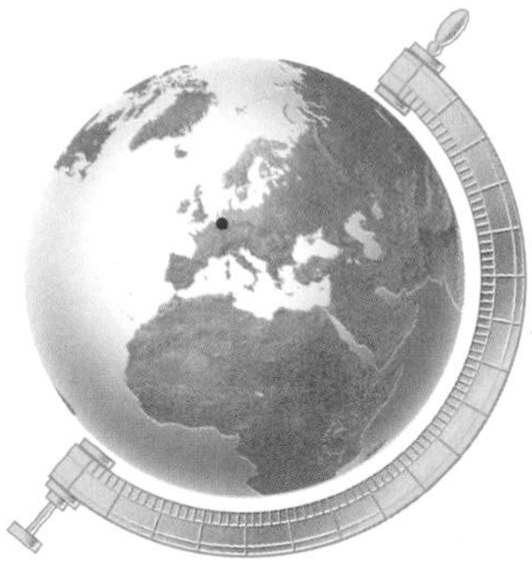

UTRECHT CATHEDRAL

The Protestant Cathedral of St Martin houses the hearts of two Holy Roman Emperors

TWO HOLY ROMAN EMPERORS

When Charlemagne was crowned Emperor of the West by Pope Leo III, a great empire was established which covered much of west and central Europe. Its leaders were powerful men and between the 11th and 13th centuries they often vied with the popes for political control.

The hearts of two of these emperors are displayed as relics in Utrecht Cathedral. Conrad II (990–1039) founded the Salian Dynasty and conquered a good part of Poland, Burgundy and northern Italy. He was Holy Roman Emperor from 1024 to 1039. Henry V (1081–1125) gained control over the German Church from the Pope, but lost the support of his bishops. He was Emperor from 1106 to 1125.

RIGHT: The octagonal tower has been separated from the rest of the cathedral since the hurricane of 1674; the church now consists of choir, transepts and two chapels off the south nave aisle.

In 1674 a violent hurricane swept over the Low Countries, causing great damage to buildings and widespread flooding. One of the structures to suffer was the great cathedral at Utrecht: the nave between the transepts and the west tower was blown down completely. When the rubble was cleared away a great gap was left between the tower and the rest of the church and, curiously, this has never been rebuilt. Today, the tower still stands apart from the rest of the cathedral.

DUTCH CATHEDRAL BUILDING

During the 7th century a small church was founded by the Franks on the site of the present cathedral. It was dedicated to St Willibrord, an Englishman who came to the Low Countries as a missionary and around 700 became archbishop of the Frisians. He spent most of his time at Utrecht. Probably nothing remained of this early church when building on the present cathedral was begun in the mid-13th century.

The Netherlands, unlike neighbouring Belgium, has a lack of good building stone, and Utrecht Cathedral is made from an attractive sandy-coloured brick.

The Reformation in Europe was a powerful influence on the churches in the Low Countries. After the Protestant triumph in Holland – which was most influenced by the teachings of the French-born John Calvin (1509–64) – there was little to encourage the founding of new cathedrals, or the enrichment of those already in existence. The Revolt of the Netherlands, that is, the struggle for independence by the Low Countries against Spanish rule, broke out in 1568 and war continued sporadically until 1648. During this time the University of Utrecht was founded, but that city's cathedral did not benefit from enlightened philosophy of architecture, and the notable absence of ornamentation and decoration deemed suitable for a Protestant cathedral tends to lend it a rather austere appearance. Despite this, there is something inspiring about the simplicity of Utrecht Cathedral.

ABOVE: The monument to Guy d'Avesnes, Bishop of Utrecht, can be found in the second south chapel, where there is also a 15th-century wall painting.

THE CHURCH AND ITS TOWER

The lack of decoration on the outside of the church is more than compensated for by the lavishly decorated choir. This part of the church rises to a height of 115 feet (35m) and architectural historians have long admired the perfect proportions of its arcades, triforium and clerestory. The choir contains some impressive tombs, including the monument to Bishop Guy d'Avesnes (died 1317) which is carved with exquisite tracery designs.

Despite the 1674 storm, the cathedral still boasts two transepts and a gorgeous, peaceful cloister. The windows in the north and south walls of the transepts are huge, stretching almost the entire height of the wall, and marked with some simple, but attractive, tracery. A chapter house was built near by but this is now part of the university.

Standing aloof from the rest of the cathedral for more than 300 years, the western tower looms 340 feet (102m) above the city. It was raised in the 14th century (probably between 1321 and 1382) after the main part of the church had been built and is said to have been a model for several similar church towers in the Netherlands.

Documentation is scanty for the early building work, but it shows that the tower was designed by Jan I van den Dom, more usually known as Magister Johannes de Hannovia. The lower part of the tower comprises tall, slender arches rising to meet a delicately wrought stone balustrade above. The middle section mirrors the lower, although it is slightly smaller. The upper part is a lovely eight-sided lantern tower, with tracery in its windows so light that it appears insubstantial. A carillon was added in the 1660s.

BELOW: The tower, which contains carillon chimes and seven bells, is said to be the tallest church tower in Holland. A climb of 465 steps is required to reach the top.

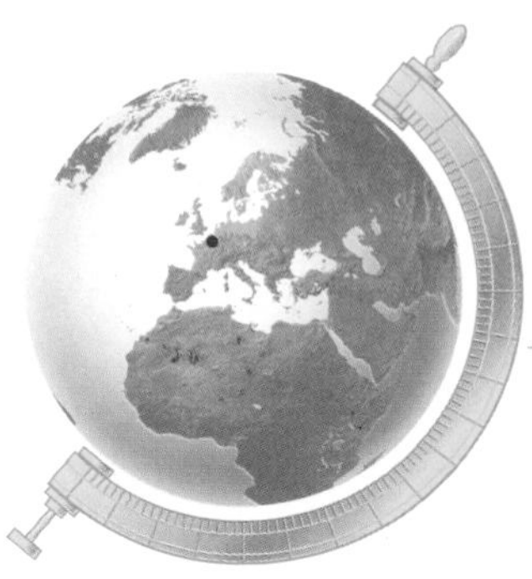

GERMANY

AACHEN CATHEDRAL

The 9th-century domed chapel of Aachen Cathedral houses the tomb of Charlemagne

CHARLEMAGNE

It was from Aix-la-Chapelle, now called Aachen, that Charlemagne (*c*742–814) administered his great empire. He was born around 742, the son of Pepin the Short, who in 751 became King of the Franks. When he was about 30 years old Charlemagne succeeded his father as king and immediately set about conquering the world. By around 800 most of western Christendom was under his control and it is a tribute to his power that he was crowned first Holy Roman Emperor by Pope Leo III.

Charlemagne spent most of the remainder of his reign consolidating his domain, building many cathedrals, churches and palaces, including those at Aachen.

He was a great patron of the arts and Christianity, and his reign is sometimes known as the 'Carolingian Renaissance'.

BELOW: Charlemagne's throne in the Palatine Chapel is constructed of simple slabs of marble.

In 814 Charlemagne, the first Holy Roman Emperor and King of the Franks (see panel), died. Some years before he had ordered his friend, adviser and biographer Einhard to build him a fine palace with its own chapel. Einhard selected the architect Odo of Metz to design something appropriately grand and in 805 the Palatine Chapel was dedicated. It was to this building that the body of Charlemagne was brought after his death, and where it remains.

A CHAPEL FOR AN EMPEROR

Einhard was a remarkable man who, besides being a gifted diplomat and writer, was also interested in the arts, especially architecture. He was familiar both with the work of the 1st-century builders of Rome and with the new style that was being developed in Italy in the form of the lovely San Vitale's chapel in Ravenna. Einhard and Odo worked together to blend sturdy Roman construction techniques with Byzantine elegance and mystery, and the result was the beautiful octagonal Palatine Chapel. This amazing building still stands, despite a turbulent history, and is incorporated into the later Gothic cathedral. It is thought work began on the chapel in around 786, and finished with its dedication in 805.

The design is a simple one, comprising an octagonal nave surrounded by a polygonal vaulted aisle with a gallery above. Separated from the nave by arches, the aisle is built in alternating bands of different coloured stone. The gallery is reached by spiral staircases on either side of the entrance porch and is separated from the nave by two tiers of colonnades made of marble and granite.

The whole chapel glimmers with the sheen of dull gold from the doors and grilles, and the walls and ceiling are richly decorated with ancient mosaics. Some of the marble pillars and slabs of stone that pave the floor were taken from ruined churches in Ravenna. Above the gallery is a free-standing clerestory that was originally given a simple conical roof but which was replaced with a tall dome and lantern in the 17th century.

LATER HISTORY

The church at Aachen, or Aix-la-Chapelle as it is known in French, has had cathedral status since the 9th century. It is best known as the coronation site for German kings, and some 30 of them were crowned here between 936 and 1531. The Palatine Chapel still has the great white marble throne said

LEFT. The octagonal design of the cathedral recalls the church of San Vitale in Ravenna; the capitals display classical influences.

to have belonged to Charlemagne himself, which was used as a coronation chair and seen as a symbol of the power of the medieval Holy Roman Emperors who sat in it.

Because the rest of the cathedral was built around the existing chapel, Aachen does not conform to the usual ground plans of European cathedrals – that is, it is neither cruciform nor a basilica. In the 14th century a Gothic choir and chancel were added to the east of the chapel. In contrast to the small, plain round-headed windows in the chapel, the choir was given 13 massive windows (84 feet/25m tall), separated by slender buttresses, that take up most of the walls and flood the interior with multi-coloured light. The original medieval glass was replaced in the 20th century.

In subsequent centuries other chapels were added in a plethora of styles and sizes. From the north, the visitor will see the steeply slanting roof of the 14th-century choir jostling with the 17th-century dome atop the Palatine Chapel, with the later steeple towering above them, in a cluster of disparate styles.

Inside is equally fascinating. The glorious bronze pulpit with its ivory carvings was a gift from Emperor Henry II in the 11th century, and the two golden reliquaries date from the early 13th century.

BELOW: The 17th-century dome is over 47 feet (14m) in diameter; hanging from it is a magnificent 12th-century chandelier.

GERMANY

MUNICH CATHEDRAL

The massive hall-church of the Cathedral of Our Lady dates from the 15th century

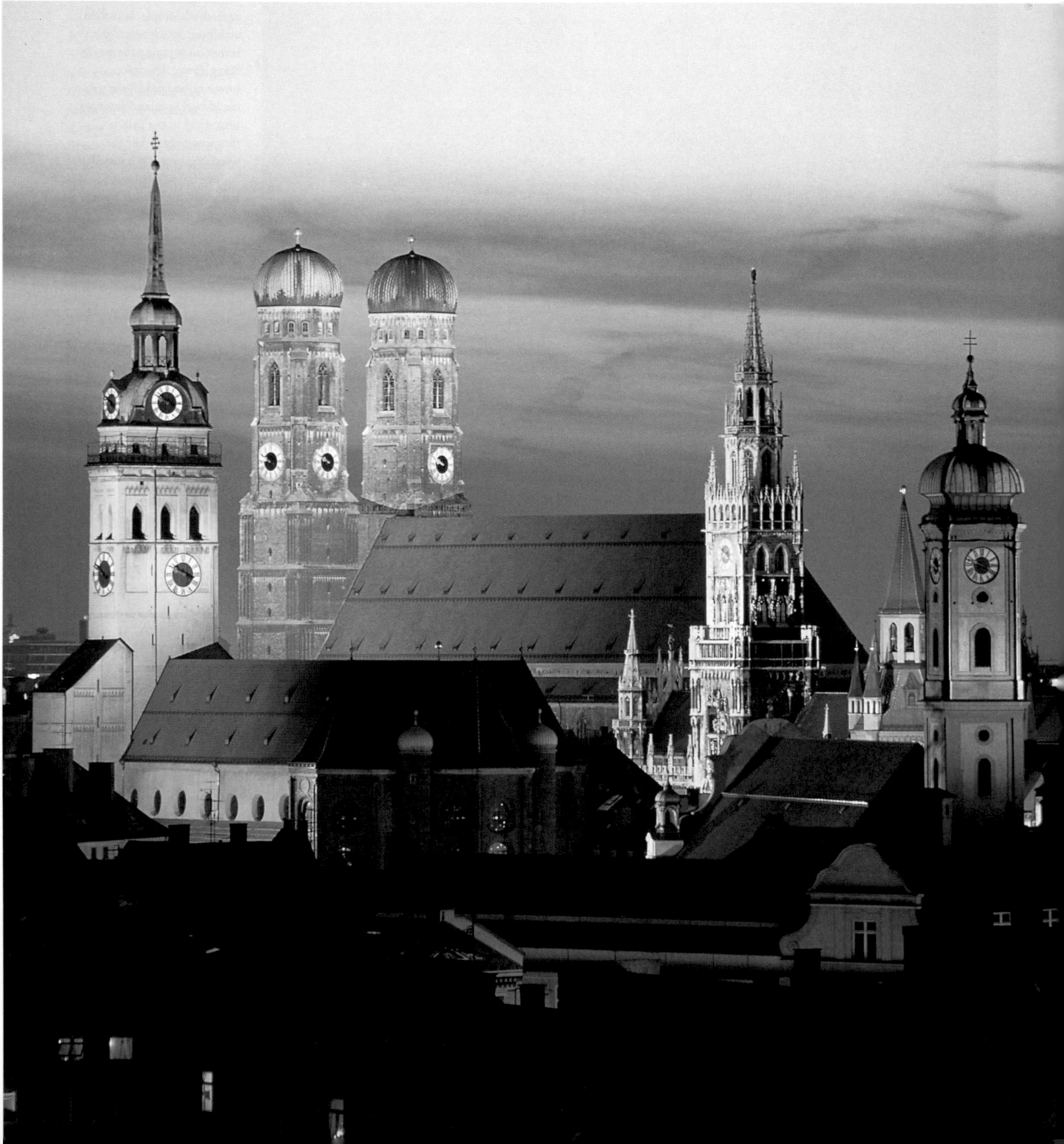

Like all major German cities, Munich (München) suffered bombing raids during World War II. The Frauenkirche, or Cathedral Church of Our Lady, was just one of hundreds of ancient buildings to be seriously damaged in Munich, but it has been so lovingly restored that it is difficult to differentiate the original parts from the sections that have been rebuilt. The cathedral is an important landmark for the people of Munich – an old building standing amid much that is modern or completely restyled. Its profile is one of the most distinctive in Germany, with its huge, steeply gabled roof and twin towers, the onion domes of which have become a symbol of the city.

The cathedral rebuilt

The first cathedral on the site was a basilica-plan church, built in the 12th century in Romanesque style. In the early 15th century, Church authorities decided to demolish the old cathedral and to build another in its place that would be larger and grander. Work began around 1468, and within 10 years the nave and aisles were virtually complete. Building continued apace and by the early 16th century the west façade and stained glass windows were finished.

The first architect responsible for the cathedral was Jörg von Halspach, known as Ganghofer. He was replaced in 1488 by Lukas Rottaler. Ganghofer's cathedral was a hall-church, with aisles as lofty as the towering nave – some 100 feet (30m) tall. The impression of height is accentuated by the length of the cathedral, which spans 358 feet (107m) from east to west, and has no transepts. An enormous crucifix hangs over the steps that lead to the high altar, but even its impressive proportions appear insignificant in the cavernous nave. The great octagonal piers (replaced after the war) dividing the nave from the aisles are totally without ornamentation and lend the great interior something of a stark feel. Cut from white stone, they rise to the ceiling which is noted for its (reconstructed) medieval star-vaulting.

From the outside

The exterior of the Cathedral Church of Our Lady, built of a deep purple-red brick, is simple and unornamented. Ten aisle windows rise almost the entire height of the wall, each one decorated with simple tracery in the form of a grid, and another five tall windows form the eastern end of the cathedral, curving round to provide an angular apse.

The simple but imposing roof slopes steeply, with its apex reaching roughly the same height as the original top of the twin towers that dominate the west façade. The upper sections of the towers, added in 1525, comprise a pair of onion domes that lend the cathedral a distinctly Russian appearance and are an intriguing piece of ornamentation on an otherwise plain exterior. Each dome is capped by a golden ball. Beneath the domes is a tier of blind arcading, while underneath again is a chamber lit by handsome, pointed-arched windows. Just above roof level are the clock mechanisms – one in each tower – that ensure the time on each of the six clock faces is the same.

Stained Glass and Furnishings

Munich Cathedral, despite an initial impression of austerity, possesses several treasures among its furnishings. The glass suffered badly in the war, although some was saved and can still be seen in the choir. The best glass is from the workshop of the glass-maker Peter Hemmel of Andlau (1420–1505), who was based in Alsace. The Window of the Annunciation dates from 1392, while the Three Kings Window was completed in 1430. All the windows are vividly coloured in yellows, reds, green and blues. Those in the aisles are 20th century. Some of the choir stalls have exquisite carvings, although they were not removed for safe-keeping during the war and many were irreparably damaged and replaced by copies.

The Teufelstritt

As visitors enter the cathedral they will see a large footprint stamped into the stone floor. This is the 'Teufelstritt', or 'Devil's Footprint'. There are many stories associated with the footprint, one of which is that the Devil challenged the architect to build the cathedral without windows. He responded to the challenge by placing his tall windows so that they could not be seen from the footprint.

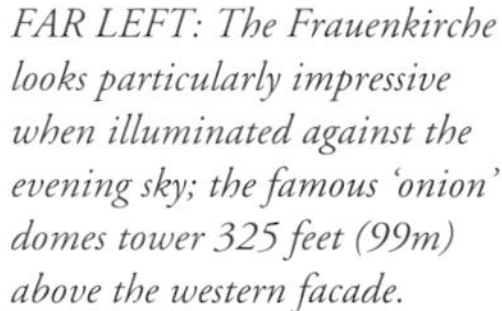

FAR LEFT: The Frauenkirche looks particularly impressive when illuminated against the evening sky; the famous 'onion' domes tower 325 feet (99m) above the western façade.

LEFT: The octagonal pillars of the nave form a continuous line hiding the aisles, which are lit by tall stained glass windows. The cathedral houses 24 wooden busts of apostles, saints and prophets, thought to be the work of the 15th-century sculptor Erasmus Grasser.

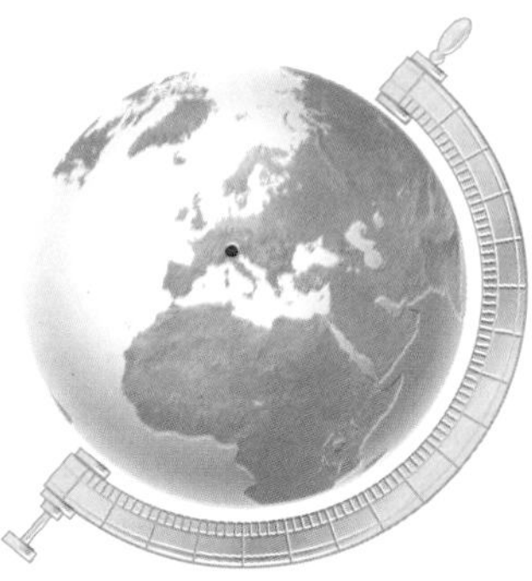

Germany

Trier Cathedral

A mighty fortress-cathedral with a beautiful baroque interior

ABOVE: The cathedral boasts a splendid modern organ which resembles a swallow's nest; it dates from 1974.

Many of Germany's finest cathedrals can be found in the western part of the country. They range from Xanten, with its simple but noble Romanesque façade, to glorious Cologne with its exuberant Gothic pinnacles and flying buttresses (see page 92). The cathedrals in this region are also ancient – Aachen (see page 80) dates from the late 8th century, and Worms, Xanten and Cologne were built in the 1200s – but none have antecedents like Trier Cathedral. It incorporates parts of a church dating from 324 to 348, and remnants of the basilica founded by Emperor Gratian (375–85) can still be seen in the walls.

A collection of buildings

The military features of Trier enhance, rather than detract from, its attraction. It also has one of the finest 11th-century façades in Europe, a celebration of Romanesque dominance and grandeur.

Trier Cathedral is really a collection of buildings,

RIGHT: The original square-shaped Roman building lies at the heart of Trier Cathedral; the other surviving remains are two fallen columns which once supported the ceiling, which can be seen in the courtyard and beside the south portal.

raised at different periods in a variety of styles, centred around a basilica that stands over the remains of a 4th-century Roman palace. In the 1040s an archbishop named Poppo began to enlarge and refine the earlier church and ordered the building of a handsome west front. In the 1160s a chancel was added to the eastern end, complete with crypt, and a polygonal apse with a dwarf gallery on the upper floor. The 1220s saw the addition of the beautiful Romanesque vaulted roof in the nave. Standing next to the cathedral, but distinctly separate from it, is the early Gothic Liebfrauenkirche (Church of Our Lady), a lovely church with radiating chapels around its eastern end, like those often seen in France.

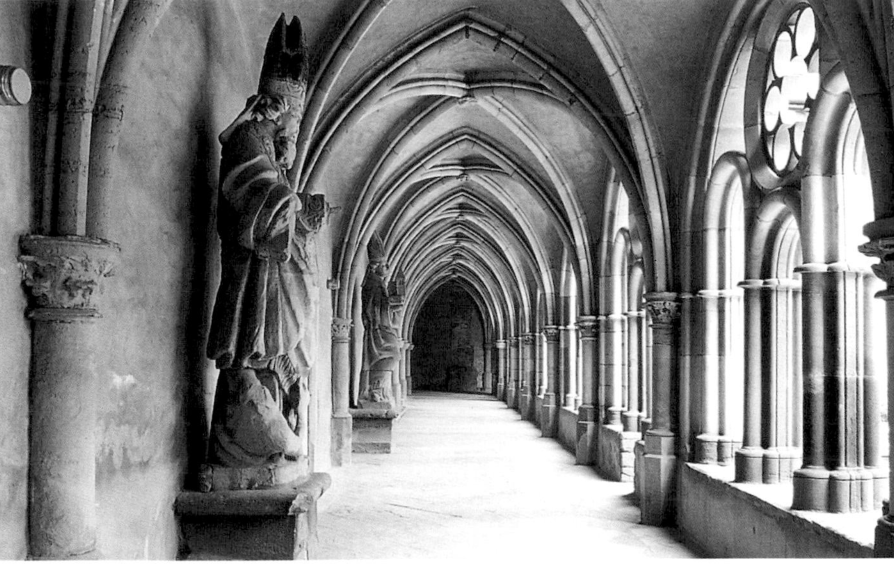

ABOVE: Statues stand guard in the 13th-century cloister; the graceful arches form a contrast to the formidable appearance of the exterior.

An imposing exterior

The dominant feature of Trier Cathedral is its imposing western façade with two towers of unequal height flanked by stair turrets with conical roofs. The fortress-like appearance of the west front is underlined by the two very small doors at the foot of each of the towers, and the tiny windows in the stair turrets. In true Romanesque fashion, the façade is plain, the only concession to decoration being blind arcades and open galleries in the towers. Some of the round-headed arches have been built in stones of alternating colours to add relief to this forbidding, powerful structure.

In Gothic times, the south tower was raised a floor and given an attractive spirelet roof and some traceried windows. The north tower has a simple pyramid roof and still looks very much as it did when it was raised in the 11th century. Between the towers is a shallow pediment above the rounded apse-like structure that dominates the façade. This is an unusual feature, and comprises three levels, the lower of which is without windows. The upper two levels possess handsome round-headed windows.

Interior features

Inside, the cathedral is rather dark due to the size of its windows but the baroque furnishings prevent it from being austere or gloomy.

During the 18th century the interior of the cathedral was considered too harsh and plain and the building underwent an overhaul. The chancel is a good example of the German baroque work conducted at this time. The cathedral was also vigorously restored between 1891 and 1910, which included a complete redecoration of the interior.

Among some of the best furnishings are the monument to Johann III von Metzenhausen, which dates from the 1540s, and the tomb of Richard von Greiffenklau, an especially splendid example of German Renaissance work. Also worth noting are the altarpieces and the fine Romanesque doorway in the south aisle. The beautiful cloisters date from the 1220s and 1230s, and in the north-west corner is a lovely statue of the Virgin Mary, called the *Virgin of Malberg.*

European fortress-cathedrals

Many cathedrals in Europe were built during periods of civil unrest and have features that are more often seen on castles than religious buildings. Trier is just one of these powerful Romanesque fortress-cathedrals with strong towers that could be used for defence. In England, Durham Cathedral (see page 112) was the mighty citadel of the prince-bishops perched on a rock above the River Wear; in France, Albi Cathedral (see page 14) – besieged several times – is a massive rectangular hall provided with thick walls and arrow slits; in Italy, Cefalù (see page 48) was built by the Normans in a recently conquered land; and in Portugal, Coimbra (see page 44) was raised while the memory of the Moorish occupation was still fresh.

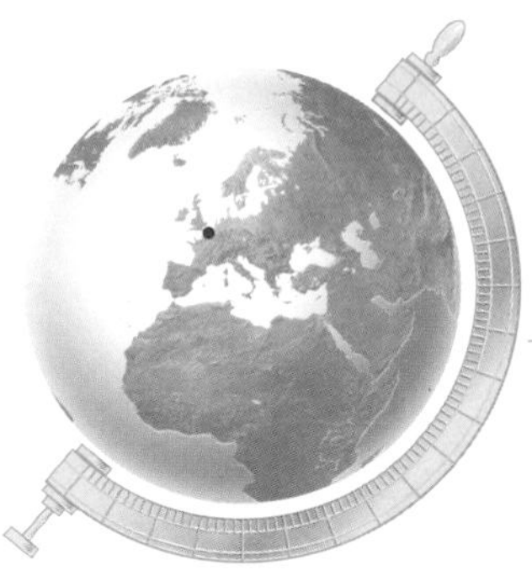

Germany

Cologne Cathedral

Twin-spired Gothic St Peter and St Mary is one of the finest cathedrals in Europe

The Shrine of the Magi

Early Christian tradition embellished the original accounts of the Three Wise Men (the Magi) who appeared at the time of Jesus's birth and gave them names – Caspar, Melchior and Balthazar. In 1164, relics reputed to be those of the Magi came into the hands of the Holy Roman Emperor Frederick Barbarossa. Barbarossa gave them to the archbishop of Cologne, who commissioned Nicholas of Verdun to build a beautiful shrine of sculpted gold in which to house them. It contains panels depicting Jesus's baptism, the Apostles, the Second Coming of Christ and the Adoration of the Magi.

Relics were an important asset in medieval times, and as a result pilgrims came to Cologne from all over Europe to pray at the Shrine of the Magi. One of the cathedral's greatest treasures, it lies behind the high altar.

In 1942 the industrial city of Cologne (Köln) was subject to bombing raids by Allied planes. Thereafter it remained a prime target right up until the crossing of the Rhine in 1945, suffering a series of devastating blitzes that resulted in 75 per cent of the city being flattened and thousands of homes destroyed. Yet, despite the thoroughness of the bombing, the cathedral survived, its massive open-work spires towering over the smouldering remains of what had been one of Germany's major industrial and commercial centres. It is said that the pilots attempted to spare the cathedral during their raids, but precision bombing in the dark was an impossible feat and it is likely the cathedral owes its survival more to luck than the beneficent intentions of the Allies.

Today, the great twin spires of Cologne Cathedral stand proud of the rebuilt city, a landmark for miles across the flat Rhineland plain.

Five centuries in the building

The east end of the cathedral was the first section to be built and it is thought that work started around 1248. It was a grand affair, with double aisles on each side and seven chapels radiating off the ambulatory. The choir was consecrated in 1322, by which time it had been decorated with medieval stained glass, and fine sculptures adorned the piers. Meanwhile, the carved misericords and seat arms were also completed. In around 1385 work was completed on the statues on St Peter's Portal and had begun on the transepts, nave and the lower stages of the towers.

Around the end of the 14th century, Church officials found that the money they had set aside for building their cathedral was insufficient and work ground to a halt. Five stained-glass windows were added in around 1500, depicting scenes from the lives of St Peter and the Virgin Mary, but no further significant building work was conducted until the 19th century.

It was not until the unsettled days of the Reformation and Lutherism had long passed that the Church authorities decided it was about time the magnificent Gothic choir was given a nave, transepts and spire. At this point, Napoleon's empire had fallen and the German states were once more independent: it was time for them to assert themselves not only politically, but artistically. King Frederick William III of Prussia was fascinated by the prospect of completing the cathedral and provided both funds and moral support for the project. The original plans for the building were unearthed from the archives, and work began.

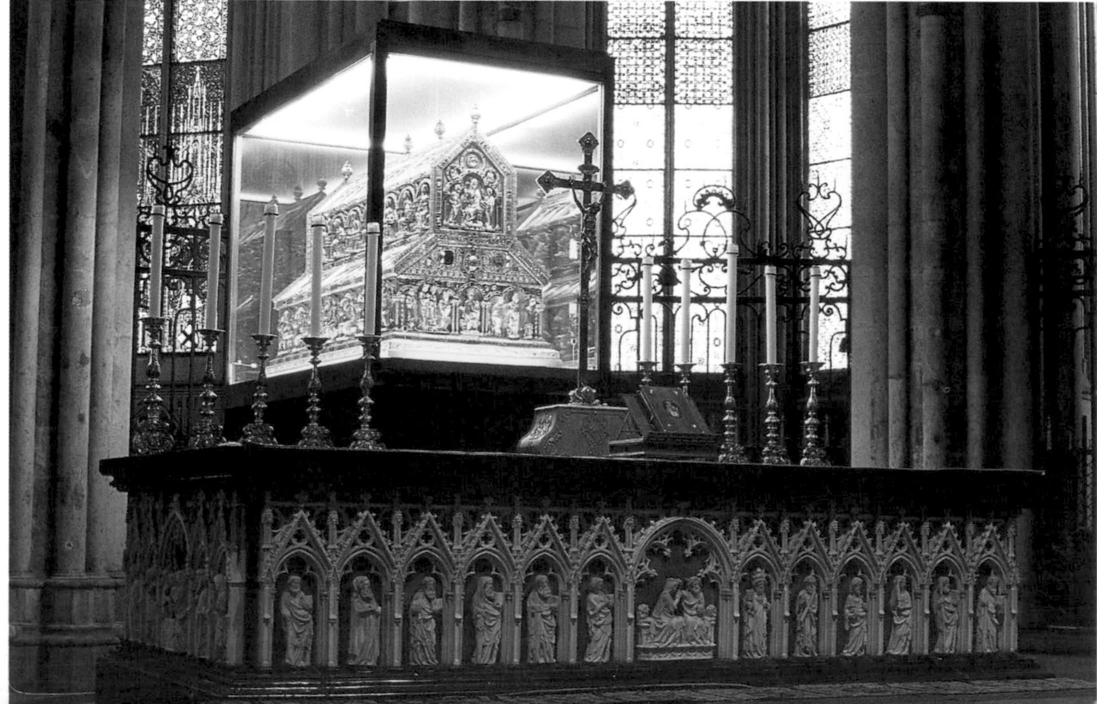

RIGHT: The cathedral houses many art treasures of great importance, including the Shrine of the Magi which is richly set with jewels and dates from 1220.

Resulting grandeur

The final result of building work that spanned five centuries is stupendous. The nave was raised to a height of 150 feet (45m) and lengthened so that the entire cathedral is 468 feet (140m) long. In addition, the two towers were topped with elegant traceried spires that soar 515 feet (155m) above the ground. These magnificent spires dominate the west façade, with its three handsome portals and triangular gables. The transepts were extended to measure 275 feet (83m) from north to south and are supported by graceful flying buttresses.

It is almost impossible to describe the sheer grandeur of the interior of Cologne. The piers in the nave leap upwards to the graceful point of the vaulted ceiling, while the long windows of the clerestory serve both to enhance the feeling of height and to allow light to bathe the nave. At the eastern end, slender fingers of window at triforium and clerestory level illuminate the choir and the high altar. Among the cathedral's many treasures is a life-sized 10th-century crucifix that belonged to Archbishop Gero, considered to be one of the oldest such crosses surviving from medieval times.

BELOW: Cologne Cathedral reflects the very peak of Gothic architecture, when builders sought to create symbols of the Heavenly Jerusalem in their complex façades and towers reaching ever higher.

ROSKILDE CATHEDRAL

Generations of Danish kings and queens are buried at St Lucius' Cathedral

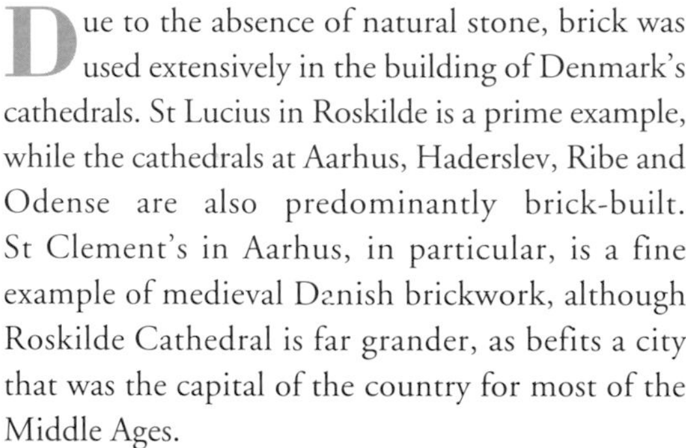

Due to the absence of natural stone, brick was used extensively in the building of Denmark's cathedrals. St Lucius in Roskilde is a prime example, while the cathedrals at Aarhus, Haderslev, Ribe and Odense are also predominantly brick-built. St Clement's in Aarhus, in particular, is a fine example of medieval Danish brickwork, although Roskilde Cathedral is far grander, as befits a city that was the capital of the country for most of the Middle Ages.

BELOW: The cathedral boasts a fine gilded altar screen as well as a graceful pulpit made of alabaster and marble.

EARLY HISTORY

The cathedral began life in the 10th century as a small wooden church and was replaced by a stone building in the 11th century. Legend has it that the second church was built with money from King Canute to atone for the murder of his brother-in-law Ulf Jarl. Royal violence and Roskilde were closely linked for a while, as Ulf Jarl's son, Sweyn II, was banned from the cathedral after murdering some of his house guests while they were at mass.

In the 1190s a third church was built under the watchful eye of Bishop Peder Suneson, who had travelled to France and was undoubtedly influenced by the great cathedrals there. Suneson's late Romanesque cathedral, built over the remains of the earlier church, had three aisles and a choir with an ambulatory.

The cathedral was further enlarged during the 13th and 14th centuries, which included the building of the St Lawrence Chapel in the north aisle and the two small chapels at the bases of the two towers. A fire in 1443 damaged the cathedral but since King Christian was buried here five years later, repairs seem to have been carried out quickly. Between 1513 and 1529 Bishop Lage Urne covered the roof with copper and commissioned a series of paintings of the founders and benefactors of the cathedral for the interior. The twin spires that top the handsome brick towers were added in the 17th century.

ROYAL TOMBS

After the 15th century Roskilde Cathedral became the traditional burial place of Danish kings and queens and much of the remodelling that was carried out at the time was specifically designed to accommodate the increasingly elaborate tombs and monuments that were built. For example, King Christian IV built the chapel in the north aisle as a tomb between 1615 and 1620, while the burial of King Frederick V in 1772 necessitated the removal of the 14th-century Lady Chapel.

The tombs in the cathedral are many and varied. The earliest ones include those of Duke

LEFT: The distinctive copper roofs of Roskilde Cathedral surmount a combination of Romanesque and Gothic architecture which has been added to over the centuries.

Christopher, who died in 1363, and Queen Margaret, who was buried in Roskilde in 1412. Later tombs that are especially noteworthy include those of King Christian IV (died 1648), his first wife Queen Anna Catharina (died 1612), his eldest son Prince Christian (died 1647), King Frederick III (died 1670), and his wife Sophia Amalie (died 1685). All these lie in Christian IV's Chapel, a small section of the cathedral based partly on designs originated by the king himself.

The classical Frederick V Chapel near the south aisle contains yet more recent royal coffins, dating from Frederick (died 1766) onwards. This lovely chapel was designed by C F Harsdorff (1735–99), an architect at the Copenhagen Academy of Fine Arts.

There is also a series of interesting monuments in the cathedral. Chief among these are two carvings on pillars depicting Harald Blaatand and King Sweyn II. Blaatand died in 987 and is attributed with founding the first church in Roskilde.

LEFT: In all 38 royal tombs are housed in the cathedral, the most recent being that of Frederik IX who died in 1972. Danish monarchs have continued to be buried here even though the court moved from Roskilde to Copenhagen after 1400.

Queen Margaret

One of Denmark's greatest leaders, who succeeded in uniting Norway with Denmark in the late 14th century, was Queen Margaret. She is buried in a handsome black marble tomb – situated behind the high altar – which was designed by Johannes Junge of Lübeck and is an outstanding example of Gothic architecture.

Queen Margaret's close association with the cathedral dates from at least 1411 when she founded the Chapel of Bethlehem under the south tower. When she died, she was first buried at Soro church, but her body was exhumed and reburied at Roskilde the following year.

The altarpiece

The altarpiece is a fine example of early Renaissance carved oak. There is a story that a Dutch captain smuggled the altarpiece from Danzig (Gdańsk, see page 140), but was caught in the act. He then declared a value on the screen that was so low that Frederick II bought it for his chapel at Fredericksborg Palace. It was donated to Roskilde Cathedral by Christian IV.

Further examples of fine carving in the cathedral are the superb choir stalls and screen that date from the early 15th century.

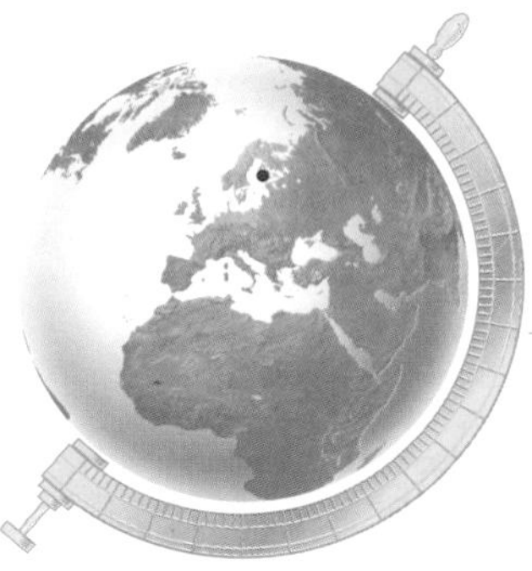

FINLAND

TURKU CATHEDRAL

Ravaged by a series of fires, the Cathedral of the Virgin Mary and St Henry still dominates Turku's Old Quarter

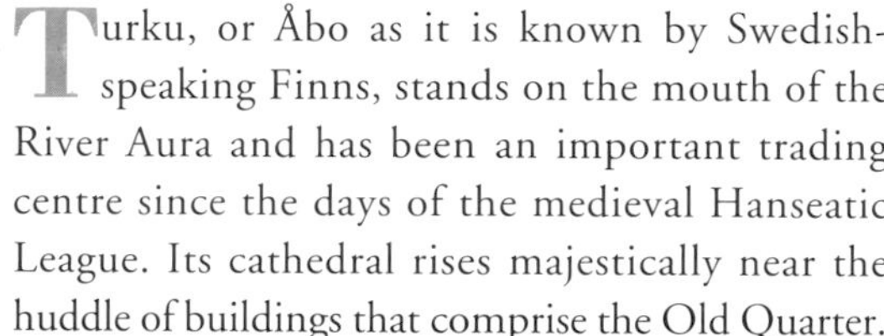

Turku, or Åbo as it is known by Swedish-speaking Finns, stands on the mouth of the River Aura and has been an important trading centre since the days of the medieval Hanseatic League. Its cathedral rises majestically near the huddle of buildings that comprise the Old Quarter.

BELOW: The focal point of the high altar is a magnificent painting depicting the Transfiguration of Christ.

FINLAND AND THE SWEDES

The original settlement in this area was 3 miles (5km) north, at the mouth of the River Aurajoki, but was transferred to its present site in the 13th century. At that time the Bishop of Finland lived in Turku and the entire country was governed from the mighty fortress south of the city. In the 1150s, the Pope ordered the neighbouring Swedes to invade Finland on a crusade and to force the country to submit to the Catholic Church (and to Sweden). In 1229 the Pope was sufficiently satisfied with the Finns' conversion to order the building of a cathedral in Turku, Finland's oldest city.

The cathedral was consecrated in 1290, although rebuilding and enlarging continued throughout the following centuries. A number of fires have raged through the cathedral, twice virtually gutting it. The second serious fire was in 1827 when the damage was so severe that a complete restoration was necessary. The same fire destroyed much of Turku and precipitated the move of the university from Turku to Helsinki, which had superseded the older city as Finland's capital some 20 years previously. The last stages of the restoration work were completed in 1929 in celebration of the cathedral's 700th birthday.

CHAPELS, MONUMENTS AND FRESCOS

Turku Cathedral is a substantial building, 286 feet (86m) long and 127 feet (38m) wide. The massive tower that so dominates the Old Quarter is about 300 feet (90m) tall. Visitors enter the cathedral through a door on the south side and are greeted by an array of chapels leading off the nave. A number of Finland's heroes are buried within the cathedral walls, or have monuments there, and the chapels are often named after them. For example, the Tott Chapel contains a monument to Ake Tott and his wife; Tott, who was known as the 'snow plough' because of his decisive military tactics, was a general serving under Gustav II Adolf (the King of Sweden) in the Thirty Years' War.

The Tavast Chapel was originally dedicated to the Sacred Body of Christ, but was renamed after

Magnus Tavast, who died in 1452. Tavast was one of Turku's most famous Catholic bishops. The lovely ornamental grille in the chapel was made on his own orders in about 1425.

The chapel to the right of the nave near the entrance contains the monument to Trosten Stålhandske ('the Hand of Steel'), a knight who made a name for himself for his bravery during the Thirty Years' War. Near the choir is the Kankainen Chapel, originally designed as a mausoleum for the noble Horn and Kurck families. When the body of Queen Karin Månsdotter, who died in 1612, was exhumed from the Tott Chapel, she was reburied here in a simple, but impressive, sarcophagus of black marble.

The beautiful frescos by R W Ekman that decorate the choir depict scenes from Finnish history. One shows the Englishman Bishop Henry of Uppsala baptising the Finns in the 12th century, while another is of linguist Mikael Agricola presenting his translation into Finnish of the New Testament to King Gustav Vasa.

MONUMENT TO INDEPENDENCE

A simple monument on the south wall of the cathedral commemorates those men of Turku who fought and died in the Finnish War of Independence. This was more a war of attrition than an out-and-out battle, and aimed to win Finland back from Russian control.

Fighting started when Finland was united with the Russian Empire in 1807, and years of bitterness and violence passed before independence was finally achieved in 1917, taking advantage of the instability that occurred after the Russian Revolution.

The monument is the work of the Finnish sculptor Yrjö Liipola. Liipola also designed the handsome statue of J J Wecksell, a Turku-born poet, that stands behind the cathedral.

LEFT: Turku is Finland's oldest town, and the brick-built cathedral is one of the nation's most important buildings, retaining traces of the original medieval church.

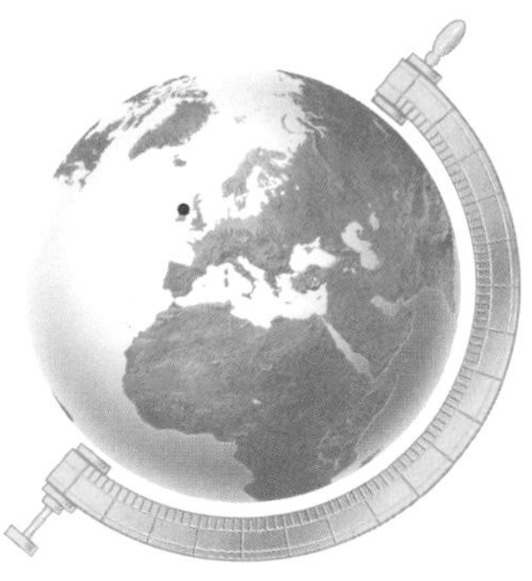

Northern Ireland

St Patrick's Roman Catholic Cathedral

The Gothic Revival Cathedral Church of St Patrick stands majestically atop a hill at Armagh

The older St Patrick's

The Church of Ireland has a cathedral in Armagh too, also known as the Cathedral Church of St Patrick. It was founded in Armagh by St Patrick himself around 445. The fact that it was the foremost site for Irish Christianity made it vulnerable to attack from all manner of assailants, and 26 lootings and burnings are recorded as occurring between 670 and 1642. A fire in 1642 caused massive devastation, but Archbishop James Margetson funded much rebuilding and conservation of the remains of the medieval cathedral out of his own pocket during the period 1663–78.

A second restoration took place during the 1760s and 1780s (although the building of the tower that was begun at this time was later abandoned), a third in the early 1800s (which included repositioning the altar and erecting a gallery for choristers and a canopied pulpit), and a fourth, massive one, entailing the virtual rebuilding of the cathedral, in the 1830s.

RIGHT: The interior of the cathedral is filled with richly coloured decorations; painted wood, marble and stonework, mosaic and stained glass all play their part.

Few cathedrals in Ireland occupy a site as impressive as the twin-spired Cathedral Church of St Patrick in Armagh, reached by a flight of 209 steps. Work on the cathedral started on St Patrick's Day in 1840, following the Catholic Emancipation Act of 1829, which allowed Catholics full civil and political rights denied since the Reformation.

Dedicated archbishops

The Archbishop of Armagh, William Crolly, returned to his diocese in 1829 and immediately began negotiations to lease a site for a new cathedral. Work began under the supervision of the architect Thomas Duff, but ground to a halt in 1848 because of the Great Famine. Crolly died shortly after and was buried in the unfinished cathedral.

Building began again in 1854, keeping to the Perpendicular Gothic style favoured by Duff. After Duff's death, the completion of St Patrick's fell to James Joseph McCarthy, one of Ireland's best-known neo-Gothic architects. McCarthy, however, preferred Early English to Perpendicular and set about changing Duff's original plans. Funds ran so low in 1855 that the Church authorities were obliged to hold a bazaar to raise money. The Pope, the Emperor of Austria and the Emperor of France donated prizes (Louis Napoleon contributed two Sèvres vases), and £7,000 was raised.

In the 1870s Archbishop Daniel McGettigan worked hard to raise the outstanding sum of money needed to complete the cathedral, and on 24 August 1873 20,000 people gathered to witness the dedication.

The archbishops who contributed to the building of the cathedral are commemorated in the impressive statues on the terrace outside the west front. As a final step, the land on which the cathedral was built was purchased from its owner, the Earl of Dartry, for £919 6*s*. The cathedral was consecrated on 27 July 1904.

A glorious achievement

Whether viewed from the inside or the outside, St Patrick's is a fine building. Externally, the walls are built of pale grey Armagh limestone, while inside the pillars and vaults are constructed of freestone and warm yellow Bath stone. Cruciform in plan, the cathedral is 211 feet (63m) long from east to west, the nave stands 110 feet (33m) tall and the transepts measure 116 feet (35m) from north to south.

The west façade is dominated by twin spires rising 210 feet (63m) above the ground. Between them is a handsome traceried window with a gallery containing 11 marble statues. A recessed portal below the statues provides the main entrance, flanked by two smaller doors at the base of the towers beneath the spires.

Between 1887 and 1904 work was carried out on the interior decoration. These years saw every inch of every wall covered in a visually stunning display of marble and mosaic. The nave is especially splendid, with great mosaic medallions depicting the faces of a host of Irish saints. An Italian artist, Oreste Amici, was commissioned to decorate the ceilings with scenes from the lives of Irish saints, and the stained glass came from Munich.

RECENT DEVELOPMENTS

Later, the Second Vatican Council of 1962–5 called for a complete redesign of the sanctuaries so that the congregation would be better able to see what was happening there during services. To this end, screens were removed and the pulpit and altar placed in different positions. However, the result of this work, although succeeding in its objective, has meant that the interior has a lack of focus and the proportions of nave and chancel seem wrong. Nevertheless, the inside of St Patrick's is highly impressive and light floods in from the arcades and nave clerestory.

BELOW: The ascent to the cathedral consists of 209 steps ranged over 7 terraces. Statues of the Apostles stand in niches above the portal, and the archbishops under whom the work on the cathedral was started and finished are commemorated by statues too.

ENGLAND

ST PAUL'S CATHEDRAL

Sir Christopher Wren's massive cathedral stands in the heart of London

A VAST MAUSOLEUM

On his death in 1723 Wren was the first person to be buried in St Paul's Cathedral. He lies under a plain slab of black marble in the crypt, above which is a Latin inscription proclaiming 'Reader, if you seek his monument, look about you'.

One or two monuments were preserved from the old cathedral and include that of the poet John Donne (died 1631). The Duke of Wellington's tomb (died 1848), designed by Alfred Stevens, is also impressive. As it is in Westminster Abbey, burial in St Paul's is regarded as a fitting tribute for people who have performed services to the nation.

BELOW: The columns of the peristyle surrounding the dome support the Stone Gallery, from where visitors can view the city; it is possible also to climb the 627 steps to the Golden Gallery.

On the night of 2 September 1666, a small fire started in a baker's shop in Pudding Lane in the City of London. As many houses at the time were built of timber and packed tightly together, the fire spread rapidly and was not brought under control until three days later. When the exhausted Londoners returned from their refuge across the River Thames, they found that around 13,000 buildings had been destroyed, along with 87 parish churches, while the great medieval cathedral of St Paul's had suffered serious damage.

The laborious task of rebuilding the ruined city began almost immediately, and the young architect, Christopher Wren (1632–1723), was at the forefront of the building programme.

CLASSICAL AND BAROQUE

When, in 1674, the decision was made to demolish the crumbling medieval St Paul's and replace it with something new, Wren was commissioned to rebuild it. Shortly before the Great Fire Wren had visited Paris and been impressed by the development of the baroque style of architecture there. Of the two designs he submitted, the one approved by Royal Warrant was neatly symmetrical, based very much on the Roman basilica style.

Wren was keen on domes and he designed a church that was Latin cross in plan, with a cupola over the central crossing. Work on the choir and nave began in 1675, with Wren very much in control. When the dome was raised, it is said that he had himself hoisted in a basket on to the dome to supervise its construction. Classical proportions and baroque ornamentation make St Paul's Cathedral one of the most significant architectural achievements of the 17th century. Work was virtually completed by 1717.

A SKILLED TEAM OF CRAFTSMEN

St Paul's is an impressive sight from any angle. Its west façade is dominated by tiers of columns rising to meet the mighty dome, which dwarfs the twin baroque western towers. Inside, the cathedral is massive, with great classical piers supporting the dome over the central crossing, and baroque ornamentation as far as the eye can see. Every wall is adorned with intricate carvings and murals in an explosion of colours and design.

Wren was determined that his cathedral should not suffer from inferior interior work and he hired the best team of craftsmen available to work on the furnishings. The Huguenot ironmonger Jean Tijou was engaged to produce the wrought-iron gates and screens, while Grinling Gibbons was commissioned to carve the stalls, screen and organ case.

The statues were designed by Caius Gabriel Cibber and Francis Bird, who also executed the relief of the Conversion of St Paul in the west façade. Since the work was carried out in durable Portland stone, the beautiful carvings of cherubs' heads, flowers and fruit have weathered well.

THE DOME

The dome that caps St Paul's and gives it its characteristic appearance is said to be among the best in the world. It comprises two sections: a brick cone supporting the delicate lantern, and an outer dome of wood sheathed in lead. The total weight of the dome is said to be 68,000 tons (69,000 tonnes), and the gold tip of the lantern tower stands 365 feet (110m) above the ground.

Inside is the famous Whispering Gallery, an acoustic feature whereby sound is carried around

the inside of the dome with absolute clarity. Thus a person whispering towards the wall can be heard by a person standing on the opposite side of the dome, a distance of some 100 feet (30m), as though he were near by.

Sir James Thornhill painted the inside of the dome, despite the fact that Wren originally envisaged a mosaic resembling those in the churches in Rome. His work depicts the life of St Paul in eight scenes.

ABOVE: The magnificent interior of St Paul's, with choir and organ case by Grinling Gibbons. The glass mosaics which adorn the vault are by Sir William Richmond.

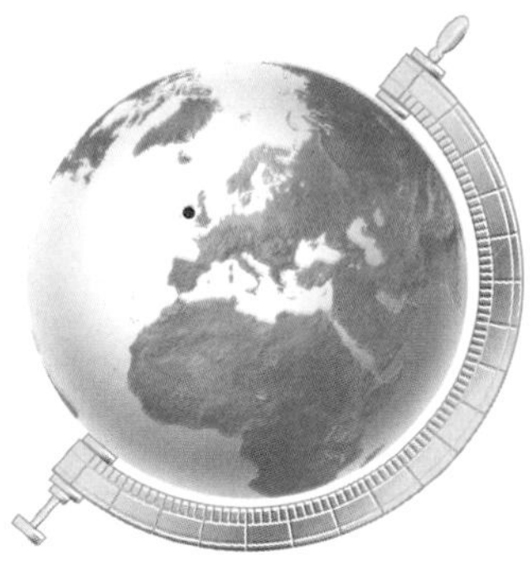

IRELAND

CORK CATHEDRAL

St Fin Barre in Cork is the finest 19th-century cathedral church in Ireland

'A SHABBY APOLOGY FOR A CATHEDRAL'

These damning words, taken from the *Dublin Builder* journal, referred to the second of Cork's cathedrals, erected on the site of a medieval building that was demolished in the 1730s. The new building was financed by a tax on coal but this proved insufficient and the money ran out before it was finished.

From contemporary accounts, lack of funding was the least of the fledgling cathedral's problems: no one liked it. It was denounced as unsightly, deformed, plain, dull and 'a shabby apology for a Cathedral that has long disgraced Cork'. Not surprisingly, this unloved building was not long for this world and on 16 January 1865 its congregation bade it farewell after a final service, during which a funeral march played on the organ seemed to be the high point.

RIGHT: The interior of the cathedral is spectacular in its variety of colour and decoration. The painted ceiling glows with luminous celestial figures, lit by a series of bright windows.

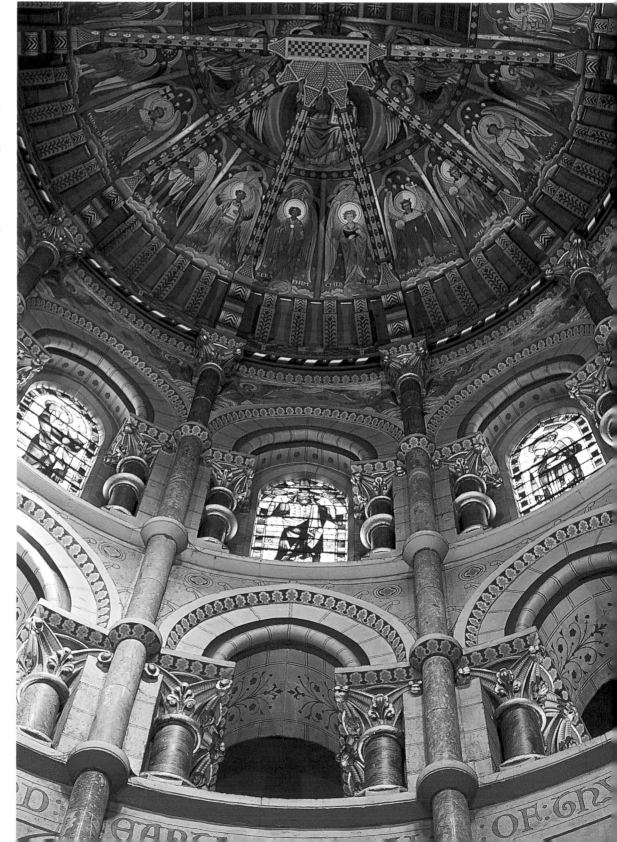

At the very beginning of the 7th century a monk from Connacht named Fin Barre (or Finbar) founded a monastery on the River Lee. After his death in 623, Fin Barre's monastery became one of the principal religious establishments in Ireland. Unfortunately, during the 10th century, this attracted the unwelcome attentions of marauding Vikings who made off with the relics of Fin Barre during a raid.

Later a cathedral church was raised on the site, probably in the 11th century, although little is known about it. By 1735 the medieval cathedral had decayed and become unsafe, partly as a result of bombardment during the Confederate wars of the 1640s, and partly due to ill-use during the Jacobite Rebellion, and was demolished. A new cathedral was raised in the 1730s but this was pulled down in 1865 to make way for a better one.

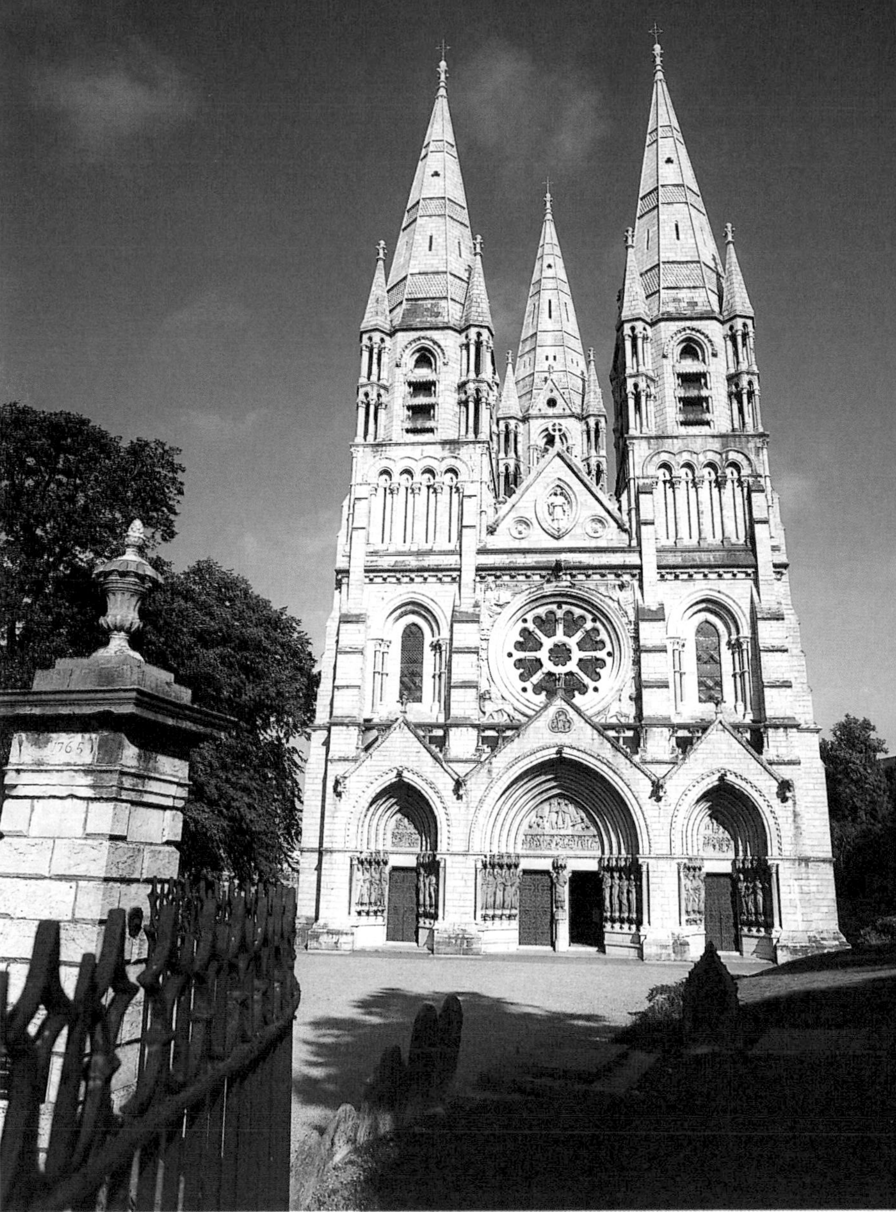

William Burges of London

Architects from all over Europe were invited to submit plans for a suitable replacement which had to seat 700 people and for which the total cost could not exceed £15,000. In the end the winning design came from a young Englishman named William Burges, despite the fact that his building costs ran to twice the stipulated amount and the cathedral would only be able to seat 466. Needless to say his competitors were furious, but the Church authorities stood fast and the foundation stone of Burges' cathedral was laid on 12 January 1865.

Almost six years later, on 30 November 1870, Cork Cathedral was consecrated, although funds for completing the spires and towers had dried up. At the consecration the bishop announced he had raised £30,000 to complete the cathedral, a statement that was appropriately greeted by an enthusiastic rendering of Handel's 'Hallelujah Chorus'. It was completed in 1879 and, although some critics deemed it 'the perfect abortion of a cathedral', it is generally admired and easily the most splendid of the many 19th-century cathedrals in Ireland.

19th-century French Gothic

The cathedral is built on a cruciform plan with a central spire, a nave, two aisles, transepts and an apsidal chapel with an ambulatory. Burges' inspiration came from the French Gothic period and comprises an elegant mixture of soaring pillars and spires and solid Norman round-headed arches. It is built of Cork limestone, a pale grey-white stone that appears an attractive silvery colour when wet.

Three recessed portals in the west front form the main entrance and provide visitors with their first view of the sumptuous interior. The pillars of the nave, crossing and apse are of red Cork marble, Bath stone, or a grey-brown stone, and rise as gracefully as those in any French Gothic cathedral. The nave ends in a low marble wall inlaid with squares of lapis lazuli, red and green porphyry and gold mosaics.

Beyond the screen is the glorious painted chancel roof, executed in 1935, and the massive bishop's throne, standing a remarkable 46 feet (14m) tall. It has wooden panels on which are carved a selection of bishops' heads, topped by a statue of St Fin Barre himself.

The sanctuary is marked by a brass screen, beyond which the high altar stands on its plinth of black marble. The reredos is a subtle blend of stone, alabaster, marble and mosaic work. The marble of the sanctuary floor was imported from the Pyrenees, and was designed by Italians working in Paris. Near the crossing, the solid brass lectern liberally decorated with rock crystals is well worth admiring. Burges originally intended this for the Cathedral of Our Lady of the Vineyards at Lille, but as he was not invited to design that cathedral, he installed it at Cork instead.

ABOVE: The elaborately carved west front features three recessed doors, each surmounted by a gable; a further gable crowns the rose window.

BELOW: This group of statues can be found adjacent to one of the doorways in the west front.

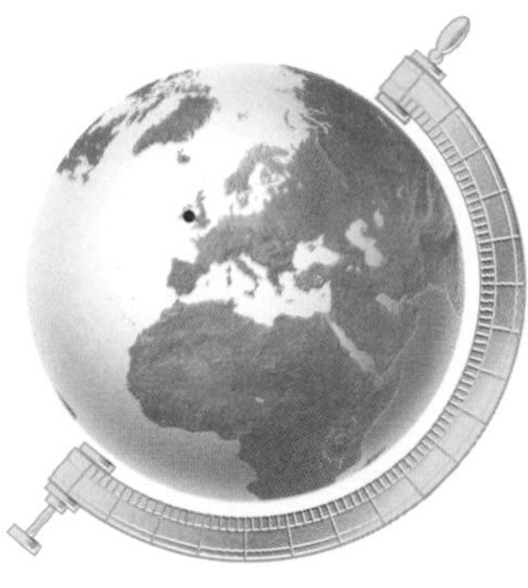

THE NATIONAL CATHEDRAL AND COLLEGIATE CHURCH OF ST PATRICK

Ancient St Patrick's in Dublin is the best-known 'cathedral' in Ireland

DUBLIN'S CATHOLIC CATHEDRAL

The Pro-Cathedral of the Immaculate Conception of the Blessed Virgin Mary, or St Mary's as it is more commonly known, is a post-Reformation Roman Catholic cathedral. It stands in Marlboro Street, in the grounds of a pre-Reformation Cistercian abbey. Building started in 1815 and the cathedral was dedicated in 1825. It is a handsome classical Revival building, the west front of which displays finely fluted pillars under a plain pediment.

BELOW: Set in spacious and attractive grounds, St Patrick's is Ireland's largest church.

Strictly speaking, the National Cathedral and Collegiate Church of St Patrick is not a cathedral: it does not have a cathedra, the throne of a bishop. The Archbishop of Dublin's throne is at Christ Church, with which St Patrick's was co-cathedral until 1871. However, having two Church of Ireland cathedrals in one city was problematic, and so it was agreed that St Patrick's should become the National Church of Ireland but be allowed to retain the title 'cathedral', because its history and importance were too significant to warrant its demotion to a mere parish church.

Dominated by its plain 14th-century limestone tower topped with a granite spire of 1749 and a neat, but pleasing, array of small pinnacles and square turrets, St Patrick's stands as a sturdy grey edifice in well-tended grounds near the city centre.

TWO CATHEDRALS AT ODDS

Like many religious foundations in Ireland, St Patrick's dates back to the 5th century when St Patrick himself is said to have baptised people in a nearby well. Nothing is known about the church until the Anglo-Norman invasion of the 1170s when a Benedictine monk called John Comyn was made archbishop. Not surprisingly, Comyn's new parishioners did not take kindly to having an Englishman foisted upon them so he promptly removed himself from Christ Church Cathedral to the more peaceful Church of St Patrick, where he could better exercise control.

However, the simple church was not grand enough for an archbishop so Comyn set about rebuilding it. The new church was dedicated in 1192 and made a cathedral in 1221. This did not please the Augustinian canons at the rival Christ Church at all, and the two cathedrals constantly fought and bickered. Even after Comyn's rebuilding, St Patrick's was still overshadowed by the larger, more impressive Christ Church. So, in the mid-13th century, work began anew and by 1316 St Patrick's boasted a spire and a tower.

ABOVE: Glowing colours bathed in soft light impart an air of tranquillity, making it hard to imagine today that in the 17th century horses belonging to Cromwell's troops were stabled in the aisles. The cathedral's present appearance dates from the 19th century.

A SERIES OF DISASTERS

The new building did not last long, however. A serious fire in 1362 damaged the tower and nave, and the spire fell down in the same century. In 1544 the roof collapsed at the western end of the nave, and between 1687 and 1795 St Patrick's was seriously flooded many times. Thus by the end of the 18th century the whole building was virtually in ruins and remained so until a major restoration programme was undertaken in the 1860s at the expense of Sir Benjamin Lee Guinness.

CONTRASTING COLOURS

St Patrick's takes the shape of a Latin cross, with a 132-foot (40-m) nave and a chancel of 56 feet (17m). The Lady Chapel behind the high altar adds another 55 feet (17m) to the overall length. The interior is simple and relatively uncluttered, so that the fluting on the pillars and the construction of the stone vaults can be clearly seen. There are, however, some fine monuments, the most obvious of which is the great black marble and alabaster creation for the 1st Earl of Cork's second wife (1631). There is also a bust of Jonathan Swift, author of *Gulliver's Travels* and Dean of St Patrick's from 1713 to 1745; he is buried in the nave.

The interior is characterised by contrasts of colour and design. The Lady Chapel has four slender pillars of dark grey stone, while the vault is a pale grey-blue with the ribs picked out in cream. Five lancet windows shed blue light on to the white stone altar. By contrast, the little baptistry, the oldest part of the cathedral, has plain stone ribs and stark, white vaulting. The walls are decorated with a geometric design of dark blue while the three lancet windows are predominantly yellow and red. With its medieval floor tiles and plain rectangular font, this is a particularly atmospheric corner.

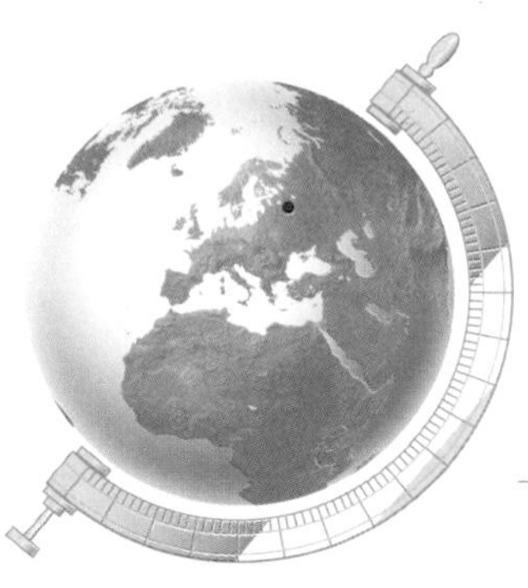

Cathedral of St Basil the Blessed

An explosion of multi-coloured onion domes dominates Moscow's renowned Red Square

Ivan the Terrible

Ivan IV, the founder of St Basil's Cathedral, was born near Moscow in 1533 and was the first of the Russian leaders to assume the title of tsar. He did much to improve Russia's commercial standing, reinforced a just legal code and developed more efficient local administration. However, his achievements are usually overlooked in the light of his brutality to his people and his family.

In 1564 he was betrayed by one of his counsellors and began to see treachery everywhere. He embarked on a reign of terror, aimed principally at the aristocracy, but culminating in the murder of thousands of his subjects. In a fit of pique, he also murdered his son in 1581. Fortunately for his people, Ivan died three years later and was succeeded by the gentler Fedor I.

The Cathedral of St Basil the Blessed is the best-known of the six magnificent cathedrals in the centre of Moscow (Moskva), and is also one of the finest. There are four cathedrals inside the Kremlin: the Cathedral of the Assumption, identifiable by its five golden domes, and dating from the 15th century; the Cathedral of the Annunciation, also 15th century, and sporting nine cupolas; the Cathedral of the Archangel Michael, dating from the 16th century and the burial place of Russian tsars; and the Cathedral of the Twelve Apostles, 17th century and formerly the Patriarch's private church. Near by, in the Novodyevichi Convent, is the 16th-century Smolensky Cathedral. And then there is the Cathedral of St Basil – sometimes called the Cathedral of the Intercession – an array of onion domes overlooking Red Square that is instantly recognisable.

The cathedral's history

In 1552, Ivan IV (see panel) won a great victory over the Mongols and captured the Kazan capital.

RIGHT: The colourful painting of the domes dates from the 17th century; before that time the towers were white and the domes gilded.

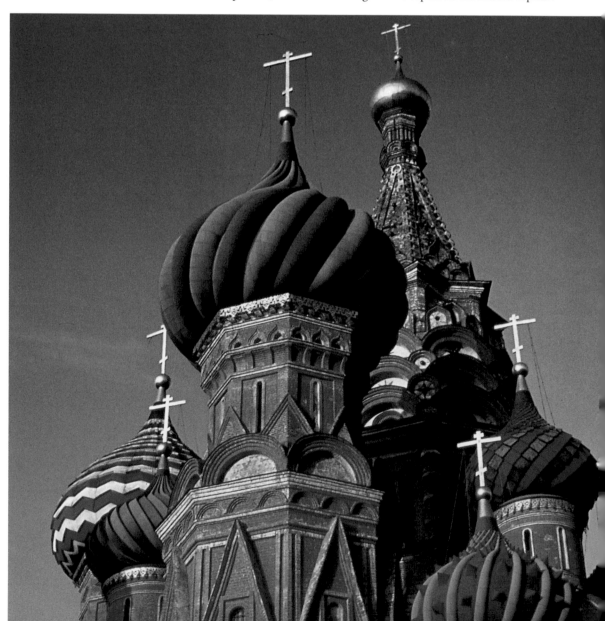

By way of celebration he ordered the building of a magnificent cathedral. There were already three cathedrals in the Kremlin, and one at the Novodyevichi Convent, but Ivan's word was law and work began between 1555 and 1560. Ivan died long before his cathedral was completed, but even in its early stages the building must have been eye-catching. It is an ingenious collection of nine small churches, rather than a unified structure – eight small chapels being placed equi-distantly around a larger one.

About 120 years after the cathedral was started the final details were completed. A hiccup in the building programme had occurred in 1611 when the cathedral was attacked by Polish forces, who sacked it. In 1812, Napoleon's troops arrived in Moscow and, finding the city deserted, used St Basil's as a stable for their horses. When Napoleon decided to abandon Moscow he ordered one of his generals to ensure the cathedral was destroyed, but, fortunately, in the chaos of the French evacuation, the order was forgotten, or overlooked, and St Basil's survived.

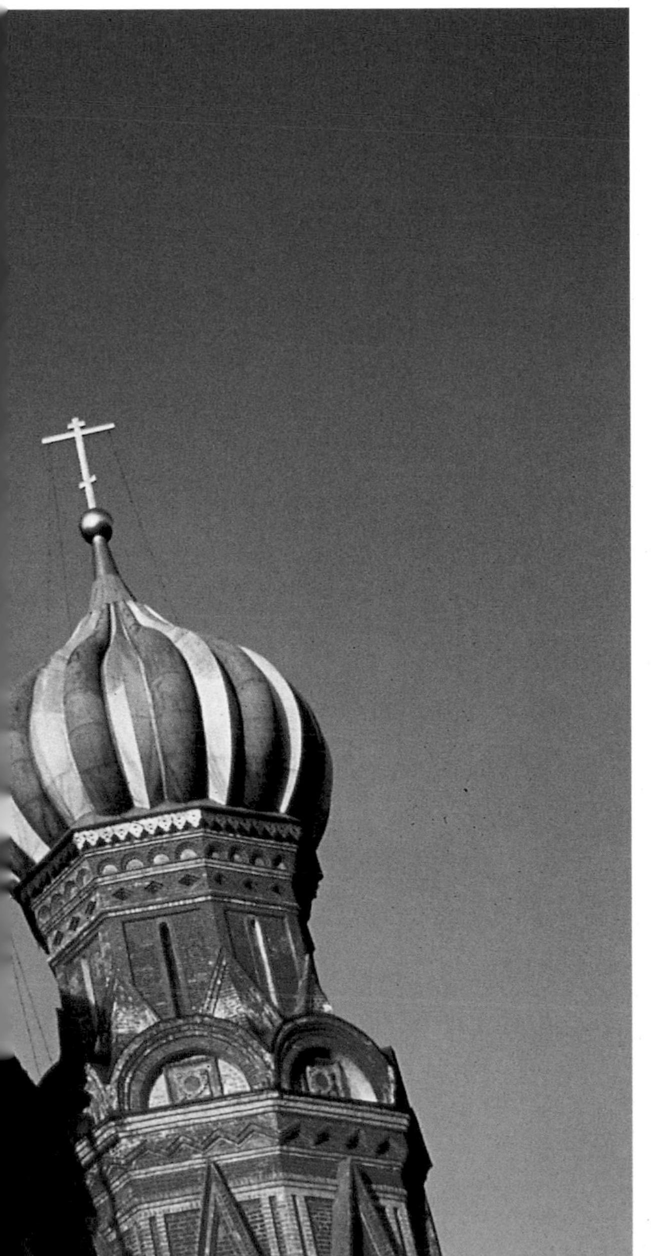

ABOVE: In general the exterior of St Basil's is more impressive than the interior, since it was originally designed as a monument celebrating the capture of Kazan's capital. This painted screen is one of the decorative items to be found within the cathedral.

From 1839 until 1845, major renovations were needed, followed by yet another period of repair in the 1950s to rectify damage sustained in World War II. During the Communist regime, the cathedral performed a secular function as a museum, containing some of the city's finest artefacts and treasures.

A Russian-Byzantine extravaganza

Indisputably Russian with its multi-shaped onion domes and fabulous external decorations, the cathedral is a riot of colour and shapes. It is said to represent the pinnacle of the process whereby Byzantine architecture was given a distinctly Russian flavour, resulting in a style of building not found in any other country.

Byzantine influence can be seen in the mosaics and frescos, and in the basic plan of a central church surrounded by subsidiary chapels. But the onion domes on the eight smaller towers are pure Russian, cleverly varied with ribs, diamond patterns, or tiles in vibrant greens, blues, reds and yellows. Although the domes appear at first to be haphazard, closer inspection reveals that there is a pattern, and that there are four tiny ones between four taller ones, all dwarfed by the massive central tower. But no two towers are the same, as though eight individual architects were given a free hand to do as they would, with no regard to the work of his neighbour. This splendid chaos is what makes St Basil's cathedral so distinctive.

The central tower is capped by an octagonal spire (although there is an onion dome atop the spire for unity), and stands about 107 feet (32m) tall. The whole complex is linked by an elevated gallery that can be clearly seen from outside.

BELOW: The building is in the form of an eight-pointed star, with the principal church in the centre. The four large chapels are aligned to the points of the compass.

ST ISAAC'S CATHEDRAL

Colossal St Isaac's Cathedral in St Petersburg dates from the 19th century

Like the other great Russian cities of Moscow and Kiev, St Petersburg (Sankt-Peterburg) boasts more than one cathedral. The Cathedral of St Peter and St Paul lies within the 18th-century fortress and is the burial place of many tsars; the Cathedral of Our Lady of Kazan was built between 1801 and 1811; the baroque St Nicholas' Naval Cathedral is a functioning Orthodox church; the Convent Cathedral of Smolny adjoins what was once a school for daughters of the nobility; and the largest of them all, St Isaac's Cathedral, stands at the heart of the city, presenting a handsome façade of granite and marble to the world.

BELOW: Light shines in through the 12 windows encircling the drum, which supports the cast-iron dome completed in 1842 by de Montferrand.

NORTHERN RUSSIA'S LARGEST CHURCH

St Isaac's Cathedral is vast. It stands like a mighty monolith in the heart of the city, dwarfing the other substantial buildings around it. Built in the shape of a Greek cross, its dimensions are impressive: 365 feet (110m) from east to west and 320 feet (96m) from north to south. Its most striking feature is its massive golden dome which looms more than 330 feet (99m) above the ground. The lantern on the top of the dome can be reached by 562 stairs.

St Petersburg was founded by Peter the Great in 1703 – a recent settlement when compared to much of Europe – and in the 1760s an Italian architect named Master Rinaldi was invited by Catherine the Great to build a cathedral in the city. However, progress was slow and his work was never completed. The next landmark was in 1816 when Tsar Alexander I invited architects from all over Europe to submit plans for a new cathedral. This competition was won by a young Frenchman named Ricard de Montferrand, who started work on the building in 1817 and continued to supervise it for the rest of his life.

An imperial building

De Montferrand's design was very much in keeping with the style of the Russian imperialists – large and imposing. Based on the classical style, it is supposed to imitate the Pantheon in Rome. Unlike most cathedrals, St Isaac's has four façades, all equally impressive, so that it presents a similar front from all sides. All have a central porch comprising thick granite columns that stand 50 feet (16m) tall. Each pillar stands on a bronze base and rises to a bronze capital, all handsomely carved, and above each set of columns is a large pediment ornamented with sculptured figures, also in bronze. A parapet decorated with more bronze sculptures runs all around the cathedral above the pediments.

Four small, open lantern towers topped with gilded domes stand on the roof dwarfed by the great central cupola which stands on a colonnaded drum, thus matching the columns below the pediments, and is topped by a small lantern. On the north and south fronts are great doors made of beaten bronze, each weighing in excess of 10 tons (10 tonnes).

A glorious centrepiece

Many eastern cathedrals boast an iconostasis, a screen separating the nave from the choir, and many display superb craftsmanship, but few are as glorious as the magnificent example which stands beneath the central dome in St Isaac's Cathedral . Built of marble, lapis lazuli and malachite, it is 225 feet (68m) in width. The malachite is carved into fluted pillars of a rich emerald green, while inlaid lapis lazuli gleams a bright blue through the gilded marble. There are 33 icons, all in mosaic, along with marble slabs on which hang paintings by famous Russian artists. Above the paintings are sculptures of Christ in glory surrounded by heavenly beings clad in gold.

The whole of the interior is a baroque explosion of colour and light, the walls richly adorned with gilded figures and mottoes, and with some superbly executed paintings.

ABOVE: Adorned with a great variety of minerals, the cathedral has been called 'the museum of Russian geology'.

To and fro ...

Hanging from the central dome is a 110-pound (50kg) pendulum of the kind that was designed by the French physicist Jean Foucault (1819–68) in 1851. It was installed in 1931 when the cathedral was used as the State Anti-Religious Museum and demonstrates how the earth rotates on its axis.

Change of name

Peter the Great's new city was initially named St Petersburg after its founder. In 1914, when war broke out with Germany, the name was changed to Petrograd by Tsar Nicholas II because it sounded more Russian than German. In 1924 it was renamed Leningrad in honour of the revolutionary leader Lenin, but reverted to St Petersburg after the fall of the Communist regime.

LEFT: The pillars of the porticos display a classical influence.

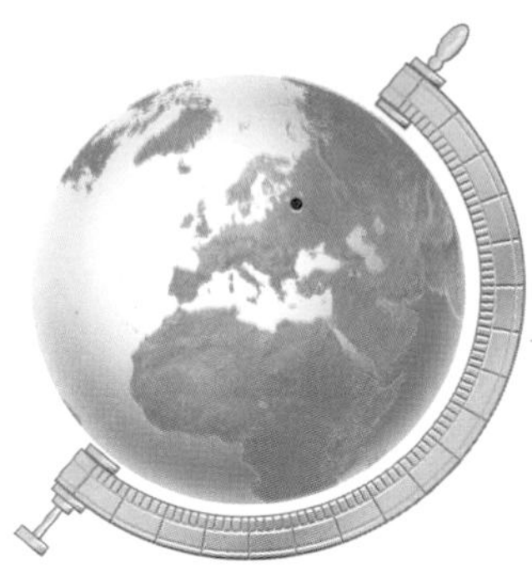

VLADIMIR CATHEDRAL

The 16th-century Cathedral of the Assumption is brilliant white with golden domes

BELOW: The white walls and golden domes of the Cathedral of the Assumption stand out dramatically against the sky.

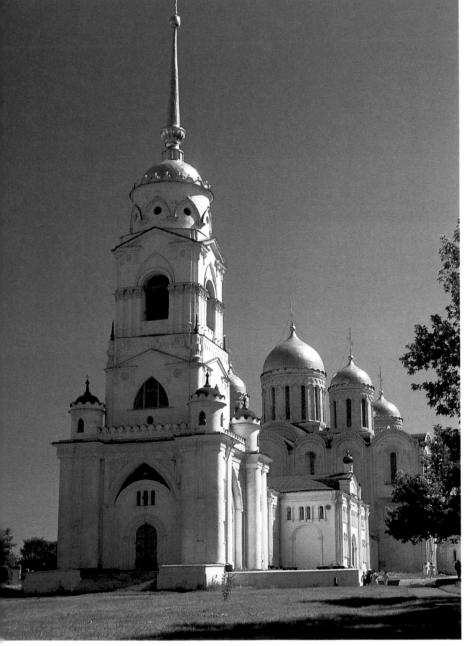

A serious problem for church builders in Russia, especially in the north, was that the traditional inverted saucer-shaped domes tended to collapse under the weight of winter snow. Thus, although Russia's most famous cathedrals are very much Byzantine in style, they lack the great shallow cupolas that characterise St Sophia's in Istanbul or Alexander Nevski Cathedral in Sophia, Bulgaria, for example. Many, such as St Basil's in Moscow and the Cathedral of the Assumption in Zagorsk, have onion domes that allow the snow to slide off before the weight damages them. Others, like the Cathedral of the Assumption in Vladimir, have small, steep-sided domes that also ensure that snow does not accumulate.

Vladimir Cathedral is an impressive sight, whether viewed in its stark whiteness in the summer sun, or seen swathed in powdery snow and surrounded by leafless trees. Standing in a pleasant park inside the citadel, on high ground near the centre of Vladimir overlooking the River Klyazma, its five domes glitter gold and green, while the west façade looms up tall and proud in a tapering series of pillars, arches and ornate decoration.

SIMPLE BEGINNINGS

Prince Vladimir (later St Vladimir) of Kiev adopted Christianity in 988 and from Kiev it spread to neighbouring kingdoms. In terms of antiquity, therefore, Vladimir is one of the oldest cathedrals in Russia. It was started around 1158 by a direct descendent of St Vladimir, Andrei Bogolyubski, who was Grand Prince of Vladimir-Suzdal. Bogolyubski's cathedral was based on a simple plan: a triple-aisled building in the shape of an oblong with a dome over the middle. Inspiration for the dome came from St Sophia's Cathedral in Istanbul (see page 152), and made use of pendentives, great triangular piers that supported a circular dome over a rectangular building.

Shortly after Bogolyubski's death a fire raged through the cathedral causing a considerable amount of damage. Bogolyubski's brother, Vsevolod, was undaunted, however, and promptly began to rebuild, envisaging a far more splendid building than Bogolyubski's.

VSEVOLOD'S CATHEDRAL

Vsevolod wanted to create a magnificent and visually stunning cathedral that would be a focus

LEFT: The interior furnishings of the cathedral are highly ornate; the numerous frescoes painted on the walls date from between the 12th and 15th centuries.

of inspiration – rather in the same way that the French Gothic architects wanted the populace to regard their cathedrals as an image of the kingdom of Heaven.

Work began around 1185 and continued for about five years. Vsevolod added two more aisles and four domes and erected a series of apsidal chapels and other buildings on all four sides. Then he ordered that gilded columns be added all around the outside and that frescoes of vivid colours should be painted on the walls inside. Vsevolod also wanted paintings to decorate the niches on the outside walls, as well as carved reliefs of various figures and animals.

Only fragments remain of Vsevolod's frescoes, but they are enough to fire the imagination about how the cathedral might have appeared in the 12th century, with every surface alive with colour.

The Mongol invasion of Russia in the 13th century resulted in the devastation of many of her cathedrals, but because Vladimir was the capital at the time it suffered more severely than most and it was not until the 14th century that the damaged cathedral was repaired. Between 1408 and 1412 the painter Andrei Rublev was commissioned to redecorate or restore the damaged frescoes. Many of his paintings survive, and are considered to be some of the best examples of religious art from the medieval period in all of Eastern Europe. One of his most skilful works is entitled *Apostles and Angels* and depicts Christ surrounded by a colourful array of heavenly beings.

A FAMOUS ICON

Icons – painted or mosaic images of Christ or saints – have formed an important aspect of Byzantine and Orthodox church history, perhaps equal in status to the relics that have abounded in western churches. The Cathedral of the Assumption in Vladimir held one of the most sacred Russian icons in existence, *The Virgin of Vladimir*. This beautiful stylised portrait of the Virgin Mary holding her infant son is thought to have been executed in Constantinople around 1125 and to have had a major influence on the development of Russian icon-making. Mary's expression is one of great tenderness and has been the inspiration for many artists. By the early 15th century *The Virgin of Vladimir* had been moved to Moscow, where she remains.

VLADIMIR'S OTHER CATHEDRAL

The graceful Cathedral of St Dimitrii was started by Prince Vsevolod between 1194 and 1197, when Vladimir was the capital of the Grand Duchy of Vladimir. Particularly outstanding is the beautiful west front with its 12th- and 13th-century carvings of scenes from a diverse array of subjects, including the Bible and classical history.

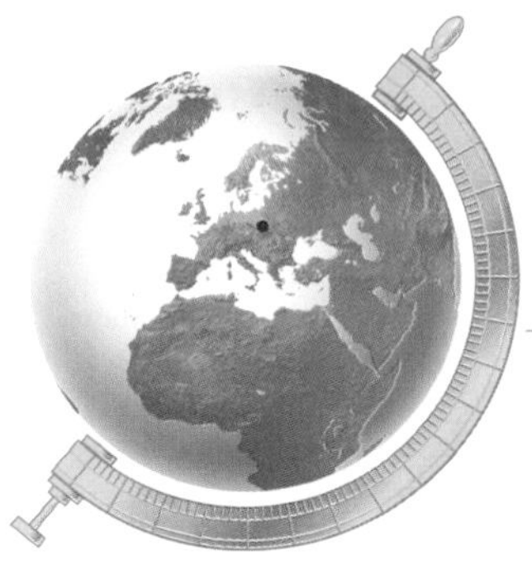

KRAKÓW CATHEDRAL

St Stanislaw, the Saviour, and St Wenceslas Cathedral – onetime burial site of Polish kings – stands on Wawel Hill

THE RENAISSANCE CHAPELS

During the 16th century two chapels, the Sigismund and Vasa, were added to the Gothic nave. Generally considered to be one of Poland's most significant pieces of Renaissance architecture, the Sigismund Chapel was commissioned in the 1520s by Sigismund I (1506–48), a great patron of the Renaissance in Poland. Sigismund employed as his architect the Florentine Bartolomeo Berecci, who designed a hexagonal chapel crowned with a gilt cupola and a lantern pierced with round windows. The interior of the chapel is richly decorated and took Berecci and his team of 30 Italian and Polish artists more than 11 years to complete. Berecci also designed the sarcophagus in which Sigismund was buried.

Kraków Cathedral and the Royal Castle have stood side by side on Wawel Hill in the beautiful city of Kraków for 1,000 years. The hill is a natural stronghold, a rocky outcrop that dominates the city and the valley of the River Vistula. Both cathedral and castle have had stormy pasts and Tartar invasions, fires and attacks by Poland's more powerful neighbours have all taken their toll. Fortunately, Kraków, unlike many European cities, was relatively unharmed during World War II and since then it has been carefully restored to provide a fitting monument to Poland's artistic and cultural history.

THE THIRD CATHEDRAL

Work on the first cathedral on the Wawel was started around 1020 by Boleslaw the Brave. It was built in sandstone, and archaeological excavations have revealed that part of the crypt and some decorated columns from this early church exist in the Renaissance part of the castle. This cathedral did not survive for long, however, and was replaced between 1090 and 1130 by a larger building in the form of a basilica with two naves and four towers. This second cathedral was severely damaged by the devastating Mongol invasion which swept across central Europe, leaving a trail of destruction in Poland, Silesia, Moravia and Hungary. Included in the city's programme of rebuilding was a third cathedral and this, along with other buildings of the period, survives today, helping to make old Kraków one of Europe's finest medieval cities.

The existing Gothic cathedral has a long, elegant nave which ends in a lovely west front carved with slender pillars and a rose window. There is much evidence of the skill of the Gothic stone masons in the cathedral as it became the traditional burial site for Polish kings during the 14th century, and their royal tombs provided the stone masons with an opportunity to show off their skills. Especially fine is the richly carved sandstone and red marble sarcophagus of Casimir the Great, built between 1370 and 1380. The wooden choir stalls also date from the Gothic period.

POLAND'S HEROES

The 17th century saw further rebuilding of the cathedral, including the mausoleum of St Stanislaw

RIGHT: Worshippers throng the cathedral for the Good Friday Mass.

which stands in the centre of the nave. Stanislaw (or Stanislaus) is the patron saint of Poland, and was bishop of Kraków in the second half of the 11th century. He was outspoken in his criticism of King Boleslaw II, and eventually excommunicated him for his cruelty and dubious private life. In response, Boleslaw had Stanislaw murdered in front of the high altar of the cathedral; Stanislaw was buried in the crypt of the first church, but later moved to the current, more prestigious, position when the mausoleum, with its delicately carved silver casket, was completed in the early 17th century. The gold reliquary dating from 1504, which is on display in the treasury, is said to contain Stanislaw's head.

Another of Poland's heroes whose bones rest in the cathedral is King John III Sobieski, whose brilliant military skills delivered Vienna from the siege of the Turks in 1683. He lies in St Leonard's crypt in the company of 13 other Polish kings, their wives and children, and such distinguished national figures as Marshall Josef Pilsudski (1867–1935), Poland's first president.

The sacristy gives access to the treasury, in which are displayed some of the cathedral's finest possessions. Perhaps best known are the lance of St Maurice, given to Poland by Emperor Otto III in 1000; the coronation sword of the kings of Poland; the 13th-century cross of King Casimir Jagiello; an 11th-century glass cup from Egypt called the Chalice of St Hedwiga; and a relic of St Florian.

BELOW: The cathedral presents a range of architectural styles with contrasting adjacent domes in green and gold.

POLAND

WARSAW CATHEDRAL

The Cathedral of St John was badly damaged in the 1944 Warsaw Uprising

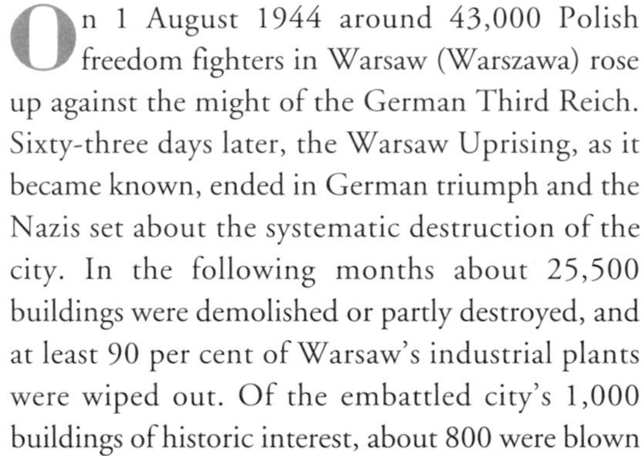

On 1 August 1944 around 43,000 Polish freedom fighters in Warsaw (Warszawa) rose up against the might of the German Third Reich. Sixty-three days later, the Warsaw Uprising, as it became known, ended in German triumph and the Nazis set about the systematic destruction of the city. In the following months about 25,500 buildings were demolished or partly destroyed, and at least 90 per cent of Warsaw's industrial plants were wiped out. Of the embattled city's 1,000 buildings of historic interest, about 800 were blown up or destroyed by fire. When Polish and Russian troops liberated Warsaw on 17 January 1945, the once-proud city was little more than a pile of smoking rubble.

BELOW: St John's is the oldest church in Warsaw, and was the place of coronation for two Polish kings.

The Cathedral of St John was just one of the historically important buildings that had been reduced to ruins. Also destroyed were the magnificent Royal Castle (Zamek Krolewski); the lovely Krakowskie Przedmiescie Street, with its elegant palaces and churches; and the old market place (Rynek Slarego Miasta).

However, daunted but determined, the Poles began to collect together old plans, photographs and details from their memories and in the following years many historical buildings of Warsaw, including the cathedral, were painstakingly rebuilt.

A CATHEDRAL IN AN ANCIENT CITY

The handsome 14th-century Gothic cathedral stands among a jumble of red-roofed houses inside the 14th- and 15th-century city ramparts, a lovely area of the city where baroque, Renaissance and Gothic architecture sit easily side by side. Next to it is the lofty, brick-built Church of the Jesuits, also completely rebuilt after 1944.

When viewed from the river the domed towers of St John's dominate the Warsaw skyline. The main tower, slender and octagonal with slatted windows on the lower half, is topped by an elegant lantern with a dome. Above this is a bright gold cross that glitters even on the dullest days. The roof is tiled and steeply pitched.

Building work on the cathedral, a simple structure with a nave and two aisles, was started in the 1330s. Various additions and restorations were carried out in the later 14th and 15th centuries, but otherwise the cathedral survived more or less in its original form until the war. The oldest surviving part is the lovely Chapel of Our Lord, built in 1339 and financed by a wealthy merchant called Baryczka.

SURVIVING TREASURES

Several items were recovered from the ruins of the cathedral before restoration work began. These include a Gothic crucifix, probably from Spain; a handsome marble slab from the 16th-century tomb of the Dukes of Mazovia, which was in the choir; and fragments of the tomb of Slanislaw Malachowski from one of the aisles. A Gothic triptych from Silesia was also recovered from the same aisle.

In the crypts underneath the cathedral are several tombs that survived the war. Among them are those of Henryk Sienkievicz (1846–1916), the novelist who wrote *Quo Vadis?*, and Gabriel Narutowicz, who was president of the Polish Republic in 1922.

The crypts have some exceptionally fine stellar vaulting (where the decorative ribs supporting the roof converge into a star-like pattern). Also worth noting are the portal and high altar designed by the Polish artist A Jablonski in 1963.

Visitors can leave the cathedral by a small side door and arcade that once linked this important religious building with the Royal Castle. Picturesque Kanonia is a lovely street named after the canons of the church who used to live in the attractive baroque-style houses there.

WARSAW'S OTHER CHURCHES

Fortunately not all the churches in Warsaw were destroyed during World War II and perhaps the finest of these is the Church of the Carmelites on Krakowskie Przedmiescie Street, which dates from the second half of the 17th century. Its elegant 18th-century façade shows a strong French influence.

On the same street is the Church of the Holy Cross which has two urns sealed in its pillars: one contains the heart of Chopin, the other the heart of novelist Ladislas Reymont (who won the Nobel Prize in 1924). The Church of the Order of the Visitation, near Victory Square, also dates from the late 18th century and has a wonderful rococo interior. Dominating the new town market square is the Church of the Sisters of the Holy Sacrament, built in 1683 by King John III Sobieski to commemorate his victory over the Turks besieging Vienna.

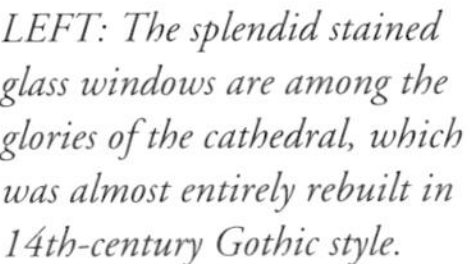

LEFT: The splendid stained glass windows are among the glories of the cathedral, which was almost entirely rebuilt in 14th-century Gothic style.

BELOW: Warsaw Cathedral witnessed the confirmation of Europe's first written constitution – the '3rd of May Constitution' of 1791.

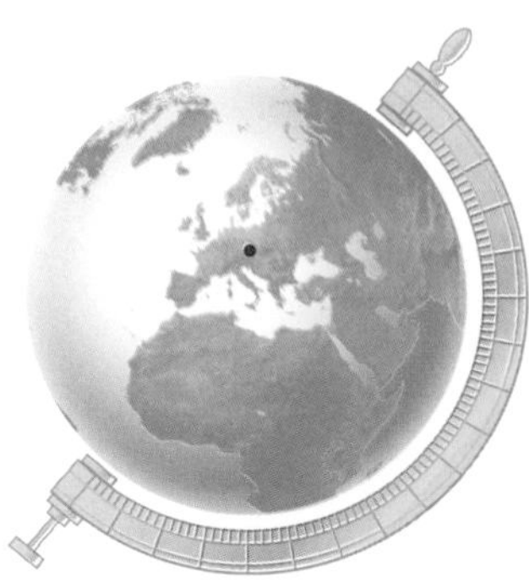

CZECH REPUBLIC

ST VITUS' CATHEDRAL

Prague's largest church, the stately Gothic cathedral, stands proud on Hradčany Hill

GOOD KING WENCESLAS

The Good King Wenceslas of Christmas carol fame is a venerable character, usually depicted in regal middle age. In reality, however, Wenceslas was a tribal chieftain murdered when he was only 26 years old by his younger brother in a church in AD929.

Wenceslas is an important figure in Czech history. He brought Christianity to his people and is the patron saint of the Czech Republic. Wenceslas Square lies at the very heart of the city, dominated by a huge romantic statue of the king clad in chain mail, brandishing a banner, and the cathedral boasts the lovely Wenceslas Chapel containing his tomb.

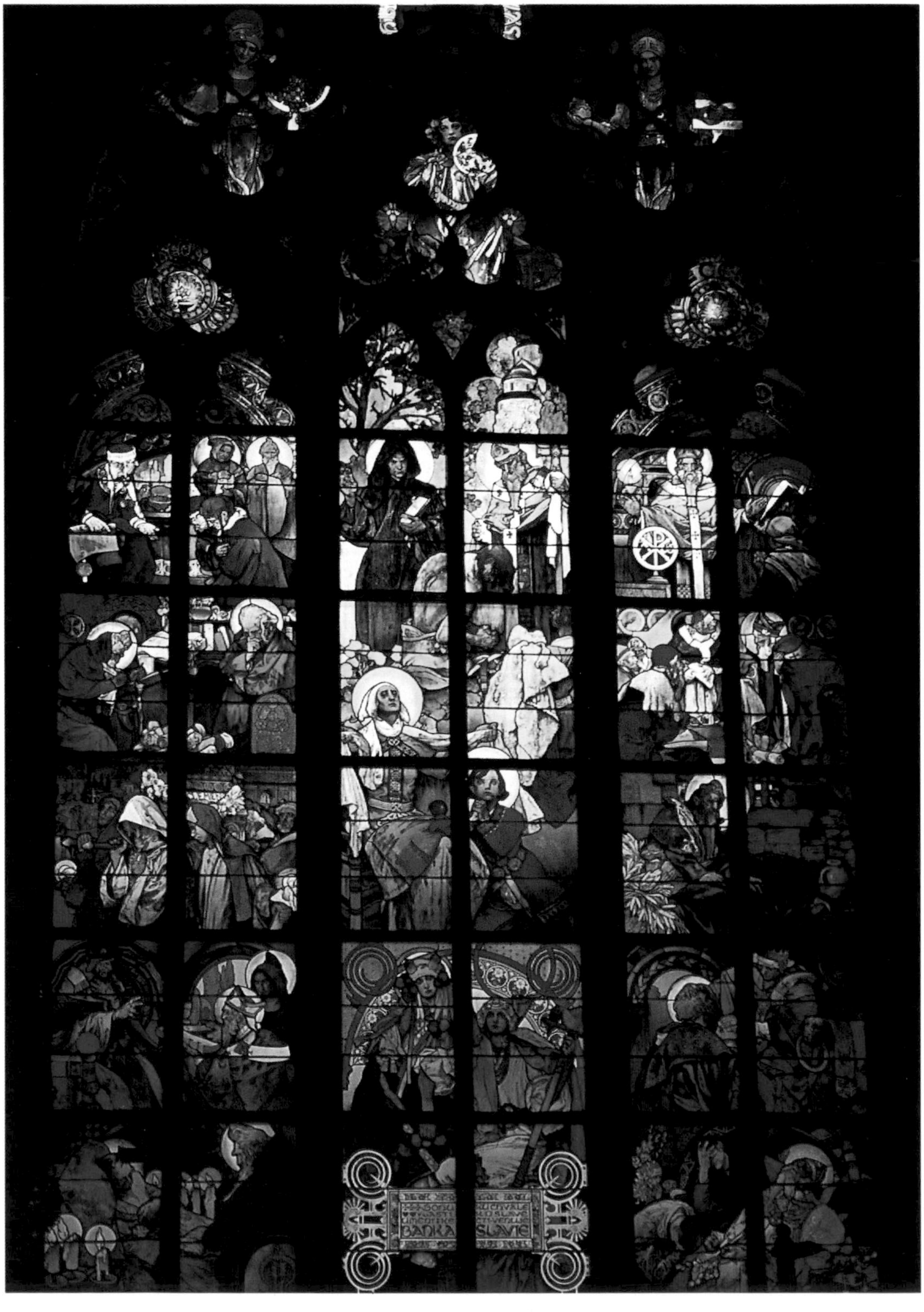

RIGHT: The delicate colours of the windows result from the designs being painted on to the glass, rather than stained. The Czech master Alfonse Mucha was among the artists who worked on the windows.

Prague (Praha), called the 'Golden City' and the 'City of a Hundred Spires', has a skyline pierced by towers and pinnacles of all shapes and sizes. But dominating all is the magnificent St Vitus' Cathedral, the great Gothic building that remains one of central Europe's finest architectural achievements. Reached by narrow cobbled streets that wind steeply up from the River Vlatva, it stands at the summit of the hill with Prague Castle, an impressive complex of palatial buildings spanning several centuries.

Wenceslas' church

The history of St Vitus' stretches further back in time than the current building. A church was founded in about 926 by King Wenceslas (see panel); it was specially designed as a rotunda to hold the arm of St Vitus which had been given to Wenceslas by Emperor Henry I as a mark of friendship. In the 11th century the constant stream of pilgrims to Wenceslas' church had become too large to be accommodated in the little building and it was incorporated into a basilica. During the following years a great many changes were made, not only to the basilica but also to the neighbouring castle. Although archaeological excavations indicate that parts of the early churches remain, most of the present cathedral dates from 1344 when a new, suitably grand cathedral was commissioned by the Bohemian Emperor King Charles IV.

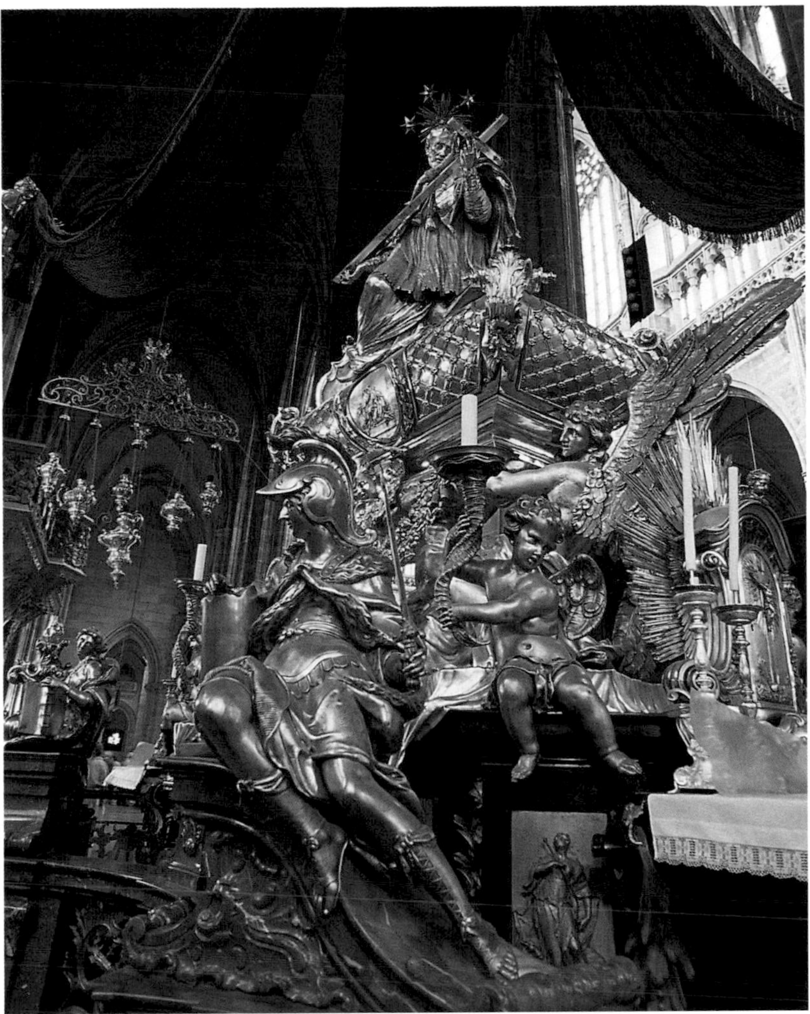

ABOVE: The sarcophagus of St John of Nepomuk in the ambulatory is by Johann Fischer von Erlach.

Charles IV's cathedral

Political upheavals before the 14th century meant that Bohemia did not have an archbishop who could crown its king and therefore Bohemian princes had to be crowned in another country. When he came to the throne Charles IV and his father set about putting an end to this demeaning state of affairs and appealed to the Pope for an archbishop of their own. This done, Charles went on to acquire the crown of the Holy Roman Empire and initiated a plan that made Bohemia one of the most powerful nations in the medieval world. The proposed cathedral at Prague played an important role in Charles' machinations, and he made certain he hired one of the best architects of the day to ensure a building as mighty as his own ambitions.

The architect was Matthew of Arras from Avignon and the cornerstone was laid on 21 November 1344. First to be built was the choir, designed specifically as a fit place for the crowning of the powerful rulers of Bohemia.

Parléř's contribution

When Arras died in 1352 he was succeeded by Petra Parléř, one of the greatest 14th-century architects in Europe. Parléř completed the eastern end of the cathedral, creating soaring pillars and huge stained-glass windows with delicate tracery, the most impressive being *The Last Judgement* in the south transept. The large windows mean that this splendid Gothic cathedral is flooded with light, allowing the visitor to appreciate the wealth of carving and the perfect proportions of the high nave.

One of the finest of Parléř's statues is that of King Wenceslas in the Wenceslas Chapel, showing a noble character wearing full armour, while the fresco on the wall behind depicts saints and kings paying homage to him. The focal point of the chapel is Wenceslas' tomb, although the wall-paintings, inlaid with semi-precious stones and gold, should not be overlooked.

Parléř also designed several of the tombs of kings, bishops and cardinals that decorate the cathedral. In the triforium there is a series of busts of various members of the royal family, and of cathedral sponsors, including Parléř himself. This fascinating gallery of portraits in stone, despite the empty, sightless eyes, manages to convey a remarkable spectrum of expressions: Anne of Schweidnitz seems amused, while John of Luxembourg glares sternly.

BELOW: The imposing pulpit is enriched with ornate decoration.

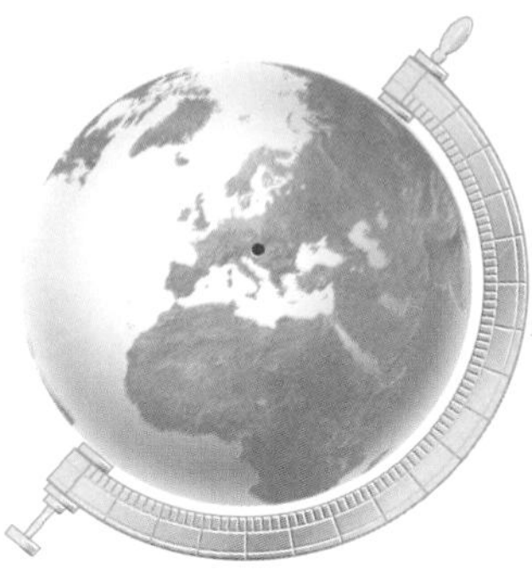

HUNGARY

ESZTERGOM CATHEDRAL

This splendid basilica, seat of the Primate of Hungary, overlooks the River Danube

BELOW: The cathedral at Esztergom is built on a massive scale; each of the eight Corinthian pillars of the portico is 72 feet (22m) tall.

At a wide and peaceful stretch of the great muddy, brown swirl that is the River Danube stands the little town of Esztergom. Visitors arriving by ferry from Budapest, or by road, will first notice the broken span of the Mária Valéria Bridge that once linked Hungary with Czechoslovakia. Destroyed in World War II, it was never rebuilt.

The vast basilica of Esztergom sits in Szent István tér on Castle Hill, a monumental building and, as the centre of Hungarian Catholicism, appropriately grand. Its imposing domes and the ornate Italianate spires of Watertown parish church contrast vividly with the heavy industry and concrete tower blocks of Slovakian Stúrovo opposite.

LEFT: The pastel-coloured interior is well-lit by the large windows in the dome.

Esztergom has been the focal point of the country's Christianity for more than 1,000 years and the Archbishop of Esztergom is still the Primate of Hungary.

Hungary's first king, Stephen, was born here in 975 and he founded a basilica, parts of which can still be seen in the palace near the present cathedral. When the Turks invaded in 1543 the archbishop fled across the Danube and the church did not re-establish itself in Esztergom for a century and a half.

The 19th-century basilica

The present building, started in 1822, was consecrated in 1856. During the service a mass composed by Franz Liszt was performed.

The proud, 236-foot (72-m), green-tinged dome of the cathedral ensures that the largest church in Hungary can be seen for many miles around. The body is equally imposing: it is 387 feet (118m) long and 131 feet (40m) wide. Its front is neatly symmetrical, with the dome towering above a massive classical porch dominated by eight slender pillars. To each side are an arch and a tower that rise almost as high as the central dome.

The gigantic proportions of the cathedral are perhaps even more evident within, as the walls sweep upwards to the coloured underside of the dome. Sparse interior decoration adds further to the sense of space. On the left of the south entrance lies the lovely red marble Bakócz Chapel, commissioned by Archbishop Tamás Bakócz (see panel) in the first quarter of the 16th century. Fortunately, the chapel survived the numerous wars and was carefully dismantled into 1,600 separate pieces and reconstructed in its current location in 1823. The chapel's main feature, other than its superb Tuscan Renaissance stone carvings, is the copy of Titian's *Assumption*, said to be the largest painting on a single canvas in the world.

The crypt

In contrast to its light and airy interior, which allows the daylight to flood in, the cathedral has a dank and gloomy crypt, a musty-smelling cavern containing candle-lit tombs. Several of these contain important figures in Hungary's turbulent history, including József Mindszenty, the archbishop who rebelled against Russian presence in Hungary by taking up residence in the American embassy in Budapest in 1956. He finally left at the request of the Pope in 1971, and died in Vienna in 1975, claiming that he would never return to Esztergom until the Russians had left Hungary. His body was brought to the cathedral in 1991. Near the crypt entrance are the relics of three priests martyred in the early 17th century in nearby Kosice.

Greedy Archbishop Bakócz

Tamás Bakócz, Archbishop of Esztergom, was a man who was determined to attain political power. Through links with the powerful Doge of Venice, Bakócz first became a cardinal, and then Patriarch of Constantinople. He hoped to become Pope, and set about securing support after the death of Julius II in 1513. However, his attempts failed and Leo X was elected instead. The new Pope then commissioned Bakócz to organise a crusade. Unfortunately for Bakócz this attempt led to a soldier by the name of György Dózsa stepping in and turning the band of crusaders into a peasant army that revolted against its overlords in 1514. The revolt was put down with brutal severity, and Dózsa was executed in the aftermath along with some 70,000 peasants. Within a decade, Bakócz had died, and shortly thereafter a Turkish military victory gave them control of Hungary.

Gold, Silver and Jewels

The treasury, on the north side of the cathedral, is crammed with ancient vestments and religious plates, chalices, patens, and other objects in a glittering display of gold and silver broken by the reds, blues and greens of precious jewels. The collection is the largest in Hungary and objects from all over the country, as well as Italy and the Byzantine Empire, can be admired. Especially lovely are the crosses, including the 13th-century Coronation Oath Cross and the Matthias Calvary Cross, dating to 1469, of delicately carved gold inlaid with enamel. The Maria Theresa Chalice is also impressive, a superb example of baroque craftsmanship.

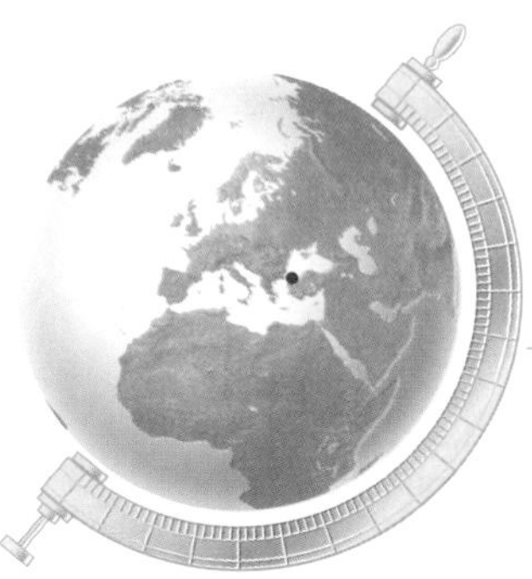

TURKEY

ST SOPHIA'S CATHEDRAL

The breathtaking cathedral at Istanbul was the greatest Byzantine cathedral in Christendom

ABOVE: The vast shallow dome of St Sophia's has made it vulnerable to earthquakes throughout its history; the enormous flying buttresses were designed in the 9th century to alleviate the problem.

Even in comparison with the most superb architectural triumphs, the fabulous Byzantine Cathedral of St Sophia (Haghia Sophia) in the centre of Istanbul cannot fail to impress. It represents the pinnacle of Byzantine architectural engineering, a vast monolith of domes and minarets standing proudly within the ancient walls of one of the most vital cities of the Middle Ages – Constantinople, known since 1930 as Istanbul.

ST SOPHIA'S GREEK ARCHITECTS

This magnificent building was designed by two Greek engineers, Isidore of Miletus and Anthemius of Tralles, who were commissioned to build a cathedral worthy to be the focus of the great Byzantine Empire. The engineers were employed by Emperor Justinian I, who ruled the Empire between 527 and 565. Justinian was lavish in his funding and employed some 10,000 labourers and craftsmen to work on the cathedral for virtually the entire period of construction (532–7). The story goes that when Justinian came to admire his new church at Christmas in 537, he exclaimed, 'Solomon, I have surpassed thee,' referring to Solomon's reputedly splendid Temple at Jerusalem.

The Great Church of the Holy Wisdom, as St Sophia's is sometimes known, was built on a square plan. The walls are a series of ascending colonnades, galleries and aisles, all drawing the eye to the massive shallow dome 107 feet (32m) in diameter which crowns the whole some 180 feet (54m) above the ground. Forty windows at the base of the dome give the impression that it floats on air when viewed from outside. Built of a combination of brick and stone, it was originally decorated with coloured marbles and mosaics, some of which survive today under the current layers of whitewash.

Inside the cathedral, under the great dome, is a huge nave some 107 feet (32m) wide and 225 feet (68m) long. It is a breathtaking spectacle of arches and colonnades, all flooded with light from the many windows. The floor, now flagged, was once covered with delicately coloured mosaics, some with gilded designs. The walls, too, were once adorned with intricate mosaics but many were plastered over

RIGHT: A detail of one of the few surviving nave mosaics, dating from the 10th century. The Virgin is flanked on one side by Constantine and on the other by Justinian, offering gifts to the Child.

when the cathedral became a mosque in 1453. Renovation of St Sophia's in the 1930s revealed some of these mosaics, including the massive Deesis mosaic in the south gallery, thought to date from the 13th century. The vast space is accentuated by chandeliers and disks bearing Islamic words suspended from the ceiling.

History

St Sophia's Cathedral lays claim to being the greatest church in Christendom for the 1,000 years between its founding and the time when it was taken over by Muslim Turks in 1453 and converted into a mosque. Before the Fall of Constantinople to the Turks, the Byzantine city had been subject to another capture – in 1204 by Christians. In 1202, Pope Innocent III had called for a crusade – the fourth since the first one in the 1090s – to go to the Holy Land. A ragged army of French and Venetian soldiers set off, but changed direction, abandoning their goal of Egypt for the more easily accessible treasures of the Byzantine Empire. The crusaders found Constantinople poorly defended and took it easily, sacking and destroying as they went. During the sacking of St Sophia's, gold and silver decorations were prised from the walls, mosaics were torn from the floors, icons were smashed and tombs were desecrated; paintings and other works of art were spirited away to France and Italy.

A Feature of Byzantine Architecture

St Sophia's has been described as an architectural miracle, because although it was one of the first buildings to be executed in the Byzantine style, it remained the finest. The biggest architectural problem encountered was how to support a dome on a square base. This was solved by the introduction of the pendentive – an inverted triangular block of masonry formed by the intersecting of a dome by pairs of arches carried on columns. This invention, carried out with such success at St Sophia's, became a dominant feature in later Byzantine churches.

Haghia Eirene: the Second Cathedral

The second largest medieval Christian place of worship in Istanbul is Haghia Eirene, dedicated to the Divine Peace, an attribute of Christ complementary to that of Divine Wisdom at St Sophia's. Pre-dating St Sophia's, it served as the cathedral of the Patriarch of the Eastern Orthodox Church from the time of Emperor Constantine until the completion of St Sophia's. Both cathedrals were burnt down in the 6th century but were rebuilt (at the same time) by Emperor Justinian. He saw them as forming the two major aspects of one religious establishment, under the same Patriarch and served by the same clergy.

LEFT: The great chandelier hanging from the centre of the ceiling was a gift from Sultan Ahmet III. The disks which crown the columns bear the names of holy and historical figures.

DOME
HANGING DISKS WITH ISLAMIC WORDS
WINDOWS AT THE BASE OF DOME
COLONNADES AND GALLERIES
SEMI-DOMES
MINARETS
BAPTISTRY
GALLERY OF THE WOMEN
HANGING CHANDELIER
FLYING BUTTRESSES

Greece

The Little Metropole

The smallest cathedral in the world is also known as Panayia Gorgoepikoos

Under the baking Mediterranean sun, in a noisy, dusty, busy capital city, stands the remarkable Little Metropolitan Cathedral of Athens, which claims to be the smallest cathedral in the world. Between 1840 and 1855 another Metropolitan cathedral was built to the north, directly behind the Little Metropole, dominating, but certainly not overwhelming, it. The new cathedral is a light and airy building and its ample interior is far more readily able to accommodate the thousands of people wanting to attend religious functions than its minuscule predecessor.

BELOW: The Great Metropole is much larger and more ornate than its miniature companion.

The legend of its founding

The Little Metropole is known variously as Panayia Gorgoepikoos (meaning 'the Virgin who is able to grant requests quickly') or Agios Elefterios. Exactly when it was founded remains uncertain, but legend

LEFT: The diminutive Little Metropole is one of Athens' most characteristic and attractive Byzantine churches. The reliefs which decorate the walls date from Classical times to the Byzantine period.

has it that the first building was raised here in 787 by the charismatic Irene, head of the Byzantine Empire and saint of the Greek Orthodox Church (see panel). No trace of this early church – if it ever existed – remains and the present building dates mainly from the 12th and 13th centuries.

UNIQUE DIMENSIONS

Lovely decorations notwithstanding, the most startling feature of the Little Metropole is its size. Built on a rectangular plan, it measures only 38 feet (11m) in length by 25 feet (8m) in width. The lower part comprises a simple rectangular room with a tiny projecting rounded apse at the eastern end. Midway along the north, west and south sides at roof level are gables with pediments pierced by double-headed round arches. Within the arches are circular window openings which are repeated in the drum below the lovely cupola that tops the building. The cupola is some 9 feet (3m) across and stands about 40 feet (12m) above the ground. Supported by four piers, the drum is cylindrical and has eight round-headed windows.

The proportions of this tiny cathedral not only seem further accentuated because of its proximity to its newer, far bigger 19th-century neighbour, but because it lies below the level of the modern pavement – visitors step down to it. Inside, the thick walls make the building seem even smaller, an impression made stronger by the fact that the little round window openings do not allow much light in. But when the cathedral is empty, and the doors closed against the continual rumble of traffic outside, its ancient stones lend an atmosphere of tranquillity often absent from larger buildings.

A GALLERY OF MARBLE

Little Metropole is built of pale cream-coloured marble and faced with an intriguing collection of Byzantine marble slabs. Some of these were taken from churches dating from the 6th to the 9th century in Athens, which were in ruins. Others came from more ancient classical Greek buildings. The result is bizarre, but fascinating. Visitors studying the walls will notice a great wealth of designs, ranging from astrological signs and mythical creatures to various geometrical carvings, zig-zags and swirls.

One of the best of these Byzantine marble reliefs is the one on the west wall depicting zodiac signs and dating from the 4th century BC. Another is the coat of arms of the Villhardouins, a powerful family that governed Athens after the Fourth Crusade (1202–4). One of the most popular themes for a Byzantine relief panel was animals facing each other to form a symmetrical design. There are several examples of this motif in the Little Metropole, the best of which is the panel of two gryphons, mythical creatures with the wings of an eagle, the body of a lion and the tail of a serpent, facing each other over a stylised tree. The design of this particular panel is thought to have originated in Persia.

IRENE, EMPRESS OF THE BYZANTINES

Irene (*c*752–803) married Leo IV, who ruled the Byzantine Empire between 775 and 780. After Leo's death, Irene acted as regent for her son Constantine VI until she was banished from court in 790. She stayed away for seven years but then returned with a vengeance. She imprisoned her son, first blinding him, and took the throne. As a precaution, she imprisoned her husband's five brothers, too.

In 730, the use of icons – painted or mosaic images of Christ or the saints – had been forbidden by a group of fanatics ('iconoclasts'). Irene, at the Council of Nicaea in 787, ordered that icons be restored but she was overthrown in 802 and exiled to Lesbos. Her stance against the iconoclasts resulted in her being made a saint of the Greek Orthodox Church.

ATHENS' FIRST CATHEDRAL

Under the 6th-century Emperor Justinian, the Parthenon was dedicated to St Sophia and then to the Virgin Mary of God. It became the Metropolitan church of Athens and its walls were said (in contemporary writings) to be covered with frescos. The vaults were used to inter dead bishops, one of whom was discovered during archaeological excavations in 1910. It was the cathedral of the Frankish Dukes, and it followed Latin rites between 1208 and 1458.

When it became a mosque, the Byzantine bell-tower at the south-west angle was converted into a minaret.

MALTA

ST JOHN'S CO-CATHEDRAL

Valletta Cathedral was built for the Knights of the Order of St John of Jerusalem in 1573

FAR RIGHT: The great barrel vault of the nave is adorned with dramatic works of art; 18 scenes from the life of St John are depicted, painted in oils directly on to the primed stone.

ST PAUL'S CATHEDRAL, MDINA

Using masons from Sicily, the first cathedral was built in Mdina in about 1100 on the site of an earlier building. It was enlarged in 1419, but was severely damaged in an earthquake in 1693 when virtually the entire structure collapsed. Lorenzo Gafà was employed to rebuild it in 1697, a task that took him five years and resulted in one of the most splendid buildings in Malta.

The cathedral reflects the fact that it was built during Malta's Golden Age. The surviving apse contains a beautiful fresco of the *Shipwreck of St Paul* by Mattia Preti, one of his finest works. Other treasures include an icon of the Virgin Mary, which is reputed to have been painted by St Luke, and a medieval silver cross said to have accompanied the knights of the First Crusade into Jerusalem.

In 1822 the splendid early baroque church of St John was made a co-cathedral with the Cathedral of St Paul in Mdina (see panel). This tiny citadel town had been a capital since Roman times and it continued to be an important stronghold until the building of Valletta commenced in the 1560s, following a long and bitter siege by the Turks. Behind the altar rails of St John's are two thrones facing each other, the Archbishop of Malta's on the left, and the British sovereign's (Malta was under British rule at the time) on the right.

THE ORDER OF ST JOHN OF JERUSALEM

The cathedral is named after John the Baptist, patron saint of the Order of St John of Jerusalem, an order closely intertwined with the history of Malta from about 1530. Orders had their origins in the crusades, when groups of monks began to form themselves into military organisations. The Hospitallers, or the Order of St John, had two duties to discharge: they were to defend the church against the Infidel, and they were to tend the sick. A series of bitter disputes with their rivals, the Templars, weakened the Hospitallers' position and they were gradually forced to retreat from the Holy Land to occupy Cyprus and then Rhodes. In the 1520s the Muslim Turks decided they had had enough of the troublesome knights and sent an invasion force to drive them away from Rhodes.

RIGHT: The three clocks on the bell-tower give the time, the day of the week, and the day of the month. The spires were removed from the towers in 1941 after bombing rendered them unstable.

The homeless knights and their followers were then offered Malta by the Holy Roman Emperor and, reluctantly, they accepted, landing at the tiny, impoverished fortified town of Birgù in 1530. Work on the new town of Valletta started in the 1560s, with the cathedral at its centre. Occupation by the Hospitallers lasted until the arrival of Napoleon in 1798.

THE EXTERIOR ...

The influence of the order and its Grand Masters is strong at the Co-Cathedral of St John. Building work started in 1573 by Grand Master La Cassière, who was so desperate to leave Birgù for his new city of Valletta that he paid for much of the building work himself. The architect was an Italian called Gerolamo Cassar. The exterior of Cassar's cathedral has been much criticised: the columns are spaced asymmetrically, and the two towers that flank the façade seem somewhat misplaced. However, Cassar died in 1586 and the building was subsequently altered and developed: the windows were enlarged to provide better light for the frescos within and the two wings were built in 1598 and 1604.

... AND THE LAVISH INTERIOR

The exterior is more than compensated for by the sumptuous interior, which draws the eye to the fabulous high altar. The building itself is a simple rectangle with the chapels of the different divisions (or *langues*) of the order ranged down each side.

The walls are richly decorated with Renaissance paintings, while the floor is paved with coloured marble slabs. Arching overhead is the magnificent ceiling painted in oils by the Calabrian genius Mattia Preti. It was commissioned by the Grand Masters Raphael and Nicholas Cotoner and was started in 1662, taking five years to complete.

The chapels off the nave house the tombs of later Grand Masters (the earlier ones are entombed in the crypt, a low-vaulted baroque room). Preti painted some of the frescos and the little chapels are crammed with treasures, including lovely silver gates on the Chapel of Our Lady of Philermos.

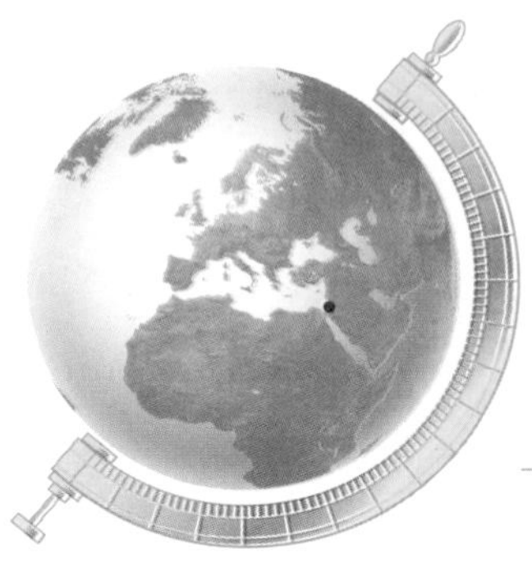

ISRAEL

CHURCH OF THE HOLY SEPULCHRE

One of the most important Christian sites in the world lies in the Old City of Jerusalem

THE CHAPEL OF THE FINDING OF THE CROSS

Thirteen uneven steps lead down to a cave that was once a cistern. Here, legend has it that Helena, the Emperor Constantine's mother, found three crosses (complete with nails) in the 320s. To identify the one used for Jesus, she touched each with a dead baby to ascertain which one restored its life. Another legend maintains the same thing was done with a dying woman, with a similarly successful result. The cross was kept at the Holy Sepulchre until the Persians came in 614, after which it was taken by the Byzantines to Constantinople. It was later divided into innumerable fragments, which appear in reliquaries all over the world, especially in churches called Santa Cruz (meaning 'Holy Cross').

In the heart of the bustling, colourful Old City in Jerusalem stands the medieval Church of the Holy Sepulchre, a pale-yellow jumble of domes, chapels and crypts. Inside is a mysterious labyrinth of incense-saturated oratories, stone-flagged passages and rooms laden with the trappings of the six diverse Christian communities that control the church.

A visit to the Holy Sepulchre is an experience indeed: small silver bells tinkle incessantly from the Armenian chapels, harsh plainsong echoes from the Greek section, all competing with the thundering Roman Catholic organ. This is no accident, for the relationship between the six communities is far from peaceful, each guarding its territory with vigorous zeal.

The six communities are Greek Orthodox, Roman Catholic (Franciscans), Armenians, Copts, Syrians and Ethiopians, with the first three holding the greater part, and the last three inhabiting a single chapel each. Disputes between the communities have traditionally been intense and, in the 1800s, relations between the Franciscans and the Greeks had degenerated to the point that they were used as a pretext for the Crimean War. An uneasy status quo has been in force since an

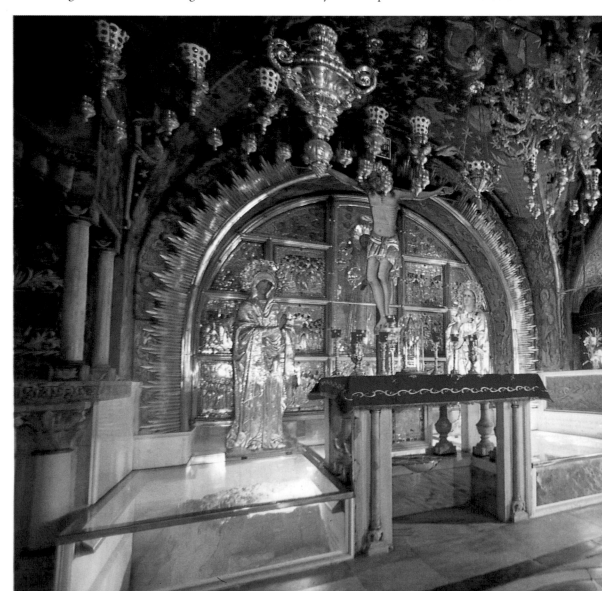

RIGHT: One of the altars in the area of the church known as 'Calvary'. The marble floor with its mosaics has been renewed during the present century.

agreement signed by all six in 1852, although the cease-fire is sometimes broken: in 1967, the Copts deliberately disrupted the Ethiopians' Easter celebrations, resulting in a disgraceful display of rioting.

A violent history

The first church to occupy the site where Jesus' tomb is said to have been located was built in 326 by Emperor Constantine. This was destroyed in 614 by Persians, then rebuilt in 629 only to be demolished yet again by Arabs in 1009. Reconstruction recommenced in 1042 with the building of a rotunda above the tomb, and the crusaders added a Romanesque church in the 12th century. A fire in 1808 did considerable damage to this, as did an earthquake in 1927. However, despite the noise to be expected of a busy pilgrim-site-cum-tourist-attraction, this atmospheric old church has retained much that is ancient.

Religious sites

One of the first things the visitor will see on entering the church is the Stone of Unction, a slab of limestone that is owned in common by all six communities. It is said that Jesus' body was anointed here before it was buried. Near by, the Place of the Three Women is where the three Marys stood by the cross (owned by Armenians). The rotunda, occupying the site of Constantine's Church of the Resurrection, is where the Holy Sepulchre stands, on the site of Jesus' rock tomb (destroyed in 1009).

Evidence that the hollow beneath the Sepulchre was where Jesus was buried has been hotly debated through the ages, and will doubtless continue to be so. It is lit by windows in the plain rotunda, which also highlights the rococo ornamentation above, added after the 1808 fire. The Sepulchre comprises two rooms: the Chapel of the Angels, containing the stone on which Mary Magdalene saw an angel sitting after Jesus' resurrection, and the tiny tomb itself. The latter is percolated by sooty holes, through which 'holy fire' is said to emerge at Easter.

Other sites in the Holy Sepulchre complex include the Chapel of the Sharing of the Raiment (Armenian), where soldiers gambled for Jesus' clothes; the Chapel of the Finding of the Cross (Greek and Franciscan); the Altar of the Crucifixion (Greek); the Tomb of Joseph of Arimathea (Ethiopian); the Chapel of Adam (Greek), where Adam's skull was said to have been discovered when Jesus was crucified; and the great Catholicon (Greek), the much-repaired nave of the Crusader church dominated by a chandelier and the 'omphalos' that represents the navel of the world.

ABOVE: The entrance to the church is through a courtyard, with the bell-tower in the north-west corner. The entrance façade dates from the time of the crusaders, and combines Romanesque and Byzantine elements. Chapels surround the courtyard.

The Ethiopian village

The Ethiopian community is housed in a curious cluster of African-style huts under the baking sun. The monks are bound by the status quo in that they cannot improve their living quarters without the consent of the other five communities, including that of their bitterest antagonists, the Copts. If they abandon these uncomfortable, miserable cells, then they risk losing their claim to the tiny Chapel of Joseph of Arimathea, the only part of the Holy Sepulchre under their control.

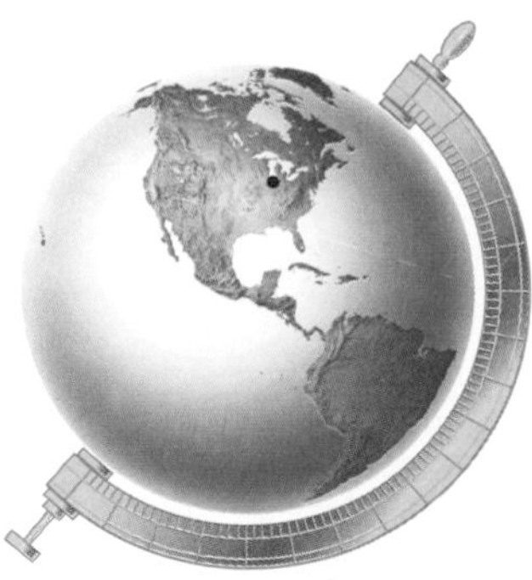

UNITED STATES OF AMERICA

HOLY NAME CATHEDRAL

This fine Catholic cathedral is associated with Chicago's first higher learning college

RIGHT: The spire of the yellow-stone cathedral soars just as high as the skyscrapers which surround it.

A COMMODIOUS EDIFICE

Keely's new cathedral, dedicated on 21 November 1875, received gushing praise from the newspapers of the time. Then the largest church west of New York, it dwarfed the nearby Jesuit Church of the Holy Family which had previously held that distinction. It is 216 feet (65m) in length, and 102 feet (31m) at its transepts, while the spire soars 210 feet (63m) above the foundations.

The great city of Chicago, founded in 1803 near the site of Fort Dearborn, expanded rapidly after the 1830s with the construction of the railways. By 1871 it was a sizeable settlement with a population made up of large numbers of immigrants from, among other places, Catholic Italy and Ireland. In that year, on the night of 8 October, a great fire raged through the city destroying virtually every building and killing several hundred people. One of the many places to disappear was the half-completed Holy Name Church, which was reported to have melted in the intense inferno within five minutes. Four years later, the foundation stone of a new cathedral was laid.

CHAPEL TO CATHEDRAL

Prior to the fire, the history of Holy Name Church had been anything but peaceful. It was originally built as a chapel to serve the newly founded St Mary's of the Lake University, the first establishment of higher education in Chicago, whose charter had been granted in 1844. Because the only alternative for Catholic worship in the area was the nearby German-speaking St Joseph Church, a new church was needed before long and a wooden structure was built on the junction of Superior and State streets. Soon this was bulging at the seams, and the Holy Name Church was built near by.

In 1859 James Duggan was appointed Bishop of Chicago and there followed a series of unsavoury intrigues and conflicts that resulted in the sacking of the priests of Holy Name Church and the closing down of the university and attached seminary. In a fury, Father McMullen, head of the university, stormed off to Rome to appeal to the Pope; the upshot of all this was that the fiery Bishop Duggan was placed in an asylum for the mentally ill until his death in 1899.

Bishop Duggan's successor, Bishop Foley, was of a gentler nature. When the fire deprived him of Holy Name Church he bought the Plymouth Congregational Church, but, realising that the plain dumpy building was unworthy as Chicago Diocese's cathedral, he set about raising funds and the corner stone of a new cathedral was laid on 19 July 1874. The architect was Patrick Charles Keely. After Bishop Foley died in 1879 the diocese was elevated to the status of Arch-diocese and the first Archbishop of Chicago was installed with due pomp and ceremony in Holy Name Cathedral on 8 November 1880. Some 12 years later a massive restoration programme was begun, during which wooden pillars were replaced with marble and the ceiling received intricately painted wooden panels. An enlargement of the sanctuary was completed in 1914 and in 1924 the archbishop was elevated to the status of cardinal.

THE 1968 RESTORATION

In 1968 the cathedral, found to be structurally unsafe, was immediately closed. Subsequently totally gutted, the building was underpinned with concrete and steel and the sanctuary completely rebuilt. The restoration, which included the installation of new stained-glass windows from

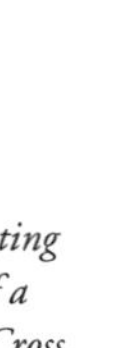

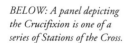

BELOW: A panel depicting the Crucifixion is one of a series of Stations of the Cross.

Milan, along with some magnificent bronze statues representing the Stations of the Cross by Goffredo Verginelli, was a tremendous success, with the new windows enhancing the effect of the elegant vaulted ceiling. The previous multi-coloured decorations were removed and statues replaced in marble or bronze to provide a unity of style absent in the older building.

During the restoration a massive lump of red-black granite was imported from Argentina specifically for the purpose of creating a new altar. This splendid piece of ecclesiastical furniture, designed by the artist Eugenio de Courten, is on a pedestal that is encircled by a beautiful sculpture in cast bronze. On 24 December 1969 the cathedral was re-opened for midnight mass.

BELOW: One of the cathedral's finest features is the vaulted roof, with its intricate cross-latticed patterns. The organ pipes rise up in front of a magnificent rose window.

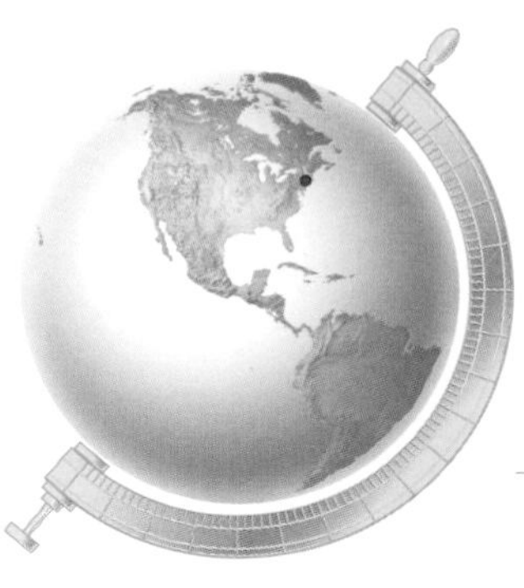

Cathedral of St John the Divine

The largest cathedral in the world is that of St John the Divine in New York

ABOVE: Work still continues on the cathedral building, and stonemasons can be seen at work in the grounds, evoking links with medieval times.

Largest, tallest, longest ...

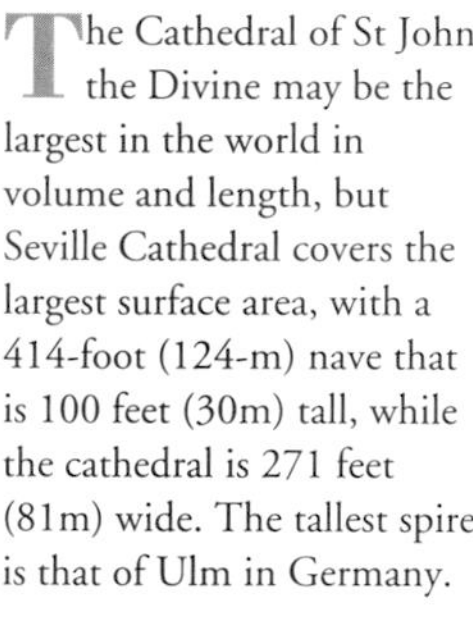

The Cathedral of St John the Divine may be the largest in the world in volume and length, but Seville Cathedral covers the largest surface area, with a 414-foot (124-m) nave that is 100 feet (30m) tall, while the cathedral is 271 feet (81m) wide. The tallest spire is that of Ulm in Germany.

RIGHT: The interior of St John's Cathedral encompasses many themes of modern times; an altar is dedicated to people who have died of AIDS, and a sculpture commemorates the deaths of 12 firefighters in 1996. There are also carvings of Nelson Mandela, and of the Manhattan skyline.

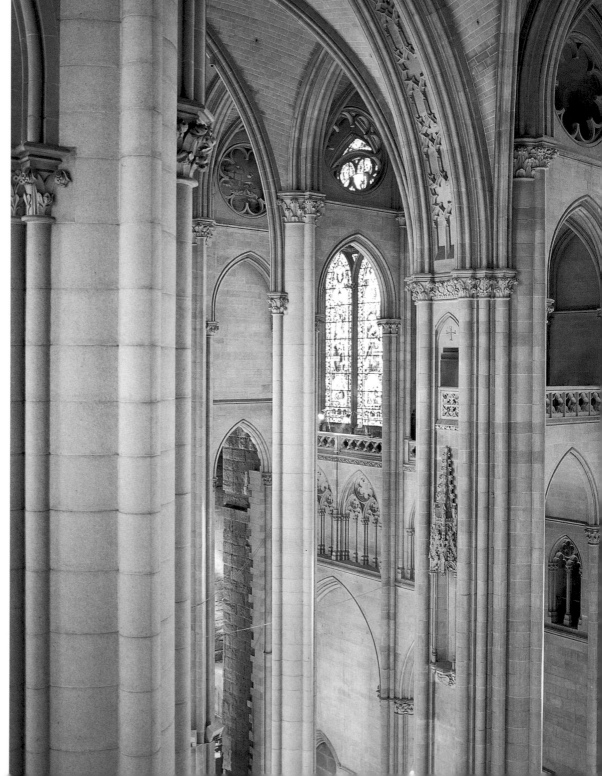

It is often said that everything is bigger in America than elsewhere, and the Cathedral of St John the Divine is no exception. It is the largest cathedral in the world, with a floor area of 121,000 square feet (11,250sq m). Its length, including the nave, choir and apsidal chapels, measures a staggering 601 feet (180m), and it is 124 feet (37m) tall and 320 feet (96m) wide at its transepts.

Romanesque to Gothic

The cathedral owes its creation to Bishop Horatio Potter, who conceived the notion of a massive Protestant church in New York in the 1870s. However, it was not until 1892 that the land was bought for it by Potter's nephew, Henry Codman Potter, also a bishop. A competition was opened for designs, and the commission was won by the architects Heins and La Farge, who had in mind a vast Byzantine-Romanesque structure. Work began in 1901 and the fine narthex and choir were completed. The choir is built of stone and tile of contrasting colours and there are seven radiating chapels (the Chapels of Tongues) off its apsidal end, each one dedicated to an ethnic group represented in the city. By 1910, both the Potters and the two architects had died and Ralph Adams Cram entered the scene.

Cram was a fanatical disciple of Gothic revivalism who firmly believed that the only imaginable style for a cathedral was High Gothic. He had already designed several impressive buildings in Boston and was keen to leave his mark on New York. He persuaded the Church authorities to let him alter the original designs from Romanesque to Gothic, and when work resumed in 1916 the style of the crossing was distinctly different from that of the choir. However, the cathedral is so enormous that the merging of the two styles at the crossing is almost unnoticeable.

Stops and starts

Lack of funds brought the work to a halt in the 1920s, but the subsequent programme of sponsorship raised $15,000,000, enabling work to begin on the great Gothic nave. This massive structure has two aisles on either side of the same height which produce the effect of a vast, dark cavern.

The west front is also breathtaking – 200 feet (60m) wide with five elegant Gothic portals of different sizes. Fine bronze doors, cast by the same company in Paris that built the Statue of Liberty, occupy the central portal. The façade is dominated by an enormous rose window 40 feet (12m) in diameter and reputedly containing more than 10,000 pieces of stained glass.

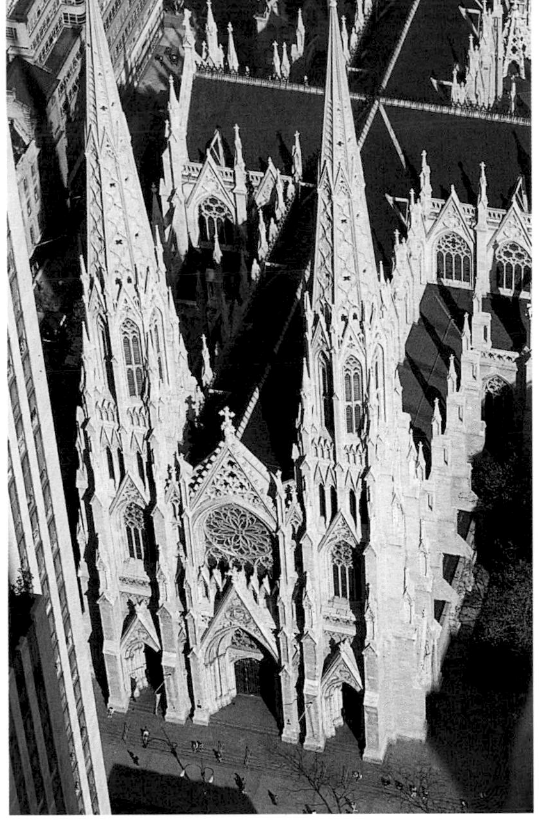

By 30 November 1941 the nave had been completed but work stopped yet again when the Japanese bombed Pearl Harbor and the United States entered World War II. Not resumed until the late 1940s, the building is still unfinished and requires finishing touches to its transepts and the two towers on the west front, while the tower over the central crossing awaits a spire. The story of the building of St John the Divine reflects that of the medieval European cathedrals, where sporadic funding and wars frequently meant that building programmes spanned many years.

A peaceful garden

An unusual feature of the cathedral is its Biblical Garden, which only contains trees and plants that are mentioned in the Bible. It is a peaceful place, and a far cry from the frenetic activity of the streets of New York.

LEFT: The proximity of St Patrick's Cathedral to the Olympic Tower provides an exciting contrast of designs.

St Patrick's Cathedral, New York

St Patrick's, the most important Catholic cathedral in the United States, stands on Fifth Avenue next to the gigantic sprawl of the Rockefeller Centre. It was conceived in 1850 and much of the work was completed by 1888 under the direction of a young architect called James Renwick. At first, there were complaints that it was too distant from the city centre, but in time New York expanded northwards and the cathedral now stands at the heart of the city. Its consecration took place in 1911.

The cathedral, cruciform in plan, is late medieval Gothic in style and has twin octagonal western towers topped by elegant spires. Among its finest features are the glorious bright blue stained-glass windows in the Lady Chapel which were made specially in Chartres.

BELOW: A peaceful atmosphere pervades the cathedral's interior, where candles glow in the many chapels and shrines.

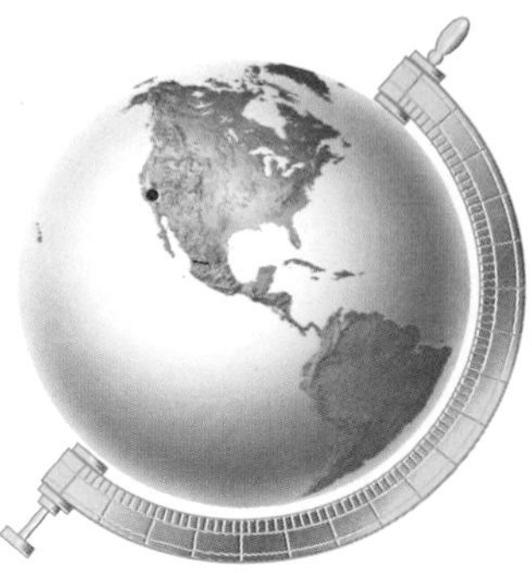

UNITED STATES OF AMERICA

GRACE CATHEDRAL

Built to withstand earthquakes, San Francisco's handsome neo-Gothic cathedral is made of steel and concrete

In 1906 a violent earthquake shook the northern Californian city of San Francisco and caused devastating damage. There had been previous earthquakes, but none had caused such widespread destruction. Much of the city was reduced to rubble and the citizens were faced with a massive rebuilding project that lasted many years.

The cathedral that was eventually built is a splendid neo-Gothic structure, similar to those in northern Europe dating from the great cathedral-building period of the 13th to the 15th centuries – the only difference being that Grace Cathedral was designed to withstand earthquakes

BELOW: Grace Cathedral was built on the site of the Crocker Mansion on Nob Hill; the house was destroyed in the 1906 earthquake. The name 'Nob' is derived from the Indian 'Nabob'.

DECADES OF BUILDING

In 1910, just four years after the earthquake, the foundation stone was laid for Grace Cathedral in a part of the city called Nob Hill, a site selected by the Bishop of San Francisco himself. However, building proper did not get started until 1928. The first parts of the cathedral to be completed were the chancel, with its eye-catching Chapel of Grace, and the transepts. Once work was well underway, the building of the nave was begun, starting at the central crossing and working east.

With the Wall Street Crash of 1929 funds were suddenly frozen and the cathedral authorities had little choice but to board up the incomplete nave and make do with the completed chancel end.

Then in 1938 a carillon of 44 bells was presented to the cathedral by a Cornish-born millionaire who also provided enough money for the north tower, in which the bells hang, to be completed. The bells ring out daily, pealing sweetly over the ever-present roar of this busy city's traffic, and providing a welcome respite from honking horns and revving engines.

By 1954 the Church authorities had raised sufficient money to complete the rest of the cathedral, which was done with astounding speed, and in 1964 the nave, transepts, west façade and south tower were completed. Grace Cathedral was consecrated on 20 November 1964.

SUBSTANTIAL PROPORTIONS

Built in the form of a Latin cross, the cathedral is approximately 320 feet (96m) in length and 165 feet (50m) wide at its transepts. There is a slender spire over the central crossing topped with a cross that soars 265 feet (80m) above the ground. The spire is substantially taller than the symmetrical twin towers of the eastern end that stand 170 feet (51m) high. Between the two towers a handsome portal is protected by a porch with a delicate pointed roof. Above the portal is a beautiful rose window filled with glass made in Chartres.

There are more than 60 slender neo-Gothic windows throughout the cathedral, each one filled

ABOVE: St Mary's Cathedral can seat 2,500 worshippers; it is designed on an open plan, intended to eliminate divisions between areas in the cathedral.

LEFT: A superb relief depicting Moses receiving the Ten Commandments.

with stained glass reminiscent of that of the very finest French Gothic cathedrals.

Earthquake precautions

The architects had learned a lesson from the earthquake of 1906 and the cathedral was constructed to withstand further quakes and tremors. Instead of being built of individual blocks of cut stone, it is constructed of concrete reinforced by steel girders. Yet considerable effort has been expended to ensure the cathedral does not have the appearance of a featureless concrete block. There are no sculptured figures on the outside – since these would crack and fall down during an earthquake – but there are many moulded pinnacles and balustrades that have been cast using sands and stones of different colours. These provide the exterior with a pleasing combination of soft yellows, pinks and greys, adding to its attraction.

Other evidence of its vulnerable position includes a lack of flying buttresses – these are not necessary given the tensile strength of the building material – and the polygonal apse, said to be stronger than a curved end.

St Mary's Cathedral of the Assumption

San Francisco has several cathedrals representing a number of different denominations. Although Grace Cathedral is the best known, St Mary's Cathedral of the Assumption is also worthy of note. There was an earlier cathedral on this site but it was almost totally destroyed by a fire in 1962. Rebuilding began immediately and by 1970 it was sufficiently complete for the first mass to be celebrated in it.

St Mary's is visually dramatic, with four great concrete pylons supporting a soaring 200-foot (60-m) tower. The tower is heightened another 50 feet (15m) by a slender steel crucifix. The main façade presents a line of glass doors under a glorious stained-glass window, in which a mystical figure hangs with arms outstretched.

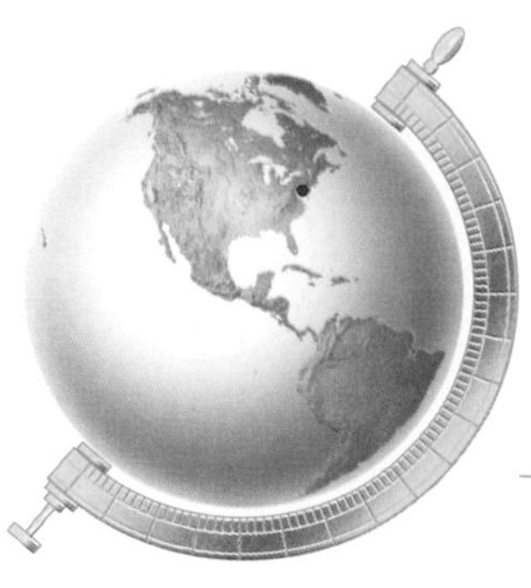

UNITED STATES OF AMERICA

WASHINGTON NATIONAL CATHEDRAL

The Cathedral of St Peter and St Paul is a handsome neo-Gothic building dating from 1907

CHILDREN'S CHAPEL

In the 1930s, the Children's Chapel was built near the south transept. One of only a few chapels in the world designed specifically for the use of children, it is characterised by its beautiful carvings intended to be of interest to the young – such as squirrels and a variety of small animals. The chapel is dominated by a welcoming statue of Christ with open arms.

Like many of the world's great cathedrals, Washington National Cathedral was not built in a day. Sufficient funds were raised for building to commence on 29 September 1907, and the ceremony to celebrate the completion of the cathedral was held in 1990, although work on the stone-carvings and the stained-glass windows is still continuing.

The cathedral has two purposes: it is intended to be a place of worship open to all denominations for religious services, and it is dedicated to education through the four schools that are attached to it.

It stands near the junction of Massachusetts and Wisconsin Avenues NW, on rising ground called Mount St Alban.

CONCEPTION AND DESIGN

The charter for the cathedral was granted by Congress on 6 January 1893 and architects were invited to submit plans. The design that was accepted was controversial from the very beginning. Once the Church authorities had purchased the land of their choice, they met several times to review the plans. Head of the committee was the energetic Bishop Satterlee who proclaimed that the American public was 'weary of designs that glorify the originality of the architect'. In short, Satterlee wanted a cathedral that looked like a cathedral.

George Frederick Bodley and Henry Vaughan submitted English-style neo-Gothic designs that won Satterlee's heart. It was to be a simple Latin cross church of white marble with an octagonal baptistry attached to the south nave and a central tower of 220 feet (66m) over the crossing.

Bodley died a month after the laying of the foundation stone, and Vaughan died 10 years later. At this point, work had progressed on the Bethlehem Chapel of the Nativity, the bishop's residence, the Chapel of the Annunciation, and the choir and sanctuary.

An architect from Boston, Philip Hubert Frohman, was appointed in 1921 and he oversaw the building work for the next 50 years. Almost as soon as he started, Frohman began to alter Bodley and Vaughan's plans: he heightened the central tower to 330 feet (99m) and revised the west front no less than four times!

BELOW: Washington National Cathedral contains this glorious rose window, with its fragile tracery and delicate tints of blue, mauve and rose.

A MASSIVE MONUMENT

As befitting a national cathedral, Washington is huge. It is 525 feet (158m) in length, while the transepts span 275 feet (83m). The nave stands 100 feet (30m) tall.

On entering, visitors are confronted with neat rows of elegantly carved pillars stretching away to the distant apse and rising to the handsome vaulted roof adorned with bosses. The nave is flanked by double aisles, and the windows cast multi-coloured light on to the pale buff-coloured Indiana limestone.

Under the central crossing is the beautiful Chapel of St Joseph of Arimathea, designed in the form of a Greek cross and housing a mural of Christ's burial, painted in 1938. Four huge piers stand at each corner of the chapel which rise to support the great tower above. This tower is known as Gloria in Excelsis, and holds a carillon of 53 bells.

Windows, bosses and carvings

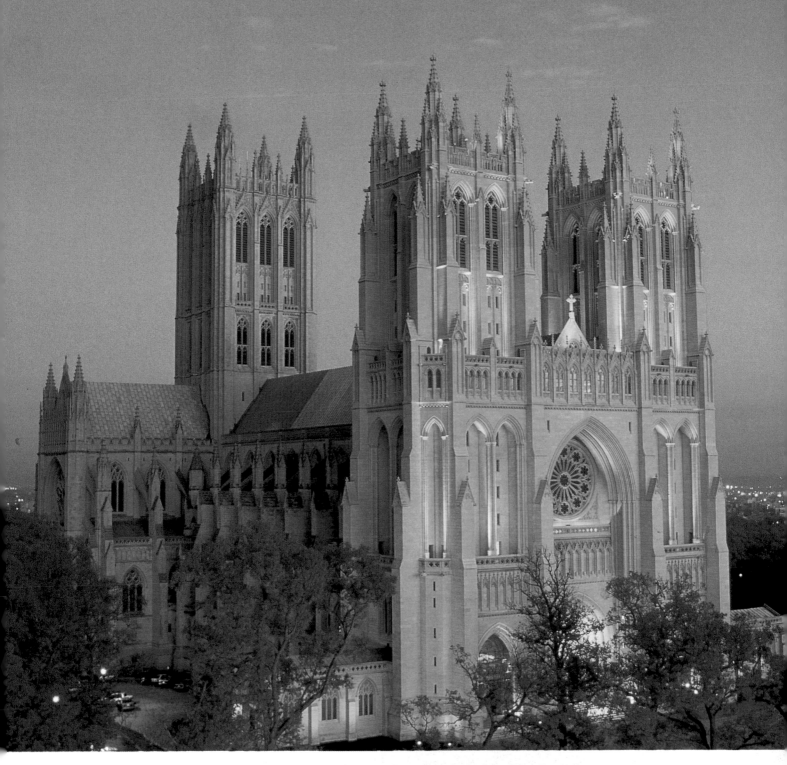

Considerable effort and thought has gone into the symbolism in the windows, bosses and carvings. There are 214 windows, each one filled with stained glass and elaborate tracery. Among the best are the magnificent rose window in the west front by Rowan LeCompte, and the fascinating Scientists' and Technicians' window (the 'Space Window'), which incorporates a fragment of rock from the moon donated by the crew of *Apollo 11*.

The cathedral's 650 vaulting bosses cover a wide range of topics from the Ten Commandments to Christian martyrs. The carvings above the west front portals, by artist Frederick E Hart, are superb, and show a swirl of half formed human creatures emerging from the primordial chaos.

ABOVE: The illuminated exterior of the cathedral appears ethereal against the evening sky.

LEFT: The vaulted roof soars to an impressive height above the nave, and is embellished with decorative roof bosses.

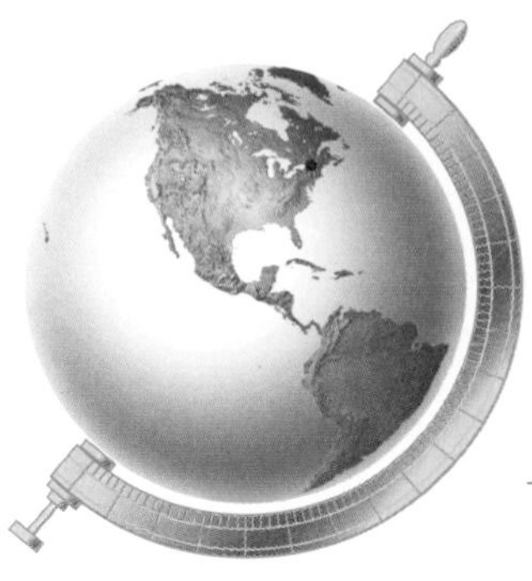

CANADA

BASILICA OF STE ANNE-DE-BEAUPRÉ

Ste Anne's is a noble 20th-century basilica near the spectacular Montmorency Falls

Legend has it that in 1650 a Breton ship was caught in a storm in the perilous waters of the St Lawrence River. The mariners prayed to Saint Anne, vowing that if she spared their lives and saved them from drowning they would build her a shrine. The storm eventually abated and the sailors duly honoured their agreement. Seven years later, settlers came and rebuilt the small wooden shrine as a wooden chapel. The story goes that one of the settlers was lame, but was desperate to take part in the building work. His wish to be healed was granted, and the first miracle had occurred.

FROM SHRINE TO BASILICA

Virtually overnight, the chapel of Ste Anne-de-Beaupré became a pilgrimage site but within a few years floods, high tides and thick river ice had destroyed it and in 1661 another wooden building was raised in its place. By 1676 the site had become too important for such a simple building and a stone church was erected. This little church served the shrine for almost 200 years, until it was demolished in 1872 to make way for the basilica. Yet it was not completely forgotten, and in 1878 its stones were used to build a commemorative chapel, in front of which is the Fountain of Ste Anne. The fountain is said to have healing powers.

BELOW: The cathedral boasts a towering twin-spired west front. Visitors can also see, on the hillside opposite, a series of cast-iron figures entitled 'The Way of the Cross'.

In 1922 a great fire raged through the basilica and, although the building was virtually destroyed, fortunately many of its treasures were rescued (see panel). The new, and latest, building was erected in 1926.

A VAST EDIFICE

Approximately one million people visit the shrine of Saint Anne each year and so the new cathedral had to be large enough to hold thousands at any one time, and grand enough to represent one of North America's premier pilgrimage sites. It can, in fact, hold 2,000 people sitting, and 8,000 standing. The basic plan of the first basilica was preserved, and what emerged is one of Canada's most impressive religious buildings.

The length of the basilica, from east to west, is 375 feet (113m), and it is 200 feet (60m) wide at the transepts. Splendid twin neo-Gothic steeples tower 300 feet (90m) to either side of the west door. The nave is long and impressive, culminating in a two-tiered apse encircled by a nest of radiating chapels.

A PLACE OF HEALING

Like Lourdes in France, Ste Anne-de-Beaupré is liberally scattered with discarded crutches, surgical shoes and braces. Through the years, many treasures have been given to the basilica from grateful pilgrims, and walking into this enormous building is like exploring a vast museum. One of the most impressive treasures is the gorgeous *Cyclorama*, a 360-foot (108-m) long canvas adorned with carefully executed religious paintings, dating from 1895. The Holy Stairs are said to be a replica of the stairs on which Christ ascended to Heaven, and pilgrims are supposed to climb them on their knees.

The altars were designed by Charles Vézina between 1702 and 1728, and were salvaged from the 1922 fire. Hanging from the ceiling is an impressive array of wooden chandeliers sculpted by the French artist François-Noël Levasseur in 1779. Visitors to the basilica are encouraged to descend the stairs to the crypt, where there is an information centre for pilgrims.

The sanctuary of the basilica holds the beautiful statue of Saint Anne standing on an onyx column. It is carved from contrasting coloured marbles from different parts of Italy: her face and hands are of white marble; her cloak is in yellow and green; and her robe is a deep purple-red. The statue is said to be able to effect miraculous cures.

ABOVE: The Virgin extends a hand in blessing, in one of the cathedral's magnificent modern mosaics.

LEFT: The nave is lit from above by tiers of richly-coloured stained-glass windows, which draw attention to the graceful angelic figures depicted on the ceiling.

TREASURES SAVED

Some of the priceless works of art that have been donated to the shrine during the 270 years since its founding are housed in the little chapel built in 1878. They include 18th-century vases engraved by the famous goldsmiths François Ranvoyzé and Laurent Amyot, and a superb collection of votive paintings. There are also religious vestments; a huge collection of chalices, patens, and silver plates; precious reliquaries; and a lovely ivory crucifix dating from 1663.

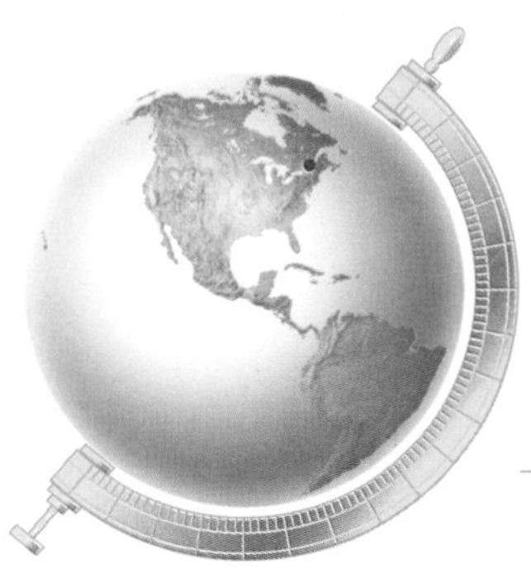

CANADA

CATHEDRAL OF NOTRE-DAME

Notre-Dame in Montréal is one of the finest Gothic Revival buildings in North America

CITY OF CHURCHES

Montréal's dual French and Anglo-Saxon cultures have ensured that it is a city especially rich in religious buildings, but perhaps best known is St Joseph's Oratory, a massive pilgrimage site opposite Mount Royal Park. In 1904 a monk named Alfred Bessette, or Brother André, obtained permission to build a small wooden oratory to the glory of St Joseph. Within a few years, word began to spread of miraculous cures effected by Brother André, and his shrine became one of the most important pilgrimage sites in North America. Funds donated by grateful penitents allowed the present splendid oratory to be built, which serves as a shrine to St Joseph and a tomb for Brother André.

Other equally fine buildings include the early 18th-century Seminary of St Sulpice and the Notre-Dame-de-Bonsecours, the oldest of the Montréal churches and known locally as the Sailors' Church.

RIGHT: The high altar stands against a background of celestial blue, with pillars painted in glowing colours, and a deep blue ceiling set with golden stars.

On the south side of the busy Place d'Armes in downtown Montréal stands the splendid Cathedral of Notre-Dame (L'Eglise Notre-Dame de Montréal). South of the cathedral lies the great muddy smear of the St Lawrence Seaway, a vast, swift-moving body of water that connects the Great Lakes to the Atlantic Ocean. Great tankers glide past, towering over the numerous cargo barges and pleasure craft that litter this enormous river. Yet, despite all this movement, noise and bustle, Notre-Dame remains a haven of peace and the visitor is able to relax from the frenzy of one of North America's liveliest cities and enjoy the stillness of this beautiful building.

BRITISH AND FRENCH RIVALRY

The first church on the site occupied by the present cathedral was built in 1656, some 14 years after Montréal was first founded. Little is known about this early church, although the population of

Montréal at the time was less than 1,000 and it was probably a simple wooden building. It was rebuilt in 1672 but was demolished to be replaced by a third building in 1823. Constructed under the supervision of the Irish architect James O'Donnell (1774–1830), this was to become one of the greatest Gothic Revival churches in the whole of North America.

In its early years Montréal was little more than a trading post, home to merchants and, seasonally, to fur traders. When the British took the settlement from the French in 1760, there followed an influx of immigrants from the British Isles which continued well into the 19th century and led to some major disputes between the French and British communities, not least those concerning differences in religion. The great neo-Gothic edifice of Notre-Dame, indisputably French in style, and distinctly Catholic in appearance, was built at the height of the bitter disputes between the French- and English-speaking citizens. Building work on the cathedral was completed by 1829.

ABOVE: The front of the Sailors' Church includes an invocation to Our Lady; since the church was founded in 1657, sailors have made pilgrimages there to give thanks for being saved from the dangers of the sea.

A vast temple

Notre-Dame is massive – one of the largest churches in North America. It is 255 feet (77m) long from east to west, and 136 feet (41m) wide at the transepts. There is sufficient room for a gathering of 12,000 people. The west front is dominated by two handsome towers, soaring some 230 feet (69m) above the Place d'Armes, known as Temperance and Perseverance. The western tower contains a fine set of bells, the largest of which is called 'Le Gros Bourdon', and weighs in at an impressive 22,000 pounds (9,980kg).

Treasures and the museum

The interior of the cathedral is sombre, with much delicately carved wood. Especially fine is the high altar, with a huge reredos of gold, decorated with elegant statues and pinnacles. Behind, the apse has been painted a deep blue, contrasting beautifully with the yellow-gold of the carvings.

There are many other features worthy of note in the cathedral, some of which are now displayed in the adjoining museum. Perhaps the finest of these are the lovely Madonna of silver that was presented by King Louis XV of France; an ivory figure of the Virgin Mary from the house of Montréal's founder Paul de Chomedey de Maisonneuve; a painting entitled *St Francis Listening to Angel Music* by Alonso Cano (1601–67); and a crucifix and chandeliers given by Louis XIV.

There is also an impressive collection of historical artefacts – sacred vestments, ancient books and a variety of *objets d'art.*

BELOW: The youthful figure of Notre-Dame-de-Bonsecours, surrounded by cherubim.

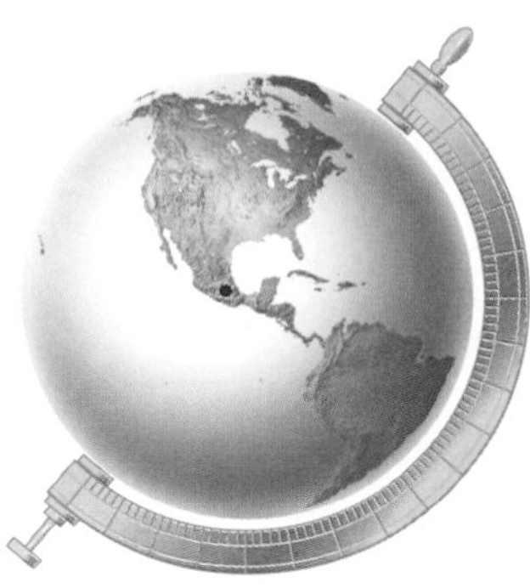

MEXICO CITY CATHEDRAL

The Cathedral of the Three Kings is the most splendid church in the country

BELOW: Much of the interior decoration of the cathedral is in the Churrigueresque style, a highly ornate 17th-century form of Spanish Baroque. The high altar, made of onyx, marble and gold, was designed by Manuel Tolsa, an architect of the colonial period.

In 1519 Hernán Cortés led a small expedition to what is today Mexico, intent on claiming the area for his native Spain. Mexico City was once the Aztec stronghold of Tenochtitlán, built in the south of the high Central Plateau of Mexico at an elevation of 7,800 feet (2,340m). By 1521, the last Aztec emperor, Moctezuma II, was dead, and his empire had become part of the Viceroyalty of New Spain. Independence, after a bitter struggle, was attained 300 years later. During this period the Spanish exerted considerable influence over many aspects of Mexican life, perhaps the most significant of which was religion. Mexico became a Catholic country and Spanish missionaries began to build a number of churches and cathedrals.

By the 1570s, the Spanish hold on Mexico had strengthened and the church in Mexico City was no longer sufficient to provide a suitably impressive focus for Catholicism in the New World. In 1573, on the ruins of an Aztec temple, the foundation stone of a new cathedral was laid by the Spanish Viceroy on behalf of King Philip II. But it was not until 250 years later that the Cathedral of the Three Kings was finally completed.

LEFT: The cathedral has sunk into the ground so that it has an uneven appearance when viewed from the square; work is in progress to make the building more stable.

An imposing structure

The cathedral was built in the form of a Latin cross with a nave and choir some 385 feet (116m) in length, and 177 feet (53m) wide at the transepts. It was built to impress – not only by its massive proportions, but by the majesty of its ornamentation. The outside is dominated by its west front, with its three baroque portals flanked by classical pillars. Over the central portal are a clock-tower and panels containing statues, fluted columns and neo-classical cornices, along with ornamented balustrades on different levels. To either side of the façade are 232-foot (70-m) tall towers surmounted by bell-shaped domes.

Mexico City Cathedral is built of a rich, warm yellow stone that seems to draw its colour from the sun itself and highlights the intricacy of the many statues and carvings that adorn the exterior. Over the central crossing is a great cupola topped with a slender lantern tower built in a whiter stone than the rest of the cathedral.

An interior to inspire

Walking into the cathedral is like entering a vast, cool cavern. It has rows of delicately carved columns along each side of the nave, rising to a small clerestory with amber windows. The overwhelming colour of the cathedral's interior is a deep yellow-gold, partly originating from the stained glass, and partly from the predominance of gold and gilt and the soft honey of the stone pillars and walls.

Beautiful 18th-century wrought-iron screens divide the nave from the choir, and the nave from the various chapels that lead off the aisles. The sacristy has some beautiful rib vaulting, while the crypt is full of the tombs of Mexican bishops dating back to the 17th century.

Chapel of the Three Kings

Sited just behind the main altar at the far end of the cathedral lies the magnificent Chapel of the Three Kings. This is easily the most opulent part of a cathedral already dripping with splendour and flamboyant decoration. It is in a style popular in Spain known as Churrigueresque, after the Churriguera family that lived in the 17th and 18th centuries (see page 37). The chapel was built between 1718 and 1737 by an architect named Jerónimo Balbas from southern Spain. It is such an astounding concoction of gilded wood pillars and statues that it defies description. The sculptures are centred around a painting of the *Adoration of the Magi* by Juárez.

LEFT: The façade of the main entrance is carved with a mass of intricate designs, which surround the statues carved in niches.

The Sagrario

During the 18th century a small building intended to be specifically for the worship of the sacrament was attached to the cathedral. Built to a design by a Spanish architect named Lorenzo Rodriguez, it is an explosion of elaborate sculptures carved into pale honey-coloured stone. This highly decorated style, common in Mexican-Spanish churches, is known as *estípite* and features carvings around a decorated pillar or column. One of the finest examples of *estípite* in Spain is in the sacristy of the Cartuja in Granada, and it is possible that it was from here that the Spanish architects derived their inspiration for the cathedrals and churches in Mexico. The *estípite* of the Sagrario is particularly fine, displaying a wealth of figures and ornamentation in luxurious high-relief.

BRASILIA CATHEDRAL

Brasilia's great, circular, ultra-modern cathedral was designed to represent the crown of thorns

THE CATHEDRAL PRECINCT

Like the great medieval cathedrals of Europe, Brasilia Cathedral does not stand alone but is flanked on three sides by ranges of buildings inside a neat, oblong enclosure. Niemeyer has ensured that these do not interfere with the prospect of the Crown of Thorns, and all are only one or two storeys high. The buildings include living quarters for the multi-denominational ministers, several chapels, offices and a museum.

OSCAR NIEMEYER

Brazil and Mexico have made rapid developments in architecture in the 20th century, under such leading figures as Lucio Costa, Affonso Reidy and José Villigrán Garcia. Oscar Niemeyer designed many of the public buildings, including the cathedral. His style is distinctive, and is often described as a 'spectacular exercise in pure geometry'.

One of the most famous of Niemeyer's buildings is the Palace of the National Congress, with its opposing concave and convex domes and twin towers. Niemeyer also designed the Alvorada Palace, the first permanent building erected in Brasilia, in which the President lives. Overlooking an artificial lake, it has marble-faced curved columns supporting a roof that overhangs the glass walls to protect them from the sun.

In 1956 the Government of Brazil decided to build a new capital in the little-populated central highlands area. This presented leading Brazilian architects with an unprecedented opportunity to express themselves and to create a style of building that was inventive, daring and, occasionally, eccentric. Brasilia emerged through the 1960s, '70s and '80s with buildings like those of no other city in the world, and to the north of it, rising like a great concrete crown, is the amazing structure of the Catedral Metropolitana Nossa Senhora Aparecida.

NIEMEYER'S CATHEDRAL ON THE PLATEAU

Brasilia stands 3,500 feet (1,050m) above sea level on the great semi-arid central plateau of Brazil. It is roughly north-west of Rio de Janeiro, a gruelling 750-mile (1,200-km) drive from the sea. Work on the cathedral under the Brazilian architect Oscar Niemeyer started in 1959 but its progress was far from smooth and building was not completed until 1980. The office of a new archbishop was created to go with the new cathedral.

Niemeyer is one of the most imaginative and creative architects of the 20th century. He wanted a cathedral that was perfectly symmetrical and as visually stunning in its own way as the magnificent Gothic cathedrals of Europe. And few people can deny that Niemeyer succeeded. The cathedral is a vast circle, the floor of which is set about 10 feet (3m) below ground level. Thus there is a 10-foot (3-m) high ring of concrete around the outside of the cathedral that forms the wall of the circular nave. This, 200 feet (60m) in diameter, is filled with chairs to accommodate those attending the cathedral's inter-denominational services. Sixteen great concrete buttresses soar out of the low nave wall, arching gracefully upwards and inwards to meet in the middle of the ceiling. Rising 102 feet (31m) above the sunken floor, this supports great hanging sculptures of angels that seem to fly.

THE CROWN OF THORNS

As the 16 concrete ribs approach the centre of the ceiling they bend upwards to end in a circle of pointed spikes, which represents the Crown of Thorns. Bursting out of the crown is a delicate golden cross. Around the corona statues of the Apostles face each other on a concrete slab about 40 feet (12m) across. The figures are large and stocky, with huge hands and strangely flat noses. Yet, despite the fact that they are so stylised, the artist has managed to impart individual facial expressions to each one. Perhaps the best is that of Matthew, who stands resolute yet serene, clutching his gospel under one arm.

Between the great buttresses is an intricate grid-work of iron filled with clear glass panels. The sunlight is intense on the central plateau and the glass serves to soften the glare, while still allowing the interior to be flooded with light. The buttresses were cast of a light-coloured substance to ensure the

even distribution of light inside the cathedral. Niemeyer has created an extraordinary effect: since the visitor can see the blue sky and white clouds through the vast concrete and glass dome that billows above, the cathedral has the feeling that it is reaching to the sky in exactly the same way as the High Gothic cathedrals of northern Europe did. Niemeyer has achieved a feeling of lightness and space, and his tapering buttresses take on the appearance of a sunburst when viewed from below.

LEFT: Looking upwards when inside the cathedral gives a remarkable sense of looking straight into the heavens, complete with flying sculptures of angels.

BELOW: Among the imaginatively grouped buildings that make up the cathedral complex is a baptistry designed in the form of a large pebble.

CUZCO CATHEDRAL

This handsome Renaissance cathedral was built on the ruins of an Inca temple

THE TEMPLE OF VIRACOCHA

Cuzco Cathedral was built over the remains of the Temple of Viracocha. Viracocha was a creator deity worshipped by the pre-Inca inhabitants of Peru and it is thought that the god entered the Inca religion at a relatively late date, possibly under the 15th-century Inca emperor who took his name. The pre-Inca peoples believed Viracocha freely wandered through his creation, teaching humans the art of civilisation. The Inca deity was perceived as a remote being who left the world to lesser deities once he had finished creating it. He was worshipped by the Inca nobility in times of crisis – it is known he was invoked when Pizarro's little army marched towards Cuzco in 1532.

AT HIGH ALTITUDES

This is the second highest cathedral in the world, standing at a height of 11,000 feet (3,300m) above sea level. The only other city with a greater altitude is La Paz, the capital of Bolivia, which stands at 11,916 feet (3,575m) above sea level, and boasts a splendid Renaissance cathedral.

RIGHT: Worshippers at prayer in Cuzco Cathedral wear bright earth-colours, contrasting with the ornate baroque paintings and furnishings which fill the interior of the cathedral.

Sprawling in a green valley below the ancient hilltop fortress of Sacsahuaman, high up in the Andean Mountains, is the modern city of Cuzco. This was the heartland of the Inca dynasty founded around 1200AD, and later its capital when the Inca empire was at its height in the 1520s. In 1532 Cuzco fell to the Spanish conquistador Francisco Pizarro, who set about transforming the city into a Spanish settlement with churches and houses with terracotta roofs.

Pizarro's architects used the foundations of the Inca temples and walls for many of their buildings, and it was these great, ingeniously matched pieces of stone that survived the devastating earthquakes that occurred in the 17th century, while the later buildings crumbled and fell.

A SPANISH CATHEDRAL ...

With the capture and eventual death of the Inca Atahualpa, the days of the great Inca empire were over. Inca Cuzco – meaning the 'navel of the world' – became a Spanish city and the temples dedicated to the sun were demolished in favour of Catholic churches. When the first cathedral at Cuzco was built is not certain, although it is likely to have been soon after the conquest. In 1650 an earthquake shook the city, damaging the fledgling cathedral. Building resumed shortly afterwards under two architects, Correa and Becerra, who had been working on the cathedral in Lima, Peru's capital city.

The cathedral is massive, impressive and dominating – a clear statement of the superior power of the Spanish over the defeated South Americans. Despite its imposing façade, it is based on a relatively simple basilica plan, with a nave and a single aisle to either side. Later, once the main parts of the cathedral were completed, two small churches were grafted on to the north and the south walls, like transepts.

The cathedral stands in the Plaza de Armas in the old part of the city, a great grey-yellow edifice that dominates the attractive square with its well-tended gardens. The west façade of the cathedral is especially imposing, and comprises a large central portal, liberally ornamented in baroque style with columns and carvings. To either side of the main

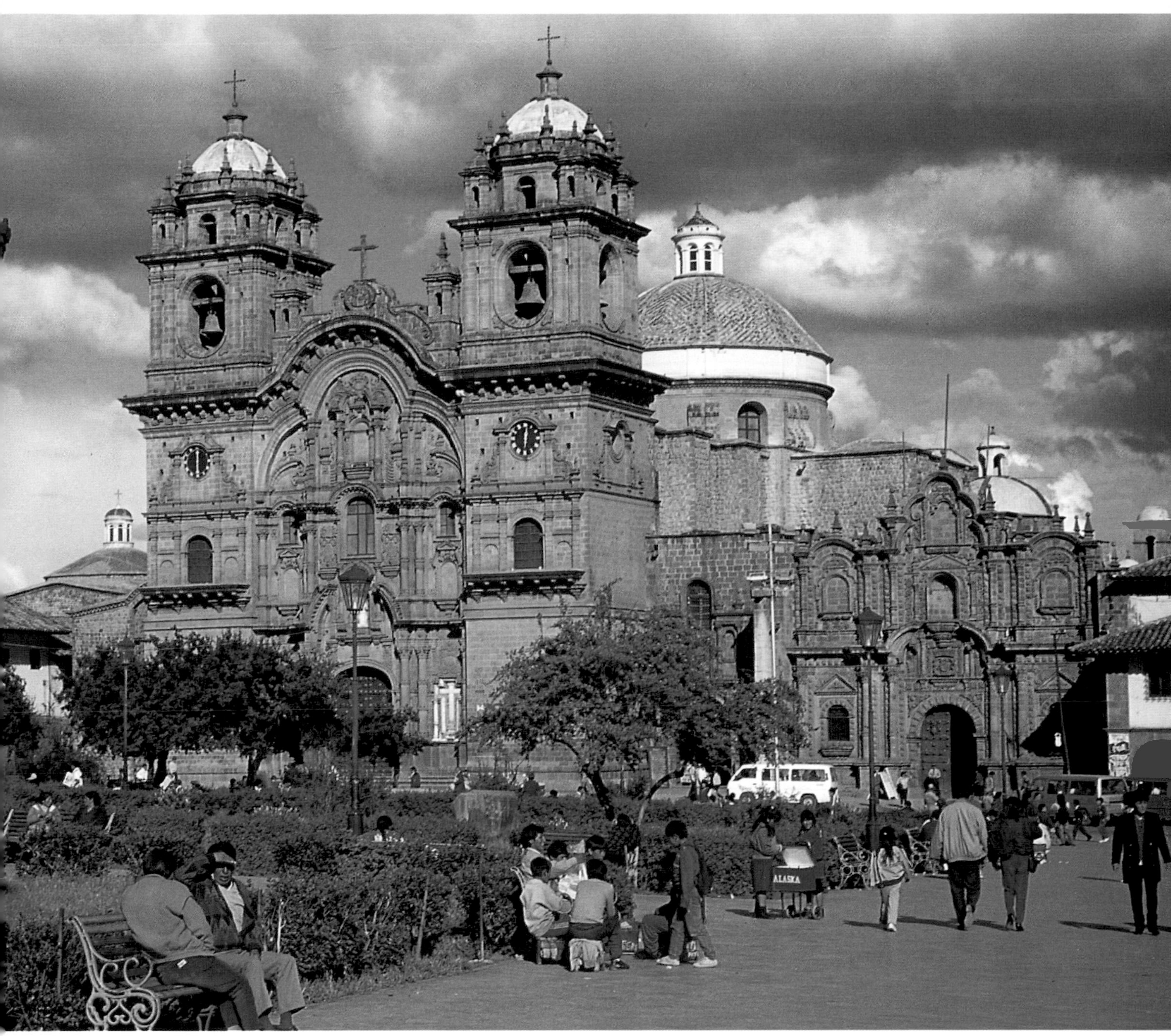

portal is a smaller door, while above is a balustrade with an unusual collection of spirelets and pinnacles. Two sturdy square bell-towers, topped with symmetrical cupolas, flank the portals.

... WITH INCA ADDITIONS

Unlike many Latin American cathedrals, Cuzco is, in general, a plain, sober structure, where ornamentation (except for the baroque panels around the central portal) is scarce. In addition, visitors to the cathedral will notice that the splendid west façade that looms over the Plaza de Armas is not purely Spanish in style. The portals have a distinctively Peruvian feel to them, especially in the patterning on the wooden doors. This is explained by the fact that it was the Peruvian Indians who provided much of the labour for the building of the west front, some of whom probably drew on their Inca ancestry for inspiration.

Another reason for the cathedral having a dual Inca-Spanish feel to it is the fact that some of the great, smooth, brown stone blocks came from Inca buildings that were destroyed when the Spanish invaded. Other stones were taken from the same quarry, but were cut by Spanish masons.

As if to compensate for the plainness of the outside, the interior is a lively riot of colour. The fine reredos in the sacristy is reputed to have been painted by Van Dyck, and many other paintings adorn the walls. The choir stalls are especially worth noting, and contain some exquisite baroque sculpture.

ABOVE: The Plaza de Armas, where the cathedral stands, was the exact centre of the Inca empire, and a focal point for religious and military ceremonies.

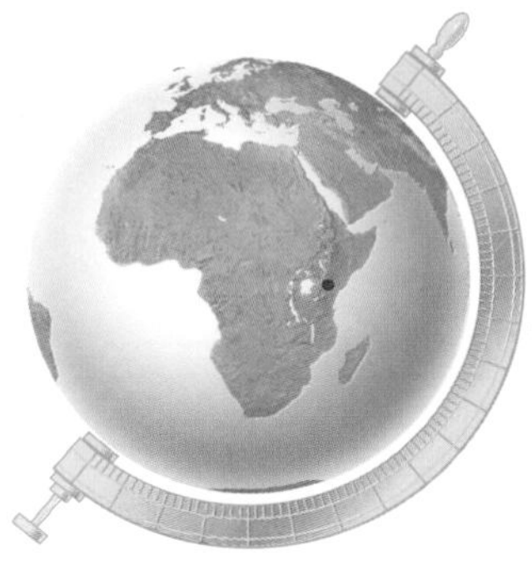

KENYA

ALL SAINTS' CATHEDRAL

The little Cathedral of All Saints in Nairobi is the mother church for the Anglicans of Kenya

AFRICA'S GREAT CATHEDRALS

Other magnificent cathedrals to be seen in Africa include the new St George's Cathedral in Cape Town, which is still not complete. Designed by Herbert Baker, the building was started in 1901 but progress has been slow. It replaces an earlier one built around 1848. When the western part of the cathedral is built it will house a fine ring of eight bells.

The cathedral's outstanding features are perhaps its beautiful clerestory windows, designed by the French glass-maker Gabriel Loire whose workshop is based in Chartres. The windows, in the vivid colours associated with Africa, describe the story of the Creation.

Another interesting feature is the ancient Coptic cross that was found on a battlefield after the destruction of Magdala in Abyssinia (Ethiopia) in 1868.

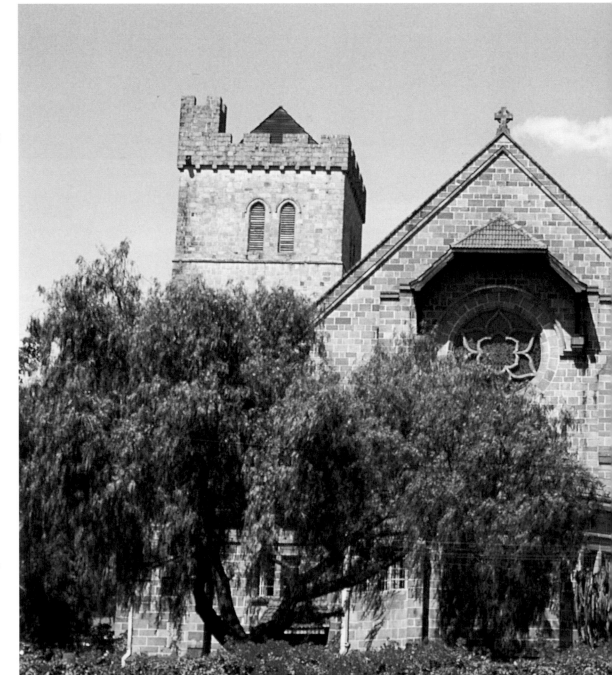

RIGHT: The grey stone of All Saints' Cathedral contrasts with the bright colours of the surrounding tropical gardens.

Before 1899 there was little except open countryside where the busy, over-populated city of Nairobi now stands. A small settlement – serving mainly as a supply depot, switching yard and campsite for the Indian labourers – was created by Europeans at Mile 327 of the East Africa Railway Line, which ran from the coast to the interior. The site was bleak and swampy, and Ewaso Nairobi was a local Masai phrase meaning 'stream of cold water'. Surprisingly, the settlement in this unappealing wilderness took root, but the wooden houses and sheds were burned down when a plague struck the community in the early years of the 20th century. The town was rebuilt and by 1907 it was of sufficient size and importance to become the capital of British East Africa. Europeans began to settle in

Nairobi in large numbers, displacing the indigenous Masai and Kikuyu people to reserves near by.

With the Europeans came their religion, creating a growing need for churches and cathedrals. By 1917, the community was large enough to warrant a cathedral, and work began on All Saints.

Thirty-five years of building

Although the foundation stone of the cathedral was laid in 1917, building work was not completed until 1952. But the lengthy building process has resulted in a fine church that, despite its very British architectural style, has retained a distinctly African feel to it.

The dominating features are the twin saddle-back towers that would perhaps be more at home overlooking a Scottish loch than an equatorial garden. They are squat, built of grey granite and topped with battlements that give the cathedral the appearance of a castle. The towers even have raised corner turrets like those on many Scottish fortified houses, and there are narrow lancet windows on each floor.

Another unusual feature is that the towers are transeptal, that is, they form the transepts of the cathedral and are not part of the western front. Offsetting the cool grey granite of the twin towers are the weathered red roof tiles below.

All Saints stands in carefully tended gardens which separate it from the city streets, and visitors can appreciate these pleasant surroundings before entering the cathedral itself.

A plain interior

In contrast to the heat and colour of the garden, the interior of the cathedral is cool and shady. The windows are small, although decorated with brightly coloured stained glass, and the pews are made of dark, polished wood.

Above the altar is a fine rose window of predominantly brilliant blue glass that allows light to flood into the eastern end of the cathedral. The star of Bethlehem is at the centre, surrounded by the crown of thorns and the cross of Jesus.

The pillars are square, undecorated, and rise to simple, but graceful, pointed arches along the nave. An unusual feature of the aisles is the row of smaller arches that abut the pillars at right angles to the nave, giving them an elegant, cloistered appearance. Whether seen during a service, when the building is humming with colour and voices, or when it is empty and offers a respite from the scorching sun and noise of the vibrant city, All Saints is worthy of fame as one of Africa's leading cathedrals.

A fateful journey

The bridge leading from Kenyatta Avenue to the cathedral grounds is named after Charles Ryall, whose claim to fame was to be fatally savaged by a lion in 1900. Ryall, travelling by train with two friends, was sleeping in the carriage when a lion leapt through the open door, grabbed him and ran off. It all happened so quickly that Ryall's horrified companions were unable to help. The carriage in question can be seen at Nairobi's railway museum.

BELOW: A multi-racial service takes place in the cathedral, reflecting the beliefs of the worshippers that all nations should strive to be one in faith.

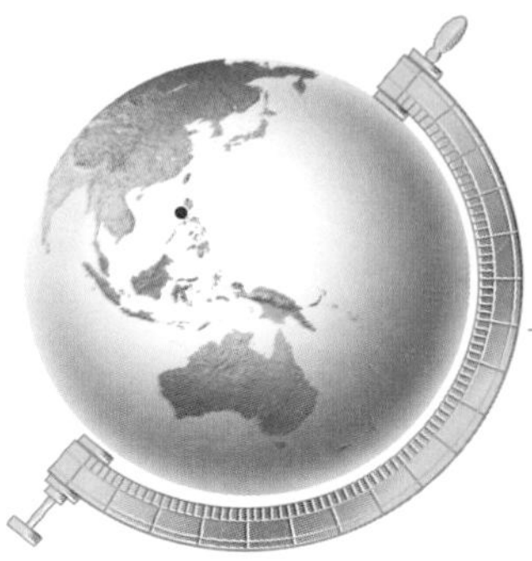

The Republic of the Philippines

Manila Cathedral

This important Asian cathedral was rebuilt after World War II with help from the Vatican

The Virgin Mary in Glass

One of the chief delights of the Cathedral of the Immaculate Conception of the Virgin Mary is its beautiful stained-glass windows. They are the work of the Filipino artist Galo Ocampo, and their theme, appropriately, is the Virgin Mary. The glass in the main body of the church depicts the life of Mary from the Annunciation by the Archangel Gabriel, through the birth of Jesus in the manger in Bethlehem, to the crucifixion and the resurrection. Other windows portray her in a variety of guises that she is said to assume in different parts of the country – such as the highly venerated statue of the Blessed Virgin of Peafrancia, brought from Spain in the 17th century. The brilliant, tropical colours of the windows are at their most vivid in the afternoon sun.

On the irregularly shaped island of Luzon in the archipelago of more than 7,000 islands that comprise the Philippines, stands Manila Cathedral, the most significant Catholic church in South-east Asia. The Republic of the Philippines is the only Christian country in Asia, with about 85 per cent of Filipinos embracing Catholicism. Religion is a vitally important element in Filipino life: almost every village has its own, often ancient, church, and religious festivals such as Christmas, Easter and saints' days are celebrated with great fervour. The Church has become a powerful political force, centring on the seat of the Archbishop of the Philippines – the Cathedral of the Immaculate Conception of the Virgin Mary in Manila.

Wars, fires and earthquakes

The history of the cathedral is closely bound up with the history of the country. Numerous cultures have invaded these beautiful islands since prehistoric times – Indonesians, Malays, great empires from India, Tang and Sung Dynasty Chinese, Japanese trader-pirates, Bornean chiefs and Arab merchants – each leaving behind traces of their visits.

In the 1520s the Portuguese navigator Ferdinand Magellan 'discovered' the Philippines and claimed them for his patron, King Philip II of Spain. On Easter Sunday 1521 a mass was celebrated on the Philippines' soil, and so began the process of converting the population to Christianity.

Miguel Lopez de Lagazapi began to colonise the Philippines in the 1560s, although the beginnings were by no means peaceful. Ten years later, Lagazapi made Manila the capital of the new Spanish colony and began to build a fortress in a Spanish-style medieval walled city – an 'Intramuros', meaning literally 'between walls'. Lagazapi founded a cathedral in 1571 within this walled city, but it only survived three years, being burned down in 1574 during a siege.

A new cathedral was hastily erected but it too burned down in 1583. Yet another building was raised, only to be demolished by an earthquake in 1600. It was rebuilt again, but tumbled down during another earthquake in 1645. The fifth cathedral raised on the site was reported to be a magnificent building, demonstrating Spanish architecture at its best, but a third earthquake brought it down in 1863. Not surprisingly, the citizens of Manila were becoming discouraged and a replacement was not built until 1879. This building stood until the terrible devastation of World War II, when Japanese soldiers fleeing from advancing American troops and Filipino guerrillas

RIGHT: The cathedral stands in a calm space amid the swirling traffic and hectic city life of Manila.

under General MacArthur holed up in the Intramuros. The fight for Manila was fierce, and victory was bought at the cost of thousands of lives and the virtual destruction of the Intramuros, including the cathedral.

The newest cathedral

Rebuilding started in 1954 and was completed by 1958 under the Filipino architect Fernando Ocampo. Funds came largely from the Vatican, and care was taken to incorporate as much of the ruined cathedral as possible; several wall sections and the basic plan survive. It is built in Romanesque style with an impressive octagonal dome that dominates the Old City, and it has a separate bell-tower. The façade, looking out across the attractive Plaza Roma, is especially handsome and has fine bronze doors with inset panels depicting the cathedral's turbulent history. Above the doors are statues of saints, mostly the work of Italian artists.

Inside, the visitor's eyes are immediately drawn to the beautiful bronze statue of the Virgin Mary on the high altar, while near by is the throne of the Archbishop of Manila, a handsome work of art sculpted in white Italian marble. The organ, which was made in the Netherlands, is the largest in Asia, with 4,500 pipes.

ABOVE: Romanesque arches are a dominant feature of Manila's cathedral, both externally and in the interior, where a wedding is shown taking place.

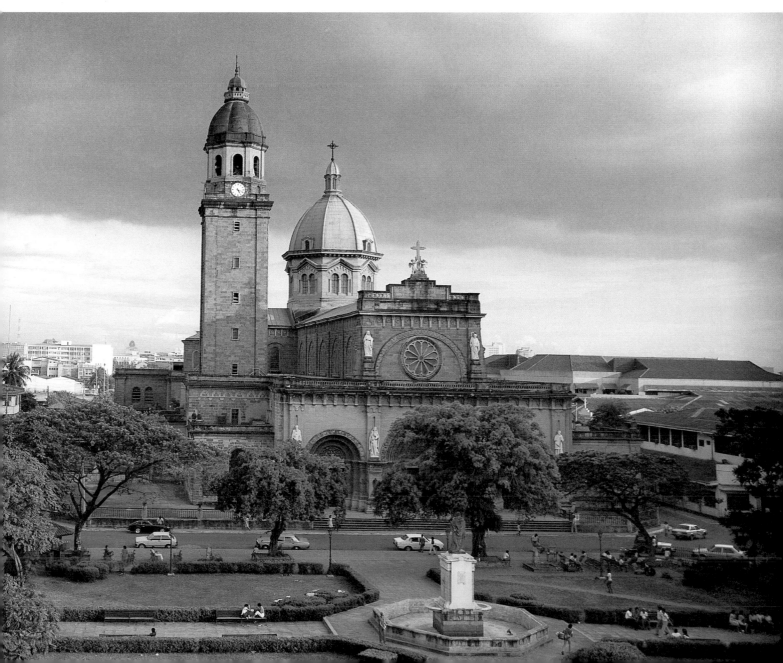

GERALDTON CATHEDRAL

The splendid Catholic Cathedral of St Francis Xavier has been described as 'a poem in stone'

AN UNUSUAL ARCHITECT

John Hawes, architect of Geraldton Cathedral, was torn between his talent for architecture and his desire to become a Franciscan. He met Bishop Kelly in Rome. Hawes drew up some sketches for the cathedral which so impressed Kelly that he offered Hawes the commission. Hawes remained in Australia until 1939, when he left for the Bahamas to become a hermit.

BELOW: The west façade recalls the style of the Franciscan missions of California.

At a small port on the rugged Western Australian coast, about 264 miles (425km) north of Perth, stands one of the finest cathedrals of the 20th century. The splendid Cathedral of St Francis Xavier is all the more impressive because it is so unexpected, and because it owes its foundation to the efforts of just one man – William Bernard Kelly, a native Western Australian who was appointed Bishop of Geraldton in 1898.

When Kelly arrived in Geraldton he found that there was very little in his scattered diocese to care for. There were some small stone churches, including little St Francis Xavier's Church near the beach, and a rough lean-to house attached, in which the resident priest lived. Despite the fact that his flock lived over a wide area, Kelly decided that his diocese needed a cathedral church and he set about raising funds from his own and neighbouring dioceses. By 20 June 1916 sufficient money had been raised for the work to commence.

SIMPLE BEAUTY

Plans for the cathedral were drawn up by priest-architect John Hawes (see panel) and the foundations were laid. The corner stone came from the seaside Church of St Francis Xavier which was demolished to make way for a railway. Work then stopped until 1926, when the crypt was built, the choir raised above it and the Sisters' Chapel built to the south. The gap between nave and choir was covered with a rough structure of wood and iron. Work ceased again until 1937, but this time continued until the entire building was completed on 28 August 1938.

Geraldton was not a wealthy diocese and both Kelly and Hawes were aware that costs had to be kept as low as possible. Thus all unnecessary decorative features were avoided, and the result is a plain but awe-inspiring building of perfect proportions. Hawes proved that a cathedral can be majestic and noble without the addition of pinnacles, statuary and tracery.

The twin western towers, with their domes, are reminiscent of the Spanish Franciscan missions of California. Between them, on top of the pediment, is a niche containing a statue of St Francis Xavier holding a crucifix and a copy of the gospels.

The dominating feature on the exterior of the cathedral is the magnificent dome, a great low saucer topped by a small lantern tower.

A colourful interior

What he could not achieve by decorative carvings, Hawes attained by clever use of banded stone. He clearly had the great Italian cathedrals at Siena and Orvieto in mind when he stipulated alternating layers of cool grey and warm orange stone. The interior has arcades of semi-circular arches, while the aisle windows have stained glass that allows more colour to filter in.

To the right of the great space underneath the dome is the elegant Lady Chapel, while opposite is the Altar of the Sacred Heart. Since the cathedral's completion, liturgical requirements have changed, and so the sanctuary to the east of the crossing no longer appears as it would have done in Hawes' day. Instead of being placed at the left side of the sanctuary, the bishop's chair now stands in the centre, behind the high altar.

Spiral stairs near the communion rail lead down to the crypt, which contains a chapel to Our Lady of Sorrows. This is a memorial to Australian soldiers who died in World War I. A piece of the True Cross is among several relics that lie in the Chapel of St Joseph.

ABOVE: The cathedral's spectacular banded stonework is sure to leave a lasting impression on the visitor.

Stained glass

Among the best of the windows here are those in the apse, which depict St Francis Xavier with St Augustine of England, St Patrick of Ireland, St David of Wales, and St Columba of Scotland. These saints were chosen to represent the countries of origin of Geraldton's first settlers.

The beautiful windows in the north aisle portray the 15 mysteries of the rosary. Those in the south aisle are based on titles of Our Lady from the Litany of Loretto. Four large circular windows, upgraded in 1988, portray in richly coloured stained glass the four evangelists – Matthew, Mark, Luke and John.

LEFT: The Chapel of Our Lady of Sorrows in the crypt is reached by a spiral staircase. The chapel is a memorial to Australian soldiers who fell in World War I.

ST PATRICK'S CATHEDRAL

The three spires of St Patrick's Catholic Cathedral in Melbourne soar into the sky

AUSTRALIA'S FINEST CATHEDRALS

Despite the relative youth of the western culture in Australia – serious settlement only began in the late 18th century – the country boasts a number of outstandingly handsome cathedrals in its cities. One of the finest is in Brisbane, which was designed by the eminent Victorian architect J L Pearson in 1901. Built in hard porphyry, it imitates the 14th-century French High Gothic style with superb ambulatory and vaulting.

OPPOSITE: In the Chapel of the Blessed Sacrament the walls and floor are highly decorative; panels behind the altar depict symbols and events relating to the life of Christ.

BELOW: Angels gaze down from the carved wooden ceiling in St Patrick's Cathedral.

Although Melbourne, a great modern metropolis, is one of Australia's largest cities, after Sydney, it was founded relatively recently. The first western settlement began to grow up around the Yarra river in the 1830s and in 1835 Melbourne was officially founded. It remained a small outpost until the gold rush of 1851 when it suddenly developed rapidly. As people flooded into the town, it became necessary to provide public buildings and services – not least churches and cathedrals. In 1901 Melbourne was made the capital of the Commonwealth of Australia, until the distinction was passed to the newly developed town of Canberra in the Australian Capital Territory.

MELBOURNE'S FIRST CATHEDRAL

Work on the Catholic Cathedral of St Patrick started in 1858, within seven years of the gold rush that so swelled the small town's population. The project was ambitious and expensive, and building was not completed until 1897. It was a design based on the High Gothic cathedrals of northern France and comprised a Latin cross with a polygonal apse at the eastern end. Its architect was William Wardell, whose elegant bluestone cathedral is said to be one of the best examples of Gothic revivalist architecture in the world.

At night, the structure is floodlit and presents an imposing landmark, standing tall and proud just behind Parliament House in Cathedral Place.

THREE SLENDER FINGERS

For 40 years the cathedral remained largely unchanged, but then the Church authorities decided to add the graceful spires included in the original design. Funds were raised and between 1937 and 1939 St Patrick's was provided with not one, but three, spires to rival those of its Anglican counterpart, St Paul's Cathedral, which had received its three spires some 11 years previously.

The spires are easily St Patrick's most dominant feature. The one over the central crossing begins as a square tower, lit by a line of slender lancet windows, then gives way to an elegant polygonal structure decorated with traceried windows and spirelets, topped by the soaring spire itself, a slim finger of deep yellow pointing straight and tall into the sky. At the west end of the cathedral the other two spires are built in much the same proportions as the central tower, but are smaller, providing the west front with a grace and elegance to rival any of the great French Gothic buildings.

CREAM AND BLUE

St Patrick's Cathedral is mainly built of blocks of bluestone, but the tracery on the windows, the decorative balustrades, and the buttresses and spirelets are of a pale cream stone that contrasts neatly with the dark walls.

The roofs of the choir, nave and transepts are tall, steeply pitched and set with tiny dormer windows. The apsidal end has radiating chapels with conical roofs, like those of the 14th-century French cathedrals, each one lit by a tall double-light window with delicate tracery at the top.

The transepts, longer than the choir, are lit by tall windows on the east and west walls and by great rose windows in the north and south walls. Among the cathedral's finest interior features are its slender, soaring pillars rising to its magnificent hammer-beam timber ceiling.

There are fine mosaics on the floor, and the marble and alabaster altar boasts beautiful glass mosaics that were made specially for St Patrick's Cathedral in Venice.

ST MARY'S CATHEDRAL, SYDNEY

Overlooking Hyde Park, Roman Catholic St Mary's Cathedral was built in Gothic style at the turn of the century

Sydney Harbour was first glimpsed by Europeans in 1788, when a ship of the First Fleet, commanded by Captain Arthur Phillip, arrived bringing convicts from England. He called it 'the finest harbour in the world', and over the next century it was transformed from the huddle of crude shacks erected by the first convicts to a thriving, profitable port with handsome Victorian buildings, one of which is the Catholic Cathedral of St Mary.

This imposing cathedral stands at the end of Macquarie Street at the junction with College Street. Overlooking the leafy haven of Hyde Park, it provides a welcome refuge from the frenetic activity of Australia's biggest city.

IRISH CONNECTIONS

The entrance in the west transept is reached by a flight of 37 steps on which stand bronze statues (both designed by sculptor Sir Bertram McKennal) of Cardinal Moran and Archbishop Kelly, two prominent, but opposing, figures in the Catholic community in Sydney in the 19th and early 20th centuries. It was Archbishop Kelly who laid the cathedral's final foundation stone on 8 June 1913.

A high percentage of the original immigrants to Sydney were Irish but they were ruled by governors who were mainly Protestant. The first cardinal of Australia, Patrick Moran, a man of considerable energy and passion, did much to promote the cause of the Catholic Church in Australia, as well as working to heal the division between Catholics and Protestants. The head of the Catholic Church in Sydney at the time was the pious Michael Kelly who spent much of his life opposing Moran. The rift between the two Irishmen continued until the death of Moran in the year 1911.

UNUSUAL GOTHIC

St Mary's was designed by an Englishman called Wilkinson Wardell (1823–99) who was employed as government architect by the Department of Works in Victoria. Space and government funding allowed Wardell to plan on a large scale, and almost all the buildings he designed are huge, St Mary's being no exception. However, his initial plans were accepted with some caution, partly because they were ambitious – a reservation that was justified in that St Mary's was never completed – and partly because of two design anomalies.

As Wardell based his plans on Lincoln Cathedral in England (see page 114) St Mary's is essentially pure Gothic, yet it has one difference. Afraid that the intense sun would cause the windows to expand and cause structural damage to the surrounding stone, Wardell limited the area of glass with the result that the cathedral interior is rather dark – unusual for a Gothic cathedral where the aim is to flood the inside

ARCHITECT AND FRAUD

St James's Church (1824), also on Macquarie Street, has an unusual history. It was originally intended to be a court of law, but, when half completed, the Sydney administration decided to convert it into a church. The building was designed by Francis Greenway, an architect who had been deported for fraud. However, the governor, Lachlan Macquarie, realised Greenway's potential and employed him to design what have turned out to be some of Sydney's finest buildings – including magnificent St James's and the elegant Hyde Park Barracks that stand near St Mary's Cathedral. Unfortunately, when Macquarie left Australia in 1822 Greenway failed to impress his successor and left to live on his farm to the north. Years later, it came to light that the deeds that proved Greenway owned this farm were a forgery.

with as much light as possible.

Another distinguishing feature of St Mary's is its orientation. Wardell was faced with a dilemma: either he could design a smaller building conforming to the traditional east–west orientation, or he could design a cathedral of impressive dimensions, the high altar of which pointed north. Given his penchant for the massive, it was no surprise that Wardell chose the latter option.

Like most Gothic cathedrals, St Mary's boasts elegant flying buttresses that spring from the arcade of the aisles to the clerestory of the nave. The doors and windows are topped with graceful pointed arches and the exterior is liberally laced with delicate pinnacles and spires, all carved from dressed honey-coloured Pyrmont stone. Wardell originally intended that the two towers at the front be topped by spires, but due to a shortage of funds these have yet to be built.

The cathedral, taking the form of a Latin cross, has a nave flanked by an east and a west aisle. The arms of the cross are formed by the transepts, the west one containing the beautiful Chapel of the Sacred Heart, and the east one containing the Chapel of the Irish Saints, plus an extension comprising the sacristies (which are not open to the public). At the far northern end of the cathedral is the ambulatory, dominated by the Blessed Sacrament Chapel and flanked by the altars of St Joseph and St Peter.

ABOVE: St Mary's is situated to the east of the city haven of Hyde Park, with its fountains, walks and formal gardens.

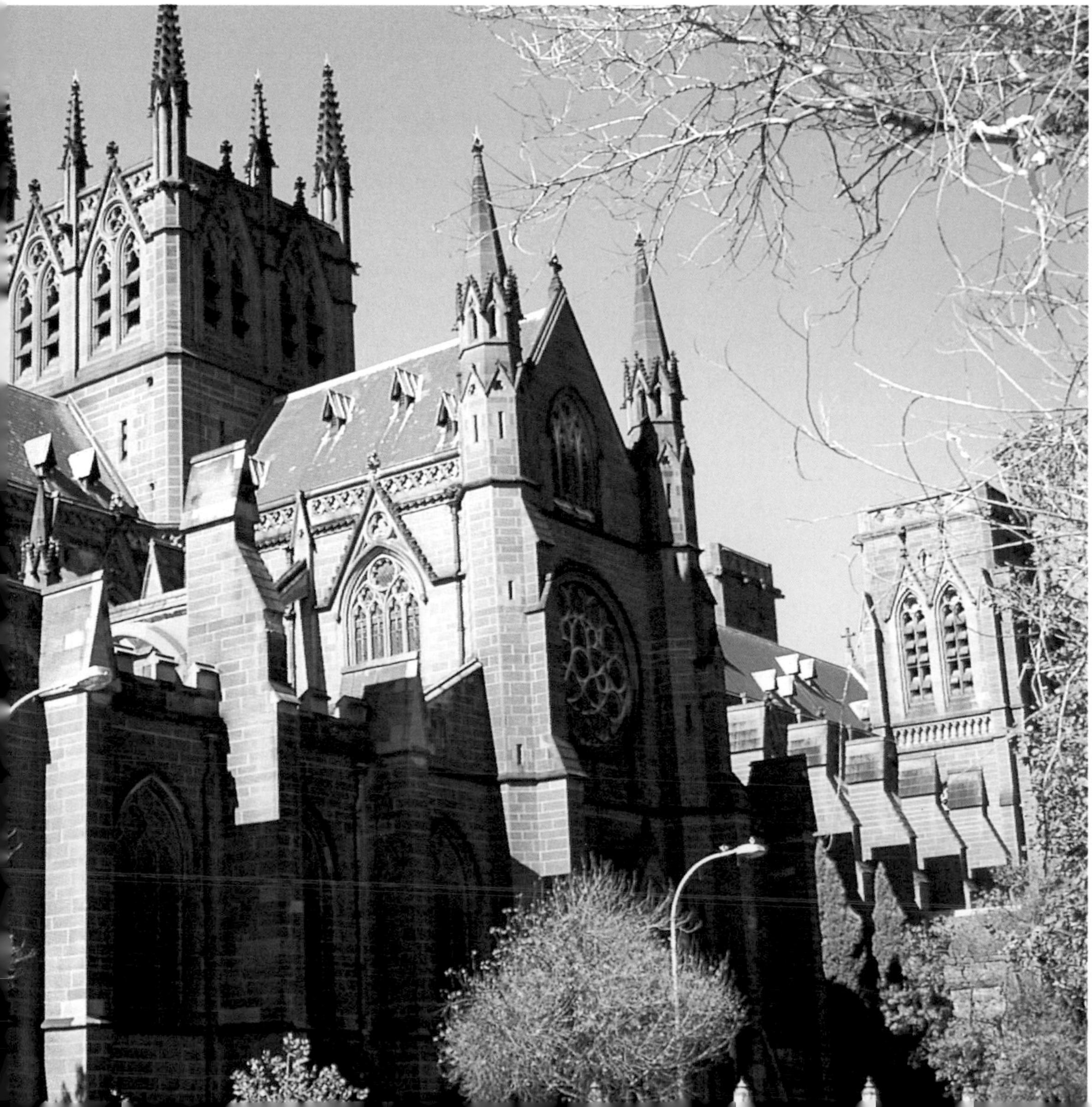

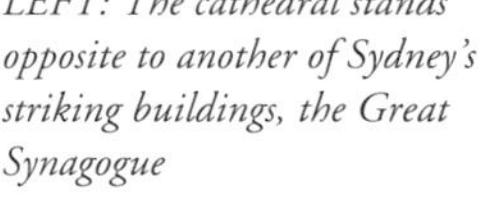

LEFT: The cathedral stands opposite to another of Sydney's striking buildings, the Great Synagogue

St Andrew's Cathedral

The Anglican cathedral of Sydney was designed by the Scottish architect James Hume. Building began in 1837 but ground to a halt five years later when funds ran out. The church remained incomplete until 1846 when Edmund Thomas Blacket – generally regarded as Sydney's 'church architect' – arrived. Work then continued for another 22 years, during which time St Andrew's was lengthened and given its distinctive twin towers and lantern.

Glossary

Aisle: a passageway that runs parallel to the nave and the choir. There are usually two, one on either side of the nave, although some cathedral s are double-aisled, with two on each side. Aisles are marked off with rows of pillars and the external wall.

Ambulatory: a walkway around the eastern end of a cathedral behind the high altar.

Apse: a semi-circular or polygonal ending. Apses are usually placed at the eastern end of a cathedral , although they can also be at the end of a transept or a chapel. The rounded end of a cathedral , including the ambulatory and chapels, is called a ***chevet*** in French Gothic architecture.

Arcade: a range of arches supported by piers or columns.

Arch: a curved structure that spans an opening. Arches can be: (1) round-headed (classical or Romanesque), (2) semi-circular, (3) pointed (Gothic), or (4) ogee (round-headed, but rising to a point at the apex).

Baptistry: a building, often separate from the main body of the cathedral , with a font used for baptisms.

Baroque: an architectural style (1600–1750) that promoted the use of flamboyant decoration and ornamentation.

Basilica: a cathedral or church with a nave, aisles, apses and narthex (entrance chamber). See diagram.

Bay: part of a nave comprising three levels: an arcade (see) on ground level, a triforium (see) on the middle level, and a clerestory (see) on the upper level. See diagram.

Blind arcade: a row of arches carved into a blank wall.

Boss: an ornamented clump of stone or wood that occurs at the intersection of the ribs on a vault. Bosses are often carved or painted.

Buttress: a mass of masonry built to add support to a wall, or to deflect pressure from an arch or vault. A **flying buttress** is a buttress in the form of an arch that absorbs the outward thrust of a pier. Flying buttresses are often carved, such as those at Chartres Cathedral .

Campanile: a bell-tower that is usually, but not always, separate from the cathedral.

Capital: the top of a column or pillar.

Carillon: a set of bells which are rung mechanically.

Chancel: the area, usually at the eastern end of a cathedral , that includes the choir and the high altar. Reserved for the clergy, it is often closed off with a stone or wooden screen or rood. The term chancel is sometimes used interchangeably with **sanctuary** and **presbytery**.

Chapter house: a separate building, or a room, used by the governing body of a cathedral for meetings.

Choir: the place where the choir sang, usually to the east of a screen. 'Choir' is often used to refer to the whole of the eastern end of a cathedral building.

Classical: using the building styles of ancient Rome and Greece.

Clerestory: the upper part of a nave, transept and choir pierced by windows. It is above the arcade (see) and triforium (see). Not all cathedrals have clerestories.

Cloisters: a covered arcade around a quadrangle, connecting the cathedral with the domestic parts of the monastery.

Colonnade: a row of columns supporting a series of arcades.

Corbel: a stone wall-bracket that supports a roof beam or a vault, or on which stands a statue.

Crossing: the part of a cruciform (see) cathedral where the nave meets the transepts.

Cruciform: cathedral that is in the shape of a cross (see diagram). There are two types of cruciform cathedral: (1) the **Greek cross**, where all four arms are of equal length, and (2) the more common **Latin cross** where the arm of the nave is longer than the choir and the transepts.

Cupola: a dome, sometimes with a lantern or turret on top.

Drum: a round or polygonal wall supporting a dome. A drum can sometimes be pierced with windows to allow light into the cathedral below.

Façade: the dominant face of a cathedral containing the main entrance. In most cathedrals, this is at the west end.

Flamboyant: the southern European Gothic style, from the 14th century onwards.

Fresco: a wall or ceiling painted with water-colours on wet plaster.

Galilee: a porch sometimes used as a chapel. These are usually at the western end of the cathedral.

Garth: the area enclosed by a cloister.

Gothic: a term used by 16th-century Italians to denote what they regarded as a barbaric style of architecture between the 12th and 15th centuries in Europe. Gothic started in France in the 1100s, and was characterised by pointed arches, elaborate vaulting, large windows with delicate tracery, clerestories and flying buttresses. In England, the Gothic occurred in three phases: (1) Early English, from late 1100s to 1200s; (2) Decorated, from 1200s to mid-1300s; and (3) Perpendicular, from mid-1300s to 1500s.

Grisaille: a method of painting, often in monochrome, to imitate sculpture.

Hall church: a church where the nave and the aisles are the same height, producing an interior like a great hall.

Lady Chapel: a chapel dedicated to the Virgin Mary, usually, but not exclusively, at the eastern end of the cathedral behind the high altar.

Lancet: a long, slim, sharply pointed window.

Lantern: a windowed turret on a cupola or a dome.

Minaret: the tall tower of a mosque used for calling to prayer. In Spain in particular, minarets were incorporated into cathedral buildings when land was taken back from the occupying Moors.

Misericord: a ledge under a hinged seat that supported monks who had to stand up for long periods. Misericords are often finely carved.

Narthex: the porch or entrance hall at the western end of a basilica (see diagram).

Nave: the main body of a cathedral west of the crossing. A nave is sometimes flanked by aisles.

Norman: the Romanesque period in Britain.

Oculus: a round window or opening (plural is oculi).

Pediment: a triangular, low-pitched gable. Pediments are features of classical architecture.

Pedentive: an inverted triangular segment supporting a circular dome over a square or rectangular base. Pedentives were first used in St Sophia's cathedral in Istanbul.

Pier: a heavy stone support or column designed to withstand vertical pressure.

Pilaster: a flat, triangular column projecting from a wall.

Portal: an ornamented doorway.

Presbytery: see Sanctuary.

Renaissance: revival of classical architecture that occurred in Europe between the 1400s and 1600s.

Reredos: a wall or screen behind the altar, usually decorated.

Retable: a picture or carving forming a backdrop to the altar.

Retrochoir: the area immediately behind the choir.

Rib: a raised band supporting the cells of a groined vault (see).

Rococo: the light, airy form of baroque that started in France in the 1700s.

Romanesque: an architectural style in Europe based on the pattern of building employed by the Romans. Romanesque was in use from the 5th century until Gothic (see) became more popular.

Rotunda: a building, or a part of a building, with a circular ground plan and a dome on top.

Sacristy: the place where sacred vessels used in Communion are stored.

Sanctuary: the area containing the main altar. Also called the presbytery.

Spandrels: the space between the shoulders of adjoining arches, or the outer edge of an arch, and the ceiling or moulding above.

Stucco: plaster that is moulded or carved.

Tracery: Gothic ornamental stonework in a window.

Transepts: the north and south arms of a cruciform (see) church.

Triforium: arcaded corridor between the arcade and the clerestory in the nave, and sometimes the choir and aisles.

Vault: arched ceiling of stone or brick. There are several different types: (1) Barrel vault – a round or pointed continuous vault like a tube; (2) Cross or groin vault – a vault formed by the meeting of two barrel vaults at right angles to each other; (3) Fan vault – a vault where ribs radiate from the wall in a fan-like pattern; (4) Lierne vault – a vault with short, secondary ribs that form a delicate pattern; (5) Star or stellar vault – a vault where the ribs meet to form a star pattern.

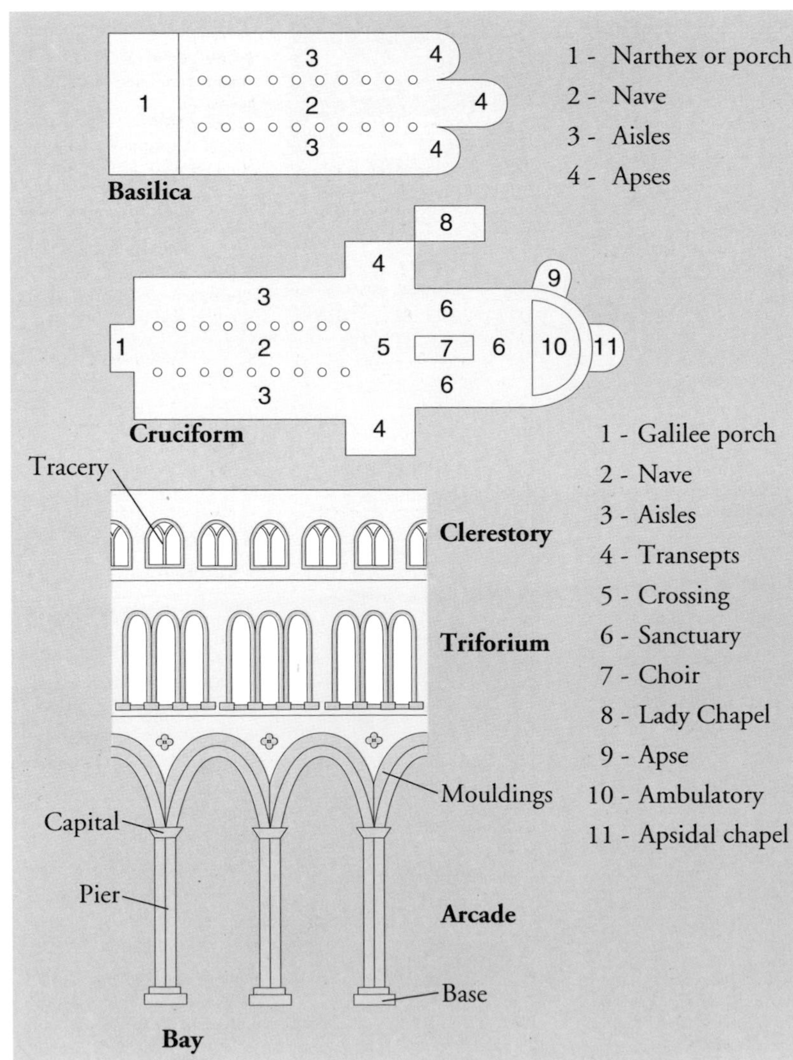

INDEX

Acknowledgements

The Automobile Association would like to thank the following photographers, libraries and associations for their assistance in the preparation of this book.

PHOTO AKG LONDON 82, 91a; J ALLAN CASH PHOTOLIBRARY 44, 45, 184; ARCAID 58/9; ARXIU MAS 36/7, 37; DR B ATWELL 188/9, 189; AUSTRIAN NATIONAL TOURIST OFFICE 62, 63 (Österreich Werbung); THE BRIDGEMAN ART LIBRARY 125a Salisbury Cathedral by John Constable (V & A Museum, London); P CASAMENTO 186, 187; CATHEDRAL OF TURKU 100; JAMES DAVIS TRAVEL PHOTOGRAPHY 34, 39, 43, 137b, 161, 175b; M GIRARD 164a; ROBERT HARDING PICTURE LIBRARY 10a, 13, 104, 105a, 105b, 106, 107, 123, 136, 150, 152a; THE HULTON GETTY COLLECTION LTD 12b; THE IMAGE BANK 3, 24, 24/5, 30/1, 31a, 35, 48, 67, 126, 137a, 164b, 165a, 178, 183; IMPACT PHOTOS 142 (S Shepheard); D K JONES/IMAGES OF AFRICA PHOTOBANK 180/1; LETICIA GRAPHICS 185a, 185b; ROGER MOSS 4a, 4c, 14/5, 15, 16, 17, 18, 19, 20, 21a, 21b, 22a, 23, 28, 29a, 29b, 31b; K NAYLOR 103; NORTHERN IRELAND TOURIST BOARD 108; PICTURES COLOUR LIBRARY LTD Front cover, 38, 97a, 101, 129a, 179; ST JOHN'S CATHEDRAL, TAMPERE 98/9, 98; THE SLIDE FILE 128, 129b; SOUTH AMERICAN PICTURES 9, 174; SPECTRUM COLOUR LIBRARY 86/7, 115b, 120, 121a, 121b, 138, 143, 182/3; TONY STONE IMAGES 169a; TRIP/N RAY 66; M VAUTIER 11a, 176/7, 177; WASHINGTON NATIONAL CATHEDRAL 168, 169b (R Burgess) P WILSON 46, 47; ZEFA PICTURES LTD 8a, 40/1, 50b, 54a, 55, 58a, 69, 81, 83, 84, 87a, 93, 96, 102, 110, 111a, 111b, 113a, 115a, 117, 122/3, 124, 125b, 127a, 127b, 130, 132, 133, 134/5, 139, 151, 153, 157, 160/1, 172/3, 173a.

All remaining pictures are held in the Association's own library (AA PHOTO LIBRARY) with contributions from the following photographers:
J N ARNOLD 135b; A BAKER 86, 90, 91b; P BAKER 116; P DAVIDSON 85; S DAY Spine, 68; J EDMUNSON 11b, 42/3; R G ELLIOTT 165b; P ENTICKNAPP 158, 159; D FORSS 131; V GREAVES 12a; A HEUMISCH 80, 80/1, 88/9, 88, 89, 92; R HOLMES 166; J W JORGENSEN 97b; P KENWARD 5; A KOUPRIANOFF 70a, 70b, 71, 72/3, 73a, 73b, 74/5, 75, 76a, 76b, 77, 78/9, 79a, 79b; S & O MATHEWS B/Cover a, c, 113b; E MEACHER 148/9, 149, 181; D MITIDIERI 59a, 152b; A MOLYNEUX 40; G MUNDY 109; D NOBLE 22b, 64b, 65; T OLIVER 1; K PATERSON 135a, 167a, 167b; J F PIN 170, 171a, 171b, 173b; C SAWYER 8b, 48/9, 50a, 50/1, 52/3, 53, 54b, 56/7, 57a, 57b; M SIEBERT 64a; B SMITH B/Cover b; A SOUTER 147b; R STRANGE 175a; R SURMAN 156; S M TAYLOR 4b, 162a, 162b, 163; L WHITWAM 112; P WILSON 32, 33; G WRONA 140, 141, 144, 145a, 145b; J WYAND 2, 146, 147a.

Cutaway illustrations on pp 26/7, 60/1, 94/5, 118/9 and 154/5 by MALTINGS PARTNERSHIP.